Social Problems in Athletics

Social Problems in Athletics

Essays in the Sociology of Sport

Edited by Daniel M. Landers

UNIVERSITY OF ILLINOIS PRESS   *Urbana Chicago London*

LIBRARY OF CONGRESS CATALOGING IN PUBLICATION DATA

Main entry under title:

Social problems in athletics.

Includes bibliographies.
1. Physical education and training—Philosophy—
Addresses, essays, lectures. 2. Sports—Philosophy—
Addresses, essays, lectures. 3. Sports—Social aspects—
Addresses, essays, lectures. I. Landers, Daniel M.,
1942–
GV342.S592   301.5′7   75–35626
ISBN 0–252–00461–2

Contents

Preface

In contemporary American society, competitive sport has come under the critical eye of the public, the academic community, and athletes themselves. At a time when sport is at the height of its popularity, it is perhaps paradoxical that considerable confusion exists regarding the educational role of sport. Alarmed by what appear to be increasing abuses in athletics, social scientists, journalists, sports revolutionaries, and concerned people in the field of physical education have begun to question whether public entertainment through sport is properly a function of education; whether interschool sports overemphasize competitive aspects of life; whether participants are becoming more dehumanized by demands for machinelike precision; whether the fun element of a game diminishes in proportion to the size of the audience; and finally, whether or not coaches teach socially undesirable behavior and develop hatred for out-groups. The relationship between education and sport is only one concern of the social science aspect of sport. Space does not permit an elaboration of other equally important concerns—sport and politics, sport and religion, sport and economics, equality of opportunity in sport, and cultural aspects of sport, to name a few.

The present anthology is an outgrowth of a conference on "Sport and Social Deviance" which was held at State University College at Brockport, New York. This conference was attended by those interested in the newly emerging interdisciplinary area concerned with the social scientific analysis of sport, play, and games. Sociologists, anthropologists, political scientists, geographers, economists, and physical educators have in recent years brought the tools of the social sciences to bear on sport. Although sport has been recognized by many scientists as an important social phenomenon, motives for such inquiry have been mixed. Some have viewed sport only as a means to test and advance social scientific theory in other more academically accepted allied areas such as sociology of education, religion, and leisure. Others have focused on sport as an important area of study in its own right.

Both views certainly have merit, but the latter is receiving more attention as the importance of sport is better understood. The study of social problems in sport and athletics now being done in physical education and sociology courses, together with the formation of interdisciplinary organizations and conferences devoted to sociology of sport, evidence the growing scholarly interest in sport. These trends make it apparent that more and more investigators are shifting to the view that sport in and of itself is deserving of scientific investigation.

The use of the term "social problems" may require some explanation. Our discussion of "problems in athletics" is not intended to convey information on techniques of taking attendance, handling student discipline, or other such routine concerns of classroom organization or management. "Social problems" refers to recurring issues for which there are no apparent or agreed-upon solutions. In this grey area the proponents of the sport establishment wage the battle for reform of American athletics. The present volume has confined its coverage to a few topics of contemporary concern, topics which represent new approaches, knowledges, and ideas. Articles in each section of the book, although touching upon problems of interest to professional educators, use the descriptive and analytic procedures of the scientific method. The potential problems stemming from these issues strike at the central values of athletics; since athletics mirrors American societal values, these social problems are believed to be associated with problems in society at large.

As with any compilation of essays originally presented at a conference, some editorial revisions were necessary. In most cases revision was minimal; in a few cases it was more substantial, but in each case revisions were either made or approved by the contributors. In addition to the prepared essays on the conference topics, reactors' comments were transcribed from tapes and developed into more formal essays.

The present anthology is intended to provide social scientists, physical educators, and others interested in the sociology of sport with an understanding of selected social problems in athletics. Such an understanding ultimately may lead to changing certain emphases, or stimulating firmer direction and control of athletic programs. The anthology is also intended for use in courses which deal with social problems in sport and athletics. Courses designed to acquaint prospective teachers, coaches, or community leaders with the social science aspects of sport all too often reflect little more than the personal experiences of the instructor. The essays in this volume may assist in filling this void.

A conference of this magnitude could not have been conducted without the cooperative efforts of many faculty members and students. The conference was initiated by the S.U.C.–Brockport department of physical education and jointly sponsored by the departments of men's and women's physical education, recreation, sociology, psychology, and anthropology as well as student clubs affiliated with these departments and the Black Student Liberation Front. Appreciation is extended to the various department chairmen and club representatives; without their encouragement and financial support the conference could not have been held. The endorsement of the conference by the International Committee for the Sociology of Sport is also acknowledged.

I must also express my gratitude to a number of individuals who assisted in various aspects of the conference. I thank Warren Fraleigh, dean of the faculty of physical education, Thomas D. McIntyre, former chairman of the sports science focus, and Dorothy Mariner of the department of sociology for their assistance in securing speakers and financial support. Other faculty members who were invaluable in hosting and conducting this conference were Gladys Evans, Merrill Melnick, Dale Hart, and Mary Livingston, as well as students Rosanne Parker, Daniel Gould, and Brenda Wright. I am particularly grateful to Penny Dorrance and my wife, Donna, for their dedication and assistance on all aspects of organizing and coordinating this conference. Last, but not least, I am indebted to the speakers, who gave their utmost in their preparation of papers.

DANIEL M. LANDERS
Pennsylvania State University

Social-Psychological Dimensions of Competition

Introduction

Many investigators have expressed the timeworn cliché that sport is a mirror of societal values. Although this is no doubt the case, very few analyses have been advanced detailing the ways in which competitive athletics reflect societal values. Such a neglect, so fundamental to a determination of social order in sport, is indeed surprising.

An analysis of societal values and values inherent in athletics is a highly ambitious undertaking; it may even be somewhat presumptuous at this stage in the development of the field. Some investigators have ignored these risks, however, and their efforts have illuminated at least one way of developing a rudimentary conceptual framework for analyzing the function of sport in society. Of the fifteen major value orientations that Williams (1960) has described as guiding the behavior of the American people, only the value of achievement orientation of a society has, to my knowledge, been related to sport. Borrowing from McClelland's analysis of *The Achieving Society* (1961), Lueschen (1967) hypothesized that the achievement orientation of a society is a causative factor explaining high levels of competitive sport involvement in West Germany. Both Lueschen and Seppänen (1970) have analyzed achievement fluctuations within and between societies by examining the dominant ideational structure of society; namely, the incorporation of the achievement value into the predominant religious or political ideology. Support has been shown for a high relationship between achievement and high-level involvement in individual sports (Lueschen 1967), as well as a nation's attainment of Olympic medals (Seppänen 1970). Although this avenue of research is encouraging in its ability to integrate seemingly diverse findings at a societal level, no follow-up investigations have been made at a macro level to determine whether the achievement value causes high-level competitive sport involvement.

Another indirect source of evidence for the achievement value within society is the more prevalent analysis of subcultural differences (e.g., sex, age, social class, etc.). It is important to be aware that even where the achievement value is very pronounced in a society, social scientists certainly do not contend that all groups of people are socialized equally into achievement values. In fact, males traditionally have received more achievement training than females, and children from middle and upper socioeconomic status groups have likewise been recipients of more achievement training than children coming from lower socioeconomic backgrounds. Roberts and Sutton-Smith (1962) have shown similar parallels between high incidence of achievement training and participation in games of physical skill. A similar correspondence between achievement training and sport participation can be found in the research literature. For example, the similarity in age trends for increasing achievement motivation (McClelland 1961) and increased competitive sport involvement (Helanko 1957) are in line with the present analysis. Likewise, the greater ratio of first-born males participating in dangerous as well as nondangerous sports (Nisbett 1968) parallels the greater achievement training traditionally received by first-borns in American society. The process by which achievement values are differentially instilled in sport participants is as yet unknown, but some hypotheses have been suggested. Roberts and Sutton-Smith (1962) have advanced a conflict-enculturation hypothesis which posits that competitive games provide a "buffered learning situation" where the child, who is experiencing conflict with achievement demands from adults or peers, can learn to cope with these demands by seeking less stressful forms of achievement. These investigators indicate that buffered learning of achievement is often attained by participation in structured but make-believe game forms. Reinforcement principles derived from learning theory have also been used to explain the process whereby achievement values are differentially reinforced in children through adult and/or peer encouragement in games and sport.

Having roughly sketched a rudimentary conceptual framework in which social order in sport can be interpreted via societal achievement values, the analysis of achievement now shifts to a lower level of abstraction—the social-psychological level of the individual participant in competitive sport. Social psychologists have discerned the characteristics of the achievement-evoking situation: standards of excellence which can be evaluated in terms of success or failure. These standards can be task-related, self-related, and other-related; they can be used by the individual to assess one's competency. A situation characterized by a .50 probability of success (i.e., an intermediate risk situation where uncertainty is most apparent) is most challenging for individuals who have incorporated the achievement value as a personality disposition. The person high in achievement motivation is also characterized by persistence in pursuit of standards of excellence; such a person often will forego immediate gratification in the interests of long-range goals. The individual is assumed to desire such situations so as to satisfy an acquired drive for individual competence and eventual autonomy. More detailed analyses of the proximal and distal antecedents of achievement orientation can be found in Berkowitz (1964) and Veroff (1969).

The characteristics of the achievement situation, as described above, are also found in competitive situations. In fact, the competitive situation is one form of achievement situation which involves comparison with social and nonsocial standards. Martens's analysis begins here with the preliminary framework for a theory of competition. To provide a testable scientific theory, Martens restricts his analysis to overt competitive situations where standards of excellence are public and the achievement of the standard is evaluated "in the presence of at least one other person who is aware of the criterion for comparison and can evaluate the comparison process." This type of competition is described as inherently a social process which is typified by the end determinant of our athletic endeavors, the athletic contest. Martens's analysis does not deal with self competition or competition against inanimate objects *in the absence of the imagined, implied, or actual presence of evaluating others*. Obviously, these latter forms of competitive behavior do exist in sport, but they are usually confined to training; they are not found in the contest where objective determination of performance standards are assessed.

Underlying Martens's discussion, as well as the present discussion, is the assumption that before we can understand potential social problems in athletics, we must comprehend the underlying social order in sport; that is, how and why sport is important in certain societies and not others, how people are differentially socialized into values in competitive sport, and finally, how individual motives to participate in competitive sport develop in the person who cognitively perceives and finds satisfaction in varying types of competitive situations. Martens has sought to provide some insight into this latter problem relating to the motives of the individual participant in competitive sport. In concluding his explanation of competition, he suggests several hypotheses derived from his model of competition which, when put to test, will provide an evaluation of the viability of his competitive model. It is also assumed that through such micro analyses of sport the social-psychological dimensions of competitive behavior will be understood, and that this understanding will provide insight into departures from this general pattern where social problems may be manifest.

While Martens's primary contribution to this section has been to construct a blueprint for future researchers to accomplish a more complete understanding of competition, he has not attempted to provide information on what is currently known regarding competition. The Sherif essay fills this void. Like the Martens essay, it deals with social standards and the social context in which this type of competition occurs. In her working definition of competition, which includes the basic characteristics of an achievement situation, Sherif emphasizes that in competition the patterns of activity in pursuit of standards or goals are consistent. She also indicates that competition has an inherent selective factor; persons or groups determine who the other people shall be in the comparison process. From her previous review of the competition literature, Sherif describes what is known regarding the social context of competition. The essay is concerned with the following five themes: 1) competition is learned during socialization, and therefore there are "no born losers or born winners"; 2) competitive processes and their outcomes vary from culture to culture, group to group, sex to sex, and sport to sport according to the structure of the goals themselves, and also in means or strategies used in attaining them; 3) the individual's aspiration level, achievement, success, failure, and their psychological consequences all depend on an effective social context consisting both of the structure of standards and goals and of those persons and groups who *count* for the child; 4) previous research models for studying competition have many times ignored the social context and are therefore inadequate and probably misleading; and 5) the psychological consequences for the child generalize far beyond the specific activities themselves.

Moving from a description of what is known about competition, the next essay by Devereux takes quite a different approach by focusing upon what ought to be a desirable form of competition for young children. Devereux is critical of the Little Leaguism trend that has traditionally involved boys, but is also becoming evident among girls. The central problem here is perhaps the changing forms of competition and the questionable desirability of adults encouraging children into more advanced forms of competition at an early age. This essay represents the first of many in this volume which confront problems in competitive athletics. Many of these problems can be roughly subsumed into a model of changing complexity of game structure and magnitude of extrinsic reward. Lueschen (1967:127) has described competitive sport on a continuum midway between the poles of unstructured play, where extrinsic rewards are latent, to work where high task structure and extrinsic rewards are manifest. Intermediate points on this continuum can also be described, such as low organized games which lie somewhere between play and competitive sport, as well as big-time college sports which fall between competitive sport and the work form (professional) of competition. The latter two competitive forms differ only in degree of extrinsic reward as well as degree of rigidly imposed structural demands upon players (e.g., contracts and other legally binding forms). Many of the issues raised here and in succeeding sections are a result of structural pressures that are brought to bear upon the individual in the transition from one play, game, sport, or work form to another. The second section of this volume contains a series of potential problems in the passage of sport to work where many times the extrinsic rewards in sport become the goal. Before turning to this set of problems, we will first examine some of the problems arising from the change-over of children's unstructured games to the more structured, adult-type competitive sports.

Devereux believes that American society has impoverished children's games by robbing children not only of childish fun, but also of valuable learning experiences. Although Devereux cites some historical evidence to indicate that in America the range of children's games has narrowed over time, no evidence has been obtained to demonstrate that similar constrictions in choice have occurred in other societies. Regardless of the outcome of this empirical question, the desirability of the trend toward more adult-controlled game environments is seriously questioned. Devereux views children's games as miniature and playful models where, through a buffered learning process, a wide variety of cultural and social activities are learned. These social activities can consist of achievement values, such as competing, winning, and losing, as well as other behaviors, such as how to cope with anxiety. The constriction of game forms in American society is construed by Devereux as detrimental to the more effective learning experiences formerly provided by socialization via a wider variety of games (kick the can, backyard baseball, etc.). Little Leaguism, as a classic example of adult-controlled highly organized competitive sport for children, is accused of bankrupting most of the features (low organization, self-organization, spontaneity, and the ability to proceed at one's own pace) of games that many maintain are more effective, meaningful learning models. Devereux raises many important issues here, and he takes a stand in favor of a return to the less-structured children's games of the past.

REFERENCES

Berkowitz, L.
   1964   *The Development of Motives and Values in the Child.* New York: Basic Books.
Helanko, R.
   1957   "Sports and Socialization." *Acta Sociologica* 2:229–240.
Lueschen, G.
   1967   "The Interdependence of Sport and Culture." *International Review of Sport Sociology* 2:127–139.
McClelland, D. C.
   1961   *The Achieving Society.* New York: Van Nostrand.
Nisbett, R. E.
   1968   "Birth Order and Participation in Dangerous Sports." *Journal of Personality and Social Psychology* 8:351–353.
Roberts, J. M., and Sutton-Smith, B.
   1962   "Child Training and Game Involvement." *Ethology* 1:166–185.
Seppänen, P.
   1970   "The Role of Competitive Sports in Different Societies." *Tutkimuksia Research Reports,* Institute for Sociology, University of Helsinki, no. 151.
Veroff, J.
   1969   C. P. Smith, ed. *Achievement-Related Motives in Children.* New York: Russell Sage Foundation. Pp. 46–101.
Williams, R. M., Jr.
   1960   *American Society: A Sociological Interpretation.* New York: Alfred A. Knopf.

Competition: In Need of a Theory

RAINER MARTENS

In preparing a discussion of the social and psychological problems associated with athletic competition, I was overwhelmed by the numerous questions I could raise and the lack of information available to answer them. Just what do we know about competition and its influence on people? Can we even define what competition is? Can we define what it is not? From a research point of view, the ability to define competition broadly enough to include those situations we generally consider to be competition, and yet to define it rigorously enough to make it a useful experimental construct, has not been satisfactorily accomplished.

Few would disagree that competition is a pervasive phenomenon in our society, with antecedents and consequences of which we know incredibly little. For example, can we explain why children compete? What factors influence how competitive a child will be? Or, to put it another way, why will one child thrive on what appears to be intense competition, and another child break into tears? Does the intensity of the competitive situation influence the quality of the child's performance in the sport? Perhaps more important, does competition have more enduring influence on the child in terms of developing or modifying his motives, attitudes, personality dispositions, self-concept, and consequently his social behavior? The influence of competition on one's interpersonal behavior is just as important to study as is the influence of competition on motor behavior.

While some may dispute the statement that we know very little about competition, most of the available knowledge comes in the form of authoritative opinion or personal experience. The information obtained by the scientific method has not been extensive and has not followed any systematic propositions, theories, or models. Would not the study of competition benefit from a theory which could predict not only why we compete, but with whom we will compete, as well as the

Rainer Martens is professor in the department of kinesiology at the University of Waterloo, Ontario.

consequences of engaging in competition? Since I think such a step is essential before we can begin to resolve these issues, I shall attempt to outline the beginnings of a theory of competition which has these attributes.

Viable theories do not spring forth from the imagination. Instead, they seem to be discovered by carefully integrating existing knowledge and other theoretical propositions. The foundation for a theory of competition will rely heavily on other theories, but it is to be hoped that the intermeshing of a number of separate but related ideas will contribute to a better understanding of the competitive process. The theoretical propositions developed herein are based substantially on the social evaluation theories (Pettigrew 1967), particularly Festinger's (1954) social comparison theory, to explain why and with whom one will engage in the competitive process. I have also benefited from Myers's (1961) attempt to develop a definition of competition from social comparison theory. Finally, I have used elements from the recent work on social facilitation (Zajonc 1965; Cottrell 1968; Martens and Landers 1972) and arousal or activation theory (Duffy 1962; Malmo 1959) to explain the consequences of the competitive process.

DEFINING COMPETITION

Because of the failure of theory to guide research on competition, competition as a concept has not been defined rigorously. What is competition to one scholar is rivalry to another, cooperation to a third, and non-competition to a fourth. Although a historical review of definitions of competition will not be presented here, I shall consider the most frequently used and commonly accepted definition. This has been the reward definition, which states that competition is a social situation in which rewards to an individual are distributed unequally on the basis of performance among those participating in the activity (Church 1968; Deutsch 1949; May and Doob 1937).

Myers (1961) has criticized the "distribution of rewards" definition on two primary grounds. First, it does not attempt to describe why individuals enter into competitive or cooperative situations. Second, for a reward definition to be satisfactory, there must be consensus on the criteria for the distribution of rewards, the subjective value of the rewards, and the goal to be achieved. All of these factors become difficult to define in many situations. There are two additional inadequacies of the "distribution of reward" definitions: these definitions do not predict with whom one will compete, and the reward definition has not in forty years led to a viable theoretical statement.

Myers believed that Festinger's social comparison theory, which has lain dormant for some time, was an important theoretical statement identifying some of the antecedent conditions of the competitive process. Social comparison theory is based on the premise that within man there exists a drive to evaluate his opinions and abilities; in the absence of nonsocial means for making such comparisons, individuals will compare themselves with others. Festinger's theory implies that individuals often enter into the competitive process in order to evaluate their own abilities. Based on this theory, Myers arrived at a rather limited definition of competition:

> More specifically, competition implies the existence of two or more performances which are compared according to some criterion. It follows, then, that only those made with the performance of another individual could be competition. It would not be a condition of competition for an individual to compare his present performance against his own past performance or against some objective standard (e.g., time). An individual cannot compete against himself or against time simply because these are not social situations. Consequently, only those comparisons made to the performance of other people could produce a state of competition. (1961:6)

Myers further restricts his definition of competition by noting that not all interpersonal comparisons involve interaction. He concludes that there is no competition if there is no interaction. Furthermore, this interaction must be of a specific nature: "The performance of each individual in the situation must be used as a standard in the comparison process. In a competitive situation between two individuals, each must compare his performance with that of the other. In addition, however, it is necessary for both individuals to be aware that the other person is engaging in the comparison" (1961:6–7).

Myers concludes that it is possible to have two comparison conditions: a *bilateral comparison condition*, which is a situation where all of a specified number of individuals make a prior public commitment to a subsequent evaluation of their performance in comparison with the performance of all the other individuals in the situation; or a *unilateral comparison condition*, which is a situation where an individual makes a prior commitment either to use the performance of another individual as a standard for comparison but where no reciprocal comparison is made, or to use an idealized performance as a standard for comparison. Myers considers the bilateral comparison condition to be a state of competition; the unilateral comparison condition is not.

Although Myers's definition has the advantage of clearly specifying what condition is competitive, it excludes so much of what has been generally considered to be competition that it has the disadvantage of being somewhat narrow. When Bob Seagren, the pole vaulter, has eliminated the field of opponents, but continues to vault and strive for a new record height, is it not competition? When Craig Breedlove runs his jet-powered racing machine in the Utah salt flats in an attempt to establish a new world land speed record, is it not competition? If a salesman declares to his boss that next month he is going to sell 20 percent more than the previous month, is this not competition? It is clear that Myers's definition excludes much of what we commonly have labeled competition.

In the following paragraphs I shall attempt to define competition somewhat more broadly than Myers, but still retain the advantage of making the definition usable; i.e., it can be defined operationally, and has a theoretical base. Competition must remain a social process to be operational, but it does not need to meet all the rigorous requirements outlined by Myers. Any definition of competition is somewhat arbitrary; in developing a theory of competition, my concern is to define the concept broadly enough to include those situations we generally consider to be competitive, but rigorously enough to make it a useful experimental construct.

COMPETITION REDEFINED

Competition is a particular form of social evaluation. The basis for all social evaluation theories lies in the premise that human beings learn about themselves by comparing themselves with others. Festinger (1954) stated that there was a "drive" to evaluate oneself. I will avoid using the term "drive," because of some connotations it raises through its association with the drive reduction position. Instead, I shall refer to an acquired motive to learn about oneself. This motive, or one closely related to it, has formed the basis of other theories. For example, White's (1959) competence theory is concerned with the motivation of behavior in order that the individual can learn how to competently interact with his environment. To do so will certainly require considerable social evaluation. Similarly, McClelland (1961) has elaborated upon an achievement motive, which also places considerable stock in an individual comparing himself with others.

Evidence can be cited to further document the development of a motive to evaluate oneself. Much of the socialization literature is concerned with the development of this motive. The developmental literature has repeatedly narrated the emergence of the comparison motive in young children. The cross-cultural research on games has illustrated the importance of games as a means for training the young by giving them an opportunity to experience adult life situations. These games allow the child to evaluate himself, particularly in comparison with others.

To evaluate one's abilities, it is necessary to make a comparison between at least two elements: your own performance, and some other standard. As Myers noted, a standard can include another individual, a group, one's own past performance, or some idealized performance level. Myers limited competition to a bilateral comparison, based on a narrow conception of the term "social," which was conceived to be direct social interaction only. I shall use a broader definition of "social" and hence derive a broader definition of competition which includes unilateral comparisons under certain conditions.

A social situation includes direct social interaction, but it may also include situations where no direct interaction occurs. These social situations have received considerable attention in social psychology under the rubric of "social facilitation," which refers to the behavioral effects of the presence of other individuals in the form of observers or a passive audience and coactors. Social facilitation research has shown these social conditions to have significant influence on verbal (Cottrell 1968; Zajonc 1965) and motor (Martens 1969) behavior. More recent evidence is illuminating why the presence of others who are not engaging in direct interaction can affect behavior. It appears that it is not the mere presence of others (as suggested by Zajonc) which affects behavior, but that social facilitation or inhibition occurs when the others are in a position to *evaluate* the performance of the person (Cottrell 1968; Martens and Landers 1972). Hence I see no reason not to define social comparison processes as the contrasting of two elements (one being the performance of an individual) in which at least one other individual is perceived by the performer as able to evaluate the comparison process.

By broadening the definition of social comparison, the definition of a competitive situation may also be expanded to include a wider range of comparisons, particularly those which Myers referred to as unilateral comparisons. Competition, essentially, is a social comparison process with one added restriction—the criterion for comparison is known by the person who is in a position to evaluate the comparison. Although the criterion for comparison in many situations is obvious (as in most sporting contests), it is much less obvious in other situations. It is also important that the criterion for comparison be known in advance, eliminating the possibility of a post hoc decision. Competition so defined cannot be a covert activity. Therefore, *competition is a process in which the comparison of an individual's performance is made with some standard in the presence of at least one other person who is aware of the criterion for comparison and can evaluate the comparison process.*

Using the second major tenet of social evaluation theory and applying it to competition, it can be postulated that competition leads to a positive, neutral, or negative self-evaluation. Substantial evidence has shown that, when one perceives a situation where evaluation by others is possible, it is arousing (Cottrell 1968; Lowe 1973; Martens 1969). The competitive process is arousing because by definition it always has the potential for evaluation. It should be noted that this arousal is elicited before the actual competition begins, acting as an anticipatory response. In reaching self-evaluation, one will determine if the comparison was equitable or inequitable. Inequity in competition occurs when an individual perceives that the ratio of his outcomes to inputs and the ratio of outcomes to inputs for the referent individual or group are unequal (Adams 1965). If equity is perceived in the competitive process and positive evaluation is obtained, arousal will decrease and satisfaction will increase. If negative evaluation is received under perceived equity, arousal will be high and dissatisfaction will increase.

When inequity is perceived, the significance of the evaluation is neutralized, but arousal is manifested as a result of the inequity. Arousal elicited as a consequence of the competitive process will move the individual to do one or more of the following, depending upon the competitive situation: alter his inputs; alter his outcomes; distort his inputs and outcomes cognitively; leave his field; act on the referent individual or group; or change the object of his comparison.

So far I have outlined the basic elements of a theory of competition, but it is extremely unrefined. It does, however, lead to a number of testable hypotheses, some of which I shall explicate below. Furthermore, it brings to bear a considerable volume of social-psychological research related to the competitive process, and it is compatible with most of the existing empirical evidence on competition. I hope to elaborate on some of the more obvious hypotheses from the theory and to incorporate some of the findings from current research, moving toward a refinement of the theory.

THE THEORY SUMMARIZED

a. Man possesses an acquired motive to evaluate his abilities.
b. To evaluate one's abilities, it is necessary to make a comparison between at least two elements: a person's performance, and some other standard.
c. When at least one other individual is in a position to evaluate, the comparison process becomes a social comparison process.
d. When the criterion for comparison is known by the evaluator, a social comparison process becomes a competitive process.
e. The evaluation in a competitive process may lead to positive, neutral, or negative evaluations.
f. The perceived potential for evaluation of the performer is arousing. Competition elicits arousal because the competitive process always has the potential for evaluation.
g. Positive evaluation will reduce arousal and increase satisfaction; negative evaluation will increase arousal and dissatisfaction.
h. If inequity in the outcome/input ratio between the comparisons is perceived, the evaluation will be neutralized, and the inequity will be arousing.
i. After the competitive process, if arousal has been heightened by negative evaluation or by perception of inequity, the individual will act to reduce it.

SOME RELATED HYPOTHESES

1. As one's ability increases, in order to evaluate the ability, an individual will move toward competition.
2. When initially learning a skill, individuals will prefer to evaluate their ability in noncompetitive situations; as the skill becomes learned, they will prefer to evaluate their ability in competitive situations.
3. As one's ability increases, an individual will prefer to compete with individuals of similar ability.
4. When extrinsic rewards for success in competition are large, the

individual will prefer an opponent that poses a smaller threat to his success.

5. The motive for evaluation through a competitive process will be reduced if the consequences are continually dissatisfying.
6. Success in competition will strengthen the motive for further evaluation through competition.
7. Individuals who are highly motivated to achieve success will have a stronger motive for comparison through competition than individuals who are highly motivated to avoid failure.
8. Individuals who are highly motivated to achieve success prefer individual sports more than those who are motivated to avoid failure.
9. The greater the consequence of the comparison, the more arousing the competition.
10. Temporarily, competition becomes increasingly arousing as the evaluation of the comparison nears.
11. Individuals have greater interpersonal attraction for those near their own ability level.
12. There is an inverted U relationship between the intensity of competition and the quality of performance.
13. If the reward for positive evaluation is high, the tendency to observe inequity toward oneself increases, while the tendency to observe inequity toward the referent individual decreases.
14. The existence of disparate abilities in a group will lead to action on the part of members of that group to reduce the disparity.

REFERENCES

Adams, J. S.
    1965   "Inequity in Social Exchange." In Berkowitz, L., ed. *Advances in Experimental Social Psychology*. New York: Academic Press. Pp. 267–299.
Church, R. M.
    1968   "Applications of Behavior Theory to Social Psychology: Imitation and Competition." In Simmel, E. C.; Hoppe, R. A.; and Milton, G. A., eds. *Social Facilitation and Imitative Behavior*. Boston: Allyn and Bacon. Pp. 135–168.
Cottrell, N. B.
    1968   "Performance in the Presence of Other Human Beings, Mere Presence, Audience, and Affiliation Effects." In Simmel, E. C.; Hoppe, R. A.; and Milton, G. A., eds. *Social Facilitation and Imitative Behavior*. Boston: Allyn and Bacon. Pp. 91–110.
Deutsch, M.
    1949   "A Theory of Cooperation and Competition." *Human Relations* 2:129–152.

Duffy, E.
1962   *Activation and Behavior*. New York: John Wiley and Sons.
Festinger, L. A.
1954   "A Theory of Social Comparison Processes." *Human Relations* 7:117–140.
Lowe, R.
1973   "Stress, Arousal and Task Performance of Little League Baseball Players." Ph.D. dissertation. Urbana: University of Illinois.
Malmo, R. B.
1959   "Activation: A Neuropsychological Dimension." *Psychological Review* 66:367–386.
Martens, R.
1969   "Effect of an Audience on Learning and Performance of a Complex Motor Skill." *Journal of Personality and Social Psychology* 12:252–260.
————, and Landers, D. M.
1972   "Evaluation Potential as a Determinant of Coaction Effects." *Journal of Experimental Social Psychology* 8:347–359.
May, M. A., and Doob, L.
1937   "Competition and Cooperation." Washington, D.C.: National Social Science Research Council. Bulletin no. 25. April.
McClelland, D. C.
1961   *The Achieving Society*. Princeton: D. Van Nostrand.
Myers, A. E.
1961   "The Effect of Team Competition and Success on the Adjustment of Group Members." Ph.D. dissertation. Urbana: University of Illinois.
Pettigrew, T. F.
1967   "Social Evaluation Theory: Consequences and Applications. In Levine, D., ed. *Nebraska Symposium on Motivation*. Lincoln: University of Nebraska Press. Pp. 241–318.
White, R. W.
1959   "Motivation Reconsidered: The Concept of Competence." *Psychological Review* 66:297–334.
Zajonc, R.
1965   "Social Facilitation." *Science* 149:269–274.

The Social Context of Competition

CAROLYN W. SHERIF

Confession of ignorance may be a step toward wisdom. Let me confess, then: I am ignorant about the field of sports and recreation. With colleagues in psychology and other social sciences, I share great information gaps about the effects of competition on children, for gaps exist in research into these problems.

It may be, however, that if we start naively, vision unclouded by preconceptions, we can avoid blind alleys that lure the sophisticated—in this case, those knowledgeable of all the pros and cons about various sports and recreation programs, philosophies, or the virtues and hazards of specific sports. Our view is guided, instead, by research on competitive processes among children. Assuredly, the consequences of severely strenuous activity on children should be a major preoccupation for physiologists, to determine whether or not children at any age are engaging in activities so strenuous as to be detrimental to their physical growth and development.

But let us be candid. Most discussions of competition among children do not concern the strenuousness of activity; they concern the social-psychological effects of competition on the developing human personality. Furthermore, such discussions too frequently bog down in irreconcilable controversy after the first few words are spoken. The participants almost always start with preconceived judgments about the effects of competition that no amount of talk can alter. To some, competition is regarded as natural, healthy, and essential for building character. To others competition is regarded as harmful, psychologically injurious, and detrimental to cooperative activity, which is endowed with all manner of beneficial effects and seen as the highest state of human relations. The person who butts into such controversies with simple-minded observations (such as the terrifying consequences for social life if everyone competed all of the time, or the obvious fact that cooperative activities are integral to anything from a good ball game

Carolyn W. Sherif is professor of psychology at Pennsylvania State University.

to a ghastly war) is regarded as a maverick who just does not get the point.

The point of such controversies is, of course, that the proponents have axes to grind. Their arguments are tools to support schemes of social arrangements—political, economic, or even recreational. Serious analysis of competitive processes involving children has no place for such ax-grinding. First, bias inevitably hampers viable research into a sorely neglected problem of major importance in child development. Second, it prevents planning for the most felicitous contexts for the development of human personality. But do-or-die defenders of competition or of cooperation are seldom as interested in such plans as they are in defending their own assumptions.

Try to find an instance of competition that does not involve cooperation with someone. Try to find an instance of cooperation, either within a group or with another group, that involves no competitive activity. According to the dictionary, competition stems from the Latin verb meaning "to seek together." In the most general sense, therefore, competition implies its supposed obverse: cooperation.

Trying as best we can to proceed without prejudgments, our task is to examine and to study the effects of competitive processes by inquiring into the *social context* in which children come together to seek, and then to examine, the effects of such contexts on the psychological outcomes of competition.

An occupational hazard of being a professor is to gain the comfortable feeling that a high-sounding definition of a problem solves the problem. At the risk of being so interpreted, a characterization of competition is here proposed because it seems conducive to our task, and because it will permit us to integrate a variety of research findings related to that task. *Competition consists of activities directed more or less consistently toward meeting a standard or achieving a goal in which performance by a person or by his group is compared and evaluated relative to that of selected other persons or groups.*

A few words of clarification will permit us to proceed to the major points in this discussion. The clarification consists of emphasizing two words in the characterization of competition. *Consistently* emphasizes patterns of activity that, with no more than occasional diversion, weave toward a standard or goal. *Selected other persons or groups* implies that consistent patterns of activity are not compared to or assessed by everybody, or by just anybody. By its very definition, competitive activity implies a social context involving *certain* other people and a selective process determining who they are or shall be.

Research bearing on the social context of competition and its effects will be summarized in the remainder of this paper. In brief, the themes of the successive sections are as follows:

1. Very young children cannot compete; competition develops during socialization in a specific social context.

2. Competitive processes and their outcomes vary according to the structure of standards and goals which, in turn, differs enormously from culture to culture, group to group, sex to sex, and even sport to sport.

3. Aspiration levels, achievement, success or failure and their psychological consequences depend upon the social context of the competitive process, the effective social context consisting both of the structure of standards and goals and of those persons and groups who count for the child.

4. Since they neglect the social context, most research models for studying effects of competition, particularly in sports, are inadequate and probably misleading.

5. Research specifically analyzing the social context of competition over time indicates that the psychological consequences for the child generalize far beyond the specific competitive activities themselves.

By analyzing the effective social context of competitive processes, alternative plans are suggested, conducive to the widest realization of human potentialities.

In discussing each of these themes, I shall be summarizing large bodies of specific research, without embroidering the discussion with copious footnotes and references. The reader with serious research interests may find ample documentation and references in Sherif and Sherif, *Social Psychology* (1969: esp. Chs. 6, 7, 11, 12, 17, 18, 19), and in my *Orientation in Social Psychology* (forthcoming).

CHILDREN LEARN TO COMPETE

Very young children cannot compete in the sense defined here. The capacity to direct behavior consistently toward an abstract standard for performance or a distant goal develops only with age and, as Piaget has suggested, through interaction with peers. Through such interaction, especially with peers who lack the overwhelming power of adults to impose standards for behavior, the child develops the ability and the desire to attain some defined level of performance or to reach a goal that does not automatically follow a short-time sequence of action ("a cookie after you eat the spinach"). Competition involves goals that are remote in time, carry abstract reward value, and are only probably attainable.

This does not mean that little children don't play, run, throw balls, swim, wrestle, hit, kick, suffer disappointments, or bask in the warm glow of approval. Infants treat one another much as objects, but soon learn games such as "I hand the toy to you and you hand it back, and I hand it to you," and so forth. Young children's play is solitary or side by side. Interaction has little to do with improving the actual performance underway. In fact, studies have shown that the presence of another child in an activity intended by adults to be competitive may actually lower performance level. The pleasure of each other's company takes precedence over sticking to the business at hand.

Usually during the preschool years, the child becomes capable and often absorbed in role-playing games—house, cowboys and Indians, war, or (as I overheard in my own neighborhood a few years ago) "let's kill Bobby Kennedy." They have reached a new level of play. They can take the roles of others, switch roles, follow and even change the rules. The play begins to take on the outward appearance of competition as the children bicker over who gets to be mommy, daddy and baby; who gets to be on the side of the good guys and who has to be bad, all the time with each side attempting to escape or bang-bang the other dead. Seldom is such play competitive in the sense defined, or in the sense that an adult intervening to set criteria for winning or losing will have much success.

Of course, the young child will respond to praise and correction in an activity that is enjoyable, such as throwing a ball or running. He responds when that praise or correction comes from an adult, older brother or sister, or playmate whose words, smiles, and frowns count a great deal in his young life. But in these early preschool years, behavior directed consistently toward attaining a standard or reaching a goal to be compared with the performance of others is only an occasional happening. You may have heard, as I did, young children playing a game in which the rules specify winning in terms of speed, time, accuracy, or the like. The winner announced "I won," whereupon another child joyously proclaimed "I won too." Then, with the pronouncement "We all won," the children turned to another concern—in this case, a devout hope that the ice cream man would soon be on their block.

Ordinarily, by about the age of six in our society, a child can and does compete. Still, the consistency of competitive behaviors varies enormously. Research has shown, for example, that middle-class children with schoolteacher and business parents compete consistently at an earlier age than children of working-class families. Perhaps even more important for our theme, the quality and persistence in competition depends upon the nature of the activity and its significance to the child. This point was driven home to me recently by an experienced recreation major at Pennsylvania State University, who expressed regret that she had not fully considered the developmental processes in competition. Working with second graders (seven-year-olds), she organized a relay race. The children were quite mature enough to grasp the rules and to understand the criterion for victory. They had a wonderful time running the relays, followed the rules, but they couldn't have cared less who won. As a result, the relays were a fun game but a shambles from the viewpoint of anything that might be called competition.

Several implications emerge from this brief account of the development of competition among children. First, the capacity to direct behavior consistently toward abstract standards or remote, uncertain goals in which one's behavior is compared and evaluated relative to others develops with age. The crucial evidence supporting this conclusion stems from a body of research showing that not only consistently competitive behavior, but also consistently cooperative behavior, consistent helping behavior, consistent sympathetic actions at the distress of others, and—most unfortunately—consistent prejudicial hostility toward groups traditionally discriminated against in our society all emerge at about the same period in the child's development.

Second, the process of development occurs in a social context in which parents, siblings, and peers are very important in providing the medium for testing one's own performance and for learning the reciprocal nature of rules and standards. Recreation leaders and teachers are important—but all of these significant figures are surrounded, like it or not, by a cultural context that is at least equally significant for the child's development. How else are we to understand the earliest buds of competition in rivalry over who gets to be father or mother, in divisions into good guys and bad guys for bang-bang conflict when the good guys and bad guys are precisely those whom the children meet in storybooks and on television? Evidence indicates that the social context for competition is crucial; if so, it is utter nonsense to speak of "born winners and born losers." There are, and always will be, individual differences. But the winners and the losers are shaped in a variety of ways by their social context, at times obviously and at others more subtly. It is more accurate to state that winners and losers are made by their experiences in a social context of other people who, to a major degree, determine the targets for their efforts and the structure of standards and goals related to those efforts.

Finally, the social context in which competitive behavior develops affects not only its rate of development but also the targets for competition—that is, what is important to the child and what can be left to the birds. In this country, at a very early age boys learn that sports of various kinds are *the* avenue for recognition to a far greater extent than girls. As a result some boys are placed in untenable situations psychologically, and many girls simply fail to persist in sufficient physical activity to develop strong and healthy bodies. We need to inquire into the variations in the social context that may produce strikingly different outcomes in what is regarded as important for competition and the behavioral outcomes of the competitive process.

DIFFERENCES IN THE NATURE AND STRUCTURE OF STANDARDS AND GOALS

Particularly in a society such as ours, it is important to recognize that the nature of activities deemed important enough to warrant competition and the structure of the relevant standards and goals differ from culture to culture, group to group, sex to sex, and even sport to sport. Too frequently we assume that what is worthy of competition (the "good life," in our terms—athletics to build body and character) is and should be a universal norm and ideal. In fact it is not. Consideration of such differences may reveal some failings in our own society and suggest guidelines in planning for needed changes.

It is commonplace to point out that societies differ enormously in the prizes they offer for different activities, including sports and recreation. What is not so obvious is that societies that prize physical activity and health need not place enormous value on organized competitive sports. In some societies, physical fitness is prized for everyone and may be encouraged through universal physical activity, including work as well as fun and games. In others, excellence in sports is prized but rewarded indirectly through extra time for practice, opportunity to instruct, while those most outstanding are expected to be self-effacing in directing their efforts to the general improvement of physical well-being rather than personal aggrandizement and public acclaim.

Let us look at our own society. Sports compose a major value complex that the child encounters at an early age, especially if he happens to be male. Furthermore, sport is defined as competition to win. For the individual, the aim is to make the first team and, at all costs, to be on the winning team. If the varsity is winning, there is consolation even in being second or third or fourth string. Barring any of these positions, it is the rare boy who does not become absorbed as spectator of amateur and professional athletics, which may well mean that his own physical activity is limited to walking to the school bus or riding a motorbike. In our own extensive research on informal groups of adolescent boys studied in their natural habitats between 1958 and 1970 in the southwestern and eastern United States, we found only one group of teenage boys with no visible interest in sports. These were sons of recent Mexican immigrants of peasant origin. Other Chicano youths in the same city were intensely interested in sports: with the hope of making a team, one group even entered a high school reputed for its magnificent athletic teams but located halfway across the city of San Antonio. While their relatively small stature precluded this goal, the youths actually stuck to that school through thick and thin, working to maintain passing grades and walking a couple of miles back and forth each day—all for the pride of identification with those glorious winners.

With girls it is different. After about the age of twelve, they quickly learn that actual participation in sports brings little glory. Their claim to fame comes through feminine attachment to the male team members, the booster clubs, or—thrill of all thrills—being a cheerleader. We will refer to girls again in the next section. Here it is sufficient to note that, in the past, their recognition in sports came chiefly from swimming, diving, ice skating, and other such graceful (hence lady-like) activities.

Among the so-called minority groups, excepting the rare Jim Thorpes, it has been primarily the blacks who have warmed their hearts through embracing the sports complex. How long and difficult has been the struggle of those pioneers who finally made it in the terms dictated by the dominant white sports complex! Black stars and superstars register their resentment at the second-class status that plagues our black citizens, even sports demi-gods. We may well sympathize, protest, and support their efforts to alter what is but one system of a dominant-subordinate relationship that permeates our national life. However, in analyzing competition in the lives of children as the sports complex is presently organized, there are issues of larger import that affect the average boy and girl regardless of race.

These larger issues center around the extreme importance attributed to organized competitive sports in our society, and the structure of goals integral to that organization. Of course, our more intelligent, confident, and successful sports educators realize that there are problems. Joe Paterno, the Penn State football coach, has said, "I don't think society would fold up if football would disappear"; he has even declared that he sees no excuse for extramural competitive sports before the high school level. He can say such things; but, as an outsider, I cannot do likewise without risking all sorts of disapprobation. This in itself is testimony to the power, prestige, and exclusiveness of the sports complex as now organized.

As a social psychologist I can, however, point to the structure of the goals that create problems in personal development for large numbers of young people. At present, the goal structure is a win-lose (or, if you wish, zero-sum) game. The aim is to win, thereby utterly defeating the opponent. This goal structure is clear enough in organized team sports; it is equally clear in the path that the individual child must take to succeed. He (or occasionally she) must gain exclusive hegemony over all competitors for the available slots on the team.

The tragedy for black youth is not that the sport complex encourages physical activity and the improvement of skills: it is that, with a few other exceptions (music, for example), the goal structure of sports provides the major, if not the only, means for him to improve his lot. Those who do not make the first string, and do not get courted for scholarships or pro teams, are assigned to perdition if they retain their devotion to the sports complex. Someone ought to question the long-range human consequences of failing in the sports lottery, both for black and for white children. How many of those hooked on the sports complex, with all their devotion of time and energy as second- and third-string players or water boys or cheerleaders, might be first-rate politicians, writers, scientists, mechanics, artists, musicians, electronic technicians, or piano tuners if the structure of goals and social support even began to approach the compelling structure of organized sports? How many useful citizens with dreams that could become realities have lost those dreams in the hours and hours of trying, hoping, sitting, and waiting to compete in sports with "I win—you lose" goal structure?

To contend that the prevailing structure of goals is necessary, normal, or natural can be countered even within the sphere of sports and recreation activities. The win-lose, beat-everyone-out-for-the-best-slot complex may indeed be characteristic of much of American life. But it is not true in many sports activities—mountain climbing, fishing, jogging, backpacking, nature hiking, many water sports, some snow sports, modern and folk dancing, calisthenics, and a good many others. Enjoyment or even excellence in golf or tennis is not dependent on the win-lose law of the organized sports jungle.

I am concerned that more children become actively involved in sports and recreation activities for both health and pleasure. I resent the undeniable fact that somewhere early in my own development I ended up out of sports activities, feeling inadequate and therefore unworthy of trying. I would like to see sports and recreation activities a part of my life and the lives of our children. Let us learn from social-psychological research just what psychological processes are involved in the effects of competition among childen.

PSYCHOLOGICAL EFFECTS OF COMPETITION DEPEND ON ITS SOCIAL CONTEXT

Competitive activities refer to performance that is compared to standards set by certain other persons, and to the assessment of performance by certain other persons. These reference standards and persons, along with the structure of goals awarded to the competitors, are the effective social context of the competitive process.

The psychological effects of the competitive process can readily be inferred from the substantial body of literature on levels of aspiration and the experiences of success and failure. Experiencing success or failure is always relative to standards to which the child aspires. Like it or not, these standards are influenced decisively by significant adults, peers, and the images portrayed through the mass media of communication. Thus the child is seldom entirely free to establish a standard that fits his interests and abilities. He cannot remain immune to the judgments of parents, teachers, and peers in setting the level of his aspiration for performance.

Long ago William James defined the experiences of success or failure in relative terms, as the ratio between one's actual performance and his pretensions or aspirations in that field of activity. Much later Kurt Lewin, F. Hoppe, J. D. Frank, and others initiated research into the relationship between aspiration level and performance. Several findings from this substantial body of research have definite implications for the effects of competition.

First, in a given activity, there is a strong tendency to maintain the same level of aspiration regardless of actual performance. Experiences of failure are in a sense inevitable on those occasions when performance falls below the standard. This failure to adjust one's standards to actual performance (or, if you like, this rigidity of the aspiration level) is typical both of the performer and of others with personal investment in his performance. For example, in a study I conducted some years ago with children and their parents in a dart-throwing task, the parents tended to maintain a rigid aspiration level for their children, as did the children for themselves, regardless of actual performance.

Although this may not be true for the professional athlete, the child's aspiration is typically set at a level that has the peculiar and unfortunate effect of assuring the better performer more frequent experiences of success than the child whose performance is average or below. Typically, the more adequate performer sets his aspiration level slightly below his performance level and keeps it there. The average or less adequate performer, on the other hand, sets a standard considerably above his typical level of performance, thereby practically insuring a continuing sense of failure and frustration. Improvement in performance, therefore, has quite different psychological meaning for the child who is able and the child who has less aptitude.

The level at which standards of performance for an activity are set by adults or older children reflects a social norm that may or may not be realistic for the developmental level and skills of the child. Many years ago Dwight Chapman and John Volkmann, then later Leon Festinger and a number of other researchers, used carefully designed experiments to show what happens when performance is compared to that of a group too advanced or too low for the person's actual potentialities. Quite simply, if the person is told the expected level of performance for a group that he considers inferior in a specific activity, he raises the standard for his own performance. However, if the comparison group is one that he regards as superior to his own, his aspiration level is sharply lowered. An adult who holds up the performance level of the varsity high school team as a standard to sixth graders may inspire the exceptional few to work harder, but the majority will simply lower the level to which they aspire. Similarly, as Joe Paterno remarked in *Football My Way*, the standards of professional sports may instigate great efforts from the ambitious few, but for most players such standards simply remove the fun of sports by producing an aspiration level recognized as inferior, hence offering little joy when it is attained.

Thus far, the summary of research on aspiration levels and performance has been abstracted from recognition of actual attainments. Of course, this is not the case. As N. T. Feather has shown, consistent improvement in skill is tracked by consistent raising of the standard set for one's performance. Conversely, consistent trends toward decreasingly adequate performance are tracked by lowering of one's expectations. This may happen to even the best athlete when he begins to lose his stride. Much more significant for young children, however, is Feather's finding that the aspiration level tends to be maintained rigidly at a high level when the actual level of performance over time is fluctuating and least predictable. This state of affairs is highly probable for the young child, whose performance is likely to vary considerably from day to day or week to week, with the result that the child faces the continuing hazard of experiencing failure for reasons that are seldom clear to him or her.

The effects of continuing experiences of success or failure in young children have been documented, notably beginning with the research of Pauline Sears. The child who experiences success at a level approved and rewarded by significant adults and peers is able to tolerate an occasional failure or an "off day," recognizing it as such. But the child whose persistent experiences are defined as less than successful, or as failures, suffers considerably from a temporary drop and the resulting disapproval from persons significant in his or her eyes. Over time, the level of aspiration set for performance drops lower and lower, and pretensions may even vanish altogether. The child simply stops trying.

The outcomes summarized above certainly have import for the planning of sports and recreation programs. Currently, the great emphasis on interscholastic competition, varsity sports, and professionalism means that the vast majority of children are doomed to be very small frogs in enormous pools. Surely, for the developing human personality, it is important to create pools in which most children can have the experience of growing and gaining because they were not pressured to maintain a constantly rising aspiration level.

The problem suggested is compounded tenfold when we focus specifically on girls' sports and recreations. As girls approach adolescence, the double standard emerges with a vengeance. The little girl who is active and skilled may be called a tomboy, but she need not suffer unduly except from the scorn of boys who don't want a girl tagging around. If her skills are directed toward sports such as water ballet, ice skating, diving, or gymnastics, she can make it through early adolescence and beyond without detracting from what she and many of her peers and adults think of as feminine. But if these graceful and accepted feminine activities are not her forte, she faces a dilemma: be typed by peers as one of those athletic oddballs, or drop out. The vast majority choose the latter course, to the great misfortune of their health, physical development, and future enjoyment. They even develop (in the sense used by Matina Horner in her doctoral thesis) a *fear* of success. If you play tennis and like it, go ahead and play, but not too well—certainly not so well that you beat male opponents.

The girl who remains devoted and who persists during her adolescent years in improving her skills in "unfeminine" sports faces a situation analogous psychologically to that of the successful black athlete. (I emphasize the psychological effects, because the sociological causes and consequences are quite different.) By striving toward and attaining a high level of performance, she experiences success in one respect but faces failure in others—namely, in those spheres traditionally defined as feminine. For the successful black athlete, of course, this impossible feat of high self-esteem and sense of accomplishment in sports is accompanied by the denial of rights and privileges that should be available to any athlete of attainment. For the female athlete in "unfeminine" spheres, the denial is psychologically painful, but perhaps less important from an educational and sociological point of view than the statistically more frequent fact that girls simply lose interest in sports, drop out, or try hard not to succeed too well. Let me enter a plea to those involved in the improvement of the status and quality of girls' physical activity. Their opportunities should be enhanced. More girls should enter and continue in sports. However, please do not fall into the traps already set by the structure of boys' sports. In achieving greater opportunity for girls, please do not merely imitate the existing male models. The task is not to imitate, but to innovate. Who knows; perhaps the boys' sports programs will be altered to imitate the new female programs.

THE INADEQUACY OF TYPICAL RESEARCH MODELS FOR STUDYING EFFECTS OF COMPETITION

As a researcher, I shall be brief and harsh in commenting on most research available on the effects of competition in sports. Too frequently the social context of competition is ignored in the research design. It is unnecessary to cast blame for this state of affairs on researchers in sports, recreation, or the sociology thereof. My point can be made from an entirely different problem area.

Consider the vast bulk of research on juvenile delinquents. Much of this research studies a sample of youth labeled as delinquents by legal authorities (and hence by their peers, school, families, and communities) and compares certain of their personal characteristics or social relationships with those of a sample labeled nondelinquents (because legal authorities have not so labeled them). In good research procedure, one matches the two samples in certain important respects, such as socioeconomic class, sex, family size or status, etc. Almost invariably, some differences are found between the two samples—usually differences that make the nondelinquent sample seem better adjusted, better students, and so forth. I am not saying that such findings are invalid; I am saying that such a research design tells us nothing at all about why the delinquent sample became labeled delinquent, why they differ from the nondelinquents, or, for that matter, why the nondelinquents are nondelinquents.

To make the point clear, let us design studies by this model in which we could show that those who engage in sports to a significant extent do not exhibit superior personal characteristics and social skills. Select a school that, for any reason, deemphasizes competitive sports and strongly emphasizes the arts, scholarship, or scientific investigation. Compare a sample of athletes in that school with non-athletes. Or, in almost any large high school, compare the girl members of the basketball or hockey teams with a sample of nonmembers. It is highly probable that the students who are not athletes would come out looking better adjusted, more sociable, and with certain more desirable personal characteristics.

This small exercise is intended to emphasize that research into competitive sports must consider the social context as a part of the research design and must trace, over time, its role in the competitive process and its effects. For this reason Thomas D. McIntyre's "Field Experimental Study of Cohesiveness, Status, and Attitude Change in Four Biracial Small Sport Groups" (Ph.D. dissertation, Pennsylvania State University, 1970) should be read seriously by researchers. While he did not find (as he had quite frankly hoped) that participation on interracial teams greatly altered the attitudes of blacks and whites toward one another, he did discover a great deal about the effects of the social context in inhibiting and permitting the formation of biracial teams, about the development of group and team organization, about the formation of friendships across racial lines, and about the competitive process. Any researcher interested in the effects of competition, for good or for evil, must undertake investigations that include the social context and study the competitive process over time. There simply are no shortcuts or easy answers to our questions in this regard. Meanwhile, our traditional cross-sectional studies comparing selected samples of athletic participants and nonparticipants will continue to tell us that conformity to and success in a highly valued activity ordinarily brings rewards and felicitous personal experiences.

PROLONGED COMPETITION ON WIN-LOSE BASIS GENERALIZES BEYOND THE GAME

In his writings on the "split-level American family" and on the goal structures that pit child against child, age group against age group, and social group against social group, Urie Bronfenbrenner of Cornell University has made it poignantly clear that we have neglected to take the broad view of the effects of competition on children. Both he and other social psychologists who have commented on childhood in general (in contrast to simply analyzing the child at home, or the child at school, or the child in sports as though the child's development were split into compartments) have illustrated some of their main points through a series of experiments directed by Muzafer Sherif (see Ch. 11 in *Social Psychology*).

In three separate experiments conducted in natural circumstances in summer camps, Sherif and his associates demonstrated that prolonged competition on a win-lose basis between groups of children had effects that extended far beyond the specific context of the games played. It should be emphasized that these experiments used sports as a medium for prolonged competition, not as the butt of criticism. The participants in each case were American boys about twelve years old to whom sports were already of central interest, along with camping and outdoor recreational activities. To compete in sports was not only a natural but also a highly desirable activity.

The camps were organized by research personnel and arranged over time so that the structure of goals between groups of boys were systematically changed to study, first, the effects of prolonged win-lose competition and, second, the change of those effects in more creative directions. For this reason I believe that they have definite implications for the possibilities of planning and programming in sports and recreational activities.

For reasons of theory and hypothesis testing, which need not be our main concern here, the participants in each of the three experiments were carefully selected to be unacquainted with each other at the outset, well adjusted in school and on the playground, and members of stable middle-class families of similar religious and ethnic backgrounds. The choice of such a homogeneous bunch of typical, normal American boys permitted us to rule out explanations of the results of their inter-action on such possible bases as their being already unduly frustrated, insecure, poor losers, or divided by striking differences in background when they came to the camp.

Research personnel all functioned in the roles of regular camp per-sonnel, securing the research data through a variety of unobtrusive research techniques that insured that the boys were not aware that their words and deeds were being studied, and that conclusions were not based selectively on events that supported the research hypotheses. (In brief, the latter was accomplished by using a combination of re-search methods, the outcome of some being beyond the researchers' control, and then basing conclusions on these converging sources of data.) While the boys did not know that they were being constantly studied, their parents were aware of the study nature of the camps. All possible safeguards, including medical precautions, were taken to in-sure the boys' safety and welfare.

Since the research concerned group competition, the first stage (about a week in each case) focused on group formation. The selected participants were divided arbitrarily into two bunches, matched as closely as possible in terms of size, skills, and interest. The sole condi-tions for activities, most of which were actually chosen by the boys themselves, were that they focus on interaction within the developing groups and that they encourage activities requiring that all members participate actively in order to reach their goal, enjoy themselves, or whatever state of affairs described the satisfactory outcome of the ac-tivity. For example, to use a canoe left by their cabin, the boys had to figure out a way to transport it through the woods. Or, when very hungry, they were given food in bulk form—ground beef, uncut buns, a watermelon, unmixed powdered drinks—whose transformation into a meal required their division of labor and cooperation.

In each case two groups formed; each group had little contact with the other and, in the last experiment, neither group actually knew of the existence of another group in camp. The groups had distinctive organizations (leader-follower relations) and norms (customs, pre-ferred territory, nicknames for members, and names for themselves). One group developed a complex of norms centering around tough, brave masculinity that flinched at no danger and willingly endured dis-comfort, while the other (closely matched initially on an individual-by-individual basis) developed its little culture in a fashion that forbade swearing, emphasized moral uplift, and encouraged regular prayer.

The goal structure in which these groups first met was transformed to a win-lose structure very naturally when they discovered each other's presence and asked to compete in organized sports. A tournament of games was organized to accede to this request and "make it more fun"; highly attractive prizes were available for the winning group. The tournament lasted for several days, including a variety of sports events selected by the boys plus a few (tent-pitching, cabin inspection, etc.) that permitted the research personnel to keep the cumulative scores of events close to the very end. This particular structure of highly desirable goals that one group could attain only at the expense of the other's loss had a number of effects that far exceeded the bounds of the sports competition itself.

As good American boys and experienced competitors, the games started in the spirit of good sportsmanship, graceful winning and losing. However, they quickly turned into vicious contests in which the sole aim was to win and in which the competitors became increasingly seen as a bunch of incorrigible cheats, quite outside the pale of that brand of humanity identified within one's group. (In the experiment mentioned, in which the culture of one group was toughness and the other of piety, this outcome applied equally to both groups, regardless of the difference in their norms for internal group behavior.)

The prolonged competition between groups had a decided impact on the leader-follower relations, norms, and focal concerns within each group. The daily concern was developing strategy and tactics to defeat the other group. Leaders or other high-status members who shrank from the intense forms of conflict that developed were replaced; erstwhile bullies who had been "put in their place" within their own groups now became heroes of combat.

Outside the athletic competition, and against adult rulings, raids and acts of aggression were organized by the boys themselves. Such acts included messing up the rival's cabin, painting derogatory slogans on the stolen blue jeans of the opponent's leader—"The Last of the Eagles"—and hoarding small green apples to be used "in case" of attack by the other group.

Upon the victory of one group in the tournament, boys in each group possessed attitudes of extreme prejudice and hostility, universally condemning the individual characters of members of their rival group. In fact, each wanted nothing at all to do with the other group.

Appeals to moral values ("love thy enemy") had no effect at all at this point. In religious services organized separately by each group, the local minister conveyed such messages and appeals in forms which the boys appreciated and understood—but immediately afterward they turned to renewed cursing of their opponents.

Cohesiveness, solidarity, self-initiated responsibility, and democratic procedures greatly increased within each group during the conflict. However, the norms of brotherhood and supporting one's fellows which were so strikingly apparent within each group did not apply to the other group. Democratic procedure, loyalty, and friendship at home need not be transferred to the treatment of those not within the magic bounds of one's own group or team.

In the experiments, several changes in goal structure were tried in the attempt to change this dismal state of affairs. First, there was a series of events that were highly appealing to each group separately (common goals) and in which they had to participate together as equals. However, these contact situations involved no interdependence between the groups. Each could eat the greatly improved food, shoot July Fourth fireworks, use new sports equipment, see a movie, etc., side by side without so much as speaking to the other group. In fact, they did speak. While they conducted their affairs separately, they used these contact situations as opportunities for recriminations, for accusations of "who's to blame" for the existing state of affairs, for hurling invectives, and when food was present, for "garbage wars" that had to be stopped when the weapons changed from mashed potatoes and paper to forks and knives.

The change that was effective, over time, in altering the generalized state of hostility and aggression created from prolonged win-lose competition was the introduction of a series of goals, each profoundly appealing to each group but whose attainment required the participation and the resources of both groups. To distinguish these from merely "common" goals, they were termed "superordinate goals": goals urgently desired by each group but unattainable without cooperation. In the first study, this condition took the form of a "common enemy." A team from another camp competed with teams selected from both of the rival groups. The short-term effects of this common enemy were to induce cooperation for "our camp" to beat theirs. However, when the common enemy was gone, the two rivals quickly retreated to their own in-groups, still unwilling to cooperate in other activities across group lines. Further, had we continued the "common enemy" approach, we would have ended by merely enlarging the scope of the generalized effects of win-lose competition that had already occurred within our camp. In effect, we would have had a bigger war.

The superordinate goals that were effective were problem situations —an apparent breakdown in the water system at a time when outside help was not immediately available; how to get another movie when the camp was short on funds and neither group had enough canteen funds left to sponsor a movie alone; a stalled Mack truck that was the sole vehicle to go for food when everyone was hungry and which was far too large for one group to push or pull alone; food preparation at a time when everyone was very hungry, even though "separate but equal" facilities were available but less efficient; tent pitching when all were tired and when the poles and stakes had somehow gotten all mixed up.

Such superordinate goal structures did not have an immediate effect on the hostility between the groups. They induced immediate cooperation, which dissipated into separate exclusiveness once the goal had been achieved. It required a series of such goals over time for a genuine and lasting change in the relationships between the groups to occur. Such a series of superordinate goals was effective; the boys not only learned to cooperate with each other as groups, but also took initiative to do so on their own. Over time, their views of the other group's immorality and ruthlessness were altered. They learned to take turns in camp activities and actually initiated campfire entertainments in which each group alternated presenting the best and funniest of their talent.

Between the alternative structures of win-lose conflict and superordinate goals, there are many other possibilities. I offer the results of these experiments to stimulate thinking, planning and, I hope, revising of the programs of the sports and recreational competitions in which our children participate. The advantage of superordinate goals, when these are genuine for each group (not imposed by adults), is that other measures which have been tried, often vainly, to keep competitive outcomes within bounds are transformed. Information is exchanged across group lines; friendships can form; leaders of groups can initiate new programs and actions without fear of being called traitors by their own groups; the creative potentials of the groups are given the broadest possible scope.

Particularly with young children in community and school contexts, the full understanding of the meaning and the potentialities of superordinate goal structures has the possibility for building competitive sports programs in which children learn the sorts of responsibility, loyalty, skilled efforts, practice, and teamwork that we believe build character, while avoiding some of the generalized consequences that accrue from competition in actual life. If seriously translated into action, these desirable and potentially fruitful experiences for development toward adulthood could create situations in which everyone can win—if not a total victory, at least enough to lift self-esteem, skills, and experiences that may universally benefit the bodies and minds of our youth. I leave the creation of superordinate goal structures to those who know much more than I about sports and recreation. I am convinced, however, that their planning requires not sheer individual genius, but cooperation and competition among those charged with such planning to produce the most effective and viable programs. I am further convinced that many of those so charged would find great joy in the experience of trying.

Backyard versus Little League Baseball:
The Impoverishment of Children's Games

EDWARD C. DEVEREUX

In this paper I shall focus on some consequences of young children's participation in highly competitive, adult-organized and promoted athletic programs such as Little League baseball, football, Pee Wee hockey, and interscholastic sports. My critique of Little League baseball and other such major sports programs for children will be based not so much upon what participation in such activities *does* for the children as upon what it does *not* do for them. I will argue that "Little Leaguism" is threatening to wipe out the spontaneous culture of free play and games among American children, and that it is therefore robbing our children not just of their childish fun but also of some of their most valuable learning experiences.

ON THE IMPOVERISHMENT OF CHILDREN'S GAMES IN AMERICA

One way to gain insight about what is happening to contemporary America is to look at ourselves in cross-cultural and historical perspective. I recently spent two months in Japan, carrying out a survey among Japanese schoolchildren. I spent as much time as I could observing children in informal play settings such as parks, neighborhood playgrounds, schoolyards, apartment courtyards, and city streets. What struck me most forcefully was the observation that Japanese children seemed to spend very little time just "hanging around"; whenever two or more children found themselves together, they seemed to move very quickly into some kind of self-organized but rule-oriented play. Though I made no formal inventory, I was impressed with the great variety and richness of the games I observed. Although the Japanese also have Little League baseball, most of the games I observed were carried out wholly without adult instigation or supervision.

On one occasion my wife and I observed a group of a dozen kindergarten children playing ring games in a public park. I had no doubt that

Edward C. Devereux is a professor in the department of human development and family studies, Cornell University.

these children were brought to the park by some teacher or adult super-visor, and I kept waiting for some adult to appear to structure the next game for them. But during the forty-five minutes we remained in the vicinity no adult ever approached or spoke to the children. Evidently the game repertory, the motivation to play, and the ability to organize and pace their own activities were well rooted in the children's own heads.

Later I went to Israel on another research project, and again I spent as much time as I could observing the informal play activities of the Israeli children. Here also I was impressed with the enormous variety of spontaneous games and play activities. On this, we also have some impressive research documentation in the work of the Israeli psycholo-gist Rivka Eifermann (1971a). In her study, a team of 150 observers recorded the play activities of 14,000 Israeli school children, in kib-butzim, moshavim, and cities, in schoolyards, playgrounds, and streets, over a two-year period. One result of this research was the compilation of an encyclopedia of over 2,000 games the children were observed to be playing, including many bewildering variants on such well-known games as soccer, tag, and hop scotch, as well as hundreds of less well-known games, also in endless variations (Eifermann 1971b). Most of these games were being played wholly without adult instigation or supervision.

Still more impressive is the monumental evidence compiled by Iona and Peter Opie, in their monograph on *Children's Games in Street and Playground* (1969), regarding the richness of spontaneous games among English children. These authors were able to identify, describe, and classify more than 2,500 different games which possess these com-mon elements: they are played spontaneously by English children with-out any adult leadership or instigation; they require no equipment whatever—not even a ball; and they are transmitted almost entirely in the oral culture of the children themselves. Most of them have been passed along among children for generations without ever having their "rules" written down, at least until the Opies turned their hands to the task. Indeed, these authors observed that children's games tend to suffer a rapid decline in interest and popularity when adults took an interest in them and began to promote them.

All this challenges us to raise the question: What has happened to the culture of children's games in America? Looking back to my own childhood some fifty years ago, I can recall literally dozens of games which we played regularly and with enthusiasm—puss in the corner, red rover, capture the flag, one-o-cat, statues, stealing sticks, blind man's buff, croquet, leap frog, duck on the rock, prisoner's base, and many, many more. No doubt some of these are still around, in vestigial form; but my impression is that I rarely see these, or other games like them, being played spontaneously by children. Those which are played seem to be adult-instigated and supervised, in schools, camps, or other organized play settings, or in party settings in homes. And even here, our game culture has become sadly impoverished. Ask any group of children what they did at a birthday party, and nine out of ten will say they pinned the tail on the donkey. Halloween? Bob for apples and tricks or treats! What ever happened to the tricks, incidentally? We have institutionalized and sterilized Halloween, and thereby killed most of its creativity and fun. It appears that our game culture has declined in richness and vitality from lack of use and from excessive adult supervision and control. "Come on, children, we're all going to play a game now!" "Do we *have* to?" You can almost hear the groans.

On these trends, there is also some research evidence in a fascinating study by Sutton-Smith and Rosenberg (1971). These authors compare game preferences of American children as documented in four different research studies spanning a period from the late 1890's to the late 1950's. Even though these four studies are not strictly comparable, certain general trends are impressively clear. The great variety of once-popular indoor and backyard skill games, such as croquet and quoits, have all declined in interest, to be replaced by the ubiquitous ping-pong. Leader games, such as Simon says, statues, and follow the leader, are now of little interest for boys. Chasing games, like tag, are now acceptable only to very little children. Central-person parlor games, such as hide the thimble, forfeits, and twenty questions, have mostly disappeared, as have the endless varieties of ring games, such as drop the handkerchief and London Bridge, and the team guessing and acting games like charades. Individual games of skill—remember mumblede peg?—are withering away. Virtually all of the undifferentiated team games, such as hare and hound, prisoner's base, etc., have either disappeared or declined in interest as boys have devoted more of their attention to a few major sports. And even here, the authors conclude, the range of choice has narrowed significantly: ". . . trends would indicate that boys are spending more and more time on fewer sports. Bowling, basketball, and football improve in rank positions, but all other sports decline. . . . This would appear to be further evidence of the increasing circumscription of the boy's play role" (p. 47).

How can we account for this apparently very real constriction in the game culture of American children? How do American children really spend their spare time? I am tempted to say that they are all out there on the baseball and football fields, or in the hockey rinks, participating according to season in the sports programs organized for them by schools and other adult sponsoring agencies. In fact, as we all know, several hundred thousand of them are doing just that—for example, as members of the now more than 40,000 Little League baseball teams. There can be no doubt that such team activities capture a very large share of these children's time and attention. In one study reported by Skubic (1956), for example, 81 out of 96 Little League players in the Santa Maria area "reported that half to most of their leisure time during the whole year is spent on baseball" (p. 102).

But even conceding that a very large absolute number of children now participate in such organized sports, the fact remains that the vast majority of children in the eight-to-twelve age range are not. What do they do instead? A great deal of unstructured, non-rule-oriented play: bike riding, for example, still ranks very high with both boys and girls. In American homes, toys, hobby kits, and various proprietary games such as Monopoly still find wide acceptance among children. Just hanging around and talking, or very informal horseplay with friends, now occupies a very large share of the typical preadolescent's time. Finally, and by far the most important, there is television watching, to which this age group now devotes some twenty hours per week.

The availability of a mass television audience has had a lot to do with the extraordinary ascendency of Big Leaguism in America, and, perhaps indirectly, of Little Leaguism as well. By focusing the attention of millions of viewers on a handful of major sports, and on the heroic teams and individual stars within them, we have converted ourselves to a nation of spectators. For most of us, sports are something to be watched, not played—at least not by amateurs.

Personally, I doubt that very many children in the eight-to-twelve age range are television sports addicts, though some undoubtedly are. But children surely perceive where their father's interests are focused, and by the age of ten or twelve they are well aware of the extraordinary payoff of success in major sports in America. They see how the star athletes are rewarded in college and high school sports, and how pleased their fathers are at any athletic achievements of their own. I suspect that Little Leaguism for elementary school children is fostered more by the parents than by the children themselves, though for some it falls on well-cultivated ground. Here is a chance to play at something really important that parents and adults generally seem to take very seriously.

Even for children who have no special interest or competence in any major sport (probably a majority of all children), or for those who are actually alienated by the whole subculture of organized, competitive sports, the model is still present and highly salient. Against the heroic, if perhaps somewhat myopic, standards of Big League or Little League sports, who would dare propose a simple game of puss in the corner, capture the flag, or red rover? Kid stuff, unworthy of the time and attention of any red-blooded American boy past the age of seven or eight!

ON THE EDUCATIONAL FUNCTIONS OF PLAY AND GAMES

Why should we care about what has been happening to the recreational and spare-time activities of our children? In approaching an answer to this question, I would like to say just a bit about the functions of games and informal play activities in childhood and comment specifically about the kinds of learning which may occur in spontaneous, self-organized children's games. I will then go on to assess how organized, adult-sponsored competitive sports stack up against this model.

But before turning to sociological or psychological analysis, let me try to give you some notion of the appeal and fun of games as they may appear to the children themselves. On this I can do no better than to quote a few passages from the Opies' account of play and games among English children:

> Play is unrestricted; games have rules. Play may merely be the enactment of a dream, but in each game there is a contest. Yet it will be noticed that when children play a game in the street they are often extraordinarily naïve or, according to viewpoint, highly civilized. They seldom need an umpire, they rarely trouble to keep scores, little significance is attached to who wins or loses, they do not require the stimulus of prizes, it does not seem to worry them if a game is not finished. Indeed, children like games in which there is a sizeable element of luck, so that individual abilities cannot be directly compared. They like games which restart almost automatically, so that everybody is given a new chance. They like games which move in stages, in which each stage, the choosing of leaders, the picking-up of sides, the determining of which side shall start, are almost games in themselves. In fact children's games often seem laborious to adults who, if invited to join in, may find themselves becoming impatient and wanting to speed them up. Adults do not always see, when subjected to lengthy preliminaries, that many of the games, particularly those of young children, are more akin to ceremonies than competitions. (1969:2)

This last point, incidentally, exactly describes my own experiences as an observer on the Ithaca school playgrounds. At first I was distressed that children could "waste" as much as half their lunch period on the preliminaries before a game was actually begun; but ultimately I came to realize that, from the children's point of view, these all were considered as part of the game itself. Much of the fun and learning occurs during these ritualized but self-organized preliminaries.

But let me quote a bit more from the Opies' perceptive account:

> Just as the shy man reveals himself by his formalities, so does the child disclose his unsureness of his place in the world by welcoming games with set procedures, in which his relationships with his fellows are clearly established. In games a child can exert himself without having to explain himself, he can be a good player without having to think whether he is a popular person, he can find himself being a useful partner to someone of whom he is ordinarily afraid. He can be confident, too, in particular games, that it is his place to issue commands, to inflict pain, to steal people's possessions, to pretend to be dead, to hurl a ball actually at someone, to pounce on someone, or to kiss someone he has caught. In ordinary life either he never knows these experiences or, by attempting them, makes himself an outcast.
>
> It appears to us that when a child plays a game he creates a situation which is under his control, and yet it is one of which he does not know the outcome. In the confines of a game there can be all the excitement and uncertainty of an adventure, yet the young player can comprehend the whole, can recognize his place in the scheme, and, in contrast to the confusion of real life, can tell what is right action. He can, too, extend his environment, or feel that he is doing so, and gain knowledge of sensations beyond ordinary experience. . . . As long as the action of the game is of a child's own making, he is ready, even anxious, to sample the perils of which this world has such plentiful supply. In the security of a game he makes acquaintance with insecurity; he is able to rationalize absurdities, reconcile himself to not getting his own way, "assimilate reality" (Piaget), act heroically without being in danger. The thrill of a chase is accentuated by viewing the chaser not as a boy in short trousers, but as a bull. It is not a classmate's back he rides upon, but a knight's fine charger. It is not a party of other boys his side skirmishes with, but Indians, robbers, men from Mars. And, always provided that the environment is of his own choosing, he—or she—is even prepared to meet the "things that happen in the dark," playing games that would seem strange amusement if it were thought they were being taken literally: murder in the dark, ghosties in the garret, moonlight, starlight, bogey won't come

out tonight. And yet, within the context of the game, these alarms are taken literally. (1969:3–4)

So much for the appeal of games for children. But what can be said about the functions of games for child development?

It has long been recognized that children's games and play activities represent miniature and playful models of a wide variety of cultural and social activities and concerns. To take a familiar example, the activities of little girls revolving about dolls and playing house undoubtedly serve some function in the process of anticipatory socialization to future roles as mothers and housekeepers. Similarly, in the games of boys, such elemental social themes as leading and following, of capturing and rescuing, chasing and eluding, attacking and defending, concealing and searching, are endlessly recombined in games of varying complexity in what Sutton-Smith (1971) has called a syntax of play. For example, the chase-and-elude themes of tag are combined with the capture-and-rescue elements of relievo in the more complex game of prisoner's base. When the chase-and-elude themes of tag are combined with the attack-and-defend themes of dodge ball, we have the more complex game represented in football.

As Roberts and Sutton-Smith (1962) have pointed out, games of different types represent microcosmic social structures in which various different styles of competing, winning, or losing are subtly encoded. Through their participation in a wide variety of different game types, in which the various elements of skill, chance, and strategy are variously recombined in gradually increasing complexity, children find an opportunity to experiment with different success styles and gain experience in a variety of cognitive and emotional processes which cannot yet be learned in full-scale cultural participation.

I would stress, at this point, that for game experiences to serve their socialization functions effectively, it is essential that children engage in a wide variety of different types of games, and at varying levels of complexity appropriate to their stage of development. If the American game culture is becoming overly constricted, will our coping styles and success strategies as adults also become constricted? Could it be, as some journalists have speculated, that America's inability to cope with the realities of world politics stems in part from the fact that our president, a football addict, is committed to a narrow-gauge game plan and success style which is grossly inadequate to deal with those of opponents who are skilled in such sophisticated games as chess and go?

Another feature of spontaneous games renders them especially effective in serving as "buffered learning experiences" for our children: the models they embody are miniaturized and rendered relatively safe by the recreational context in which they typically occur. As Lewin (1944) noted, games tend to occur on a "plane of unreality," which renders them especially well suited as contexts in which to toy with potentially dangerous psychological and emotional problems. Thus Phillips (1960) has observed that many children's games provide a miniature and relatively safe context for gaining useful experience in the mastery of anxiety. Consider in this connection the titillating joys of peek-a-boo, the universally popular game in which infants toy with the anxieties associated with mother absence, and the happy resolution achieved in the discovery that one can bring her back by uncovering one's eyes. In playful games, older children deliberately project themselves into situations involving risk, uncertainty, and insecurity, and the tensions generated by the conflicting valences of hope and fear. Particularly where some element of chance is involved, failure is less invidious and hence more easily bearable. Similarly, in games involving mock combat, aggression may be safely expressed because, as Menninger (1942:175) pointed out, "one can hurt people without really hurting them"—and, of course, without too much danger of being really hurt in return.

I must stress in particular the point that children's games are effective as expressive models for gaining experience in the mastery of dangerous emotions very largely because of their miniature scale and their playful context. They are rendered safe by remaining on a plane of unreality, in which "reality consequences" do not have to be faced. I would like to go on to argue that "child's play," far from being a frivolous waste of time as it is so often pictured in our task-oriented, puritan culture, may in fact represent an optimum setting for children's learning.

To gain some perspective on this matter, consider what psychologists are saying about the kinds of conditions in which optimum learning may occur. In designing their famous computer-typewriter-teaching-machine, or "automatic reflexive environment," O. K. Moore and A. R. Anderson (1969) were careful to take into account what they believe to be the essential features of a really good learning environment: it should permit free and safe exploration; it should be self-pacing; it should be "agent-responsive"; it should provide immediate and directly relevant feedback; it should be "productive," that is, so structured that a wide variety of ramifying principles and interconnections can be learned; it should be "autotelic" or self-rewarding, i.e., related directly to the child's own spontaneous interests and motivations; and, finally, it should be responsive to the child's own initiatives in a way which will permit him to take a "reflexive view of himself." Otherwise put, the environment should be such that the child may alternate in the roles of active agent and patient, and at times may step back and view the whole setting from the viewpoint of an umpire.

If we take these principles seriously, it is easy to see why many children do not learn very much in traditionally structured school settings. In such traditional schools, the pupils are patients and the teacher is the active agent. The principles which are to be learned are explained, perhaps even demonstrated, by the teacher, rather than being discovered by the children themselves. Learning is defined as work, which implies that the children, left to follow their own motivations and interests freely, would rather be doing something else. The pacing of activities is rigidly controlled by the teacher, the school schedules, or the tyranny of the lesson plan. And the evaluative feedback, coming from the teacher rather than from the materials themselves, is often delayed, irrelevant, and peculiarly invidious.

These principles, so widely violated in the regular educational settings in which children are supposed to be learning, are all admirably incorporated in a spontaneous, self-organized and self-paced game of backyard baseball, and in many other children's games and play activities. Little League baseball—and other adult-organized and supervised sports—do a pretty good job of bankrupting most of the features of this, and other, learning models.

But before continuing with this line of argument, I would call your attention to another eminent child psychologist's observations about the functions of spontaneous, self-organized children's games. In his classic study of the moral development of children, Jean Piaget (1932) noted that social rules, for the young child, originally appear as part of the external situation, defined and enforced by powerful adults. At an early stage of "moral realism," the child conforms because he must, to avoid punishment and to maintain the needed goodwill of his parents. But he feels no internalized moral commitment to these rules; he had no share in defining them, they often seem arbitrary or unnecessary, and they are often imposed in an arbitrary and punitive fashion. Piaget argued that children's experiences in informal games and play activities with their own age mates play an essential role in moving them beyond this stage of moral realism. In an informal game of marbles, for example, where there is no rule book and no adult rule-imposer or enforcer, and where the players know the rules only vaguely or have differences of opinion about what they really are, the children must finally face up to the realization that some kinds of rules really are necessary. They must decide for themselves what kinds of rules are fair, in order to keep the game going, and interesting, and fun for all; they must participate in establishing the rules and must learn how to enforce them. Experiences like this, Piaget theorized, play a vital role in helping the child grow to a more mature stage of moral development based on the principles of cooperation and consent.

Along somewhat similar lines, Parsons and Bales (1955) have argued that the enormous power differentials between adults and children present serious obstacles to certain kinds of essential learning. For example, adult authority usually appears to young children to be heavily ascriptive in character; authority flows from the fact that one is a parent, a teacher, a coach, or simply an adult, possessed of awesome powers to punish or reward. But the relevance of this power is not always obvious. Within the peer group, where differences in power are on a much smaller scale, leadership is much more likely to be based on relevant, universalistic criteria. A child leader is accepted and followed only to the extent that he effectively expresses the children's own values and helps them to work or play together in self-satisfying ways. It is largely within the framework of informally organized peer groups, these authors reason, that the child learns to conceive of social relationships as being patterned on relevant, universalistic principles in which people must get along in common subjection to general rules.

Kohlberg (1964) has pointed to yet another feature of unstructured children's play for the processes of moral development. If rules are rigidly fixed once and for all by parents, teachers, coaches, or rule books, the child may learn them and perhaps accept them, but he will not gain much experience in the development of mature moral judgment. According to Kohlberg, it is only with some real experience with dissonance, as when the rules are ambiguous or when there is some cross-pressure or opinion difference about which rules should apply, that children learn to understand how certain more general moral principles must be formulated to help them decide for themselves what they should do. Much of my own recent research has tended to support the notion that informal peer group experiences and their accompanying dissonance contribute to the development of moral autonomy in children (Devereux 1970) and that authoritarian control by adults has precisely the opposite effect (Devereux 1972).

BACKYARD VERSUS LITTLE LEAGUE BASEBALL, VIEWED AS LEARNING SETTINGS

In the light of what has been said thus far, I shall now comment on what I see as some crucial differences between an informal and spontaneous version of backyard baseball and the organized and adult-controlled Little League version of the same game. Let me grant at once that the latter form of the game is obviously much better equipped, better coached, and probably also a good deal safer. No doubt Little League children really do get better training in the official rules and strategies of our national sport, and better experience in the complex physical skills of ball handling, fielding, and so on. If the purpose of the game is to serve as an anticipatory socialization setting for developing future high school, college, and professional ball players, the Little League sport is clearly the winner.

But if we look at the matter in a more general educational perspective, it appears that those gains are not achieved without serious cost. In educational terms, the crucial question must always be not what the boy is doing to the ball, but what the ball is doing to the boy. In Little League baseball this is often not the case. Almost inevitably, in a highly organized, competitive sport, the focus is on winning and the eye is on the ball. How often does the well-intentioned volunteer coach from the phys ed department really think about what kind of total experience his boys are having, including those who have warmed the bench all afternoon, or who were not selected for League competition?

Of that, more shortly. But first let me describe a typical variant of backyard baseball, as played in my own neighborhood some fifty years ago. We called it one-o-cat. There were no teams. With a minimum of five kids you could start up a game, though it was better with seven or eight; once the game got started, usually a few more kids would wander over to join in. Often these were kids of the wrong age or sex, but no matter: it was more fun with more kids, and the child population was a bit sparse back then. One base—usually a tree, or somebody's sweater or cap. Home plate, usually a flat stone. Two batters, a catcher, a pitcher, a first baseman. If other kids were available, you had some fielders, too. If someone had a catcher's mitt, we'd use a hard ball; otherwise a softball, tennis ball, or anything else. If someone had a face mask, the catcher would play right behind the batter; otherwise, way back. There was no umpire to call balls and strikes, so the pitcher was disciplined mostly by shouts of "put it over!" Fouls were balls that went to the right of the tree marking first base or to the left of a shrub on the other side; in other yards or fields, different foul markers would have to be agreed upon.

The rules of the game, as we vaguely understood or invented them, were fairly simple. Pitched balls not swung at didn't count either as balls or strikes. Three swings without a hit and you were out. In principle you could go on hitting fouls indefinitely, but after a while the other kids would complain and make you swing at a wild one. A caught fly put you out. A good hit could get you to the tree and back for a home run; a lesser hit could leave you stranded at first, to be hit in, maybe, by the other batter. Or you could be put out either at first base or at the home plate in the usual fashion. Since there were no fixed base lines, when a runner was caught between the first baseman and the catcher, a wild chase all over the yard frequently ensued. When you went out, you retired to right field and everybody moved up one notch, catcher to batter, pitcher to catcher, first baseman to pitcher, left fielder to first, etc. There were no teams and nobody really bothered to keep score, since the personnel of the game usually changed during the session anyway, as some kids had to go do their chores or as others joined in. The object seemed to be to stay at bat as long as you could, but during the afternoon every kid would have plenty of opportunities to play in every position, and no one was ever on the bench. If a few more kids showed up, the game was magically transformed to two-o-cat, now with three rotating batters and a second base somewhere near where third would have been; the runners now had to make the full triangular circuit in order to complete their run.

Maybe we didn't learn to be expert baseball players, but we did have a lot of fun. Moreover, in an indirect and incidental way, we learned a lot of other kinds of things which are probably more important for children between the ages of eight and twelve. Precisely because there was no official rule book and no adult or even other child designated as rule enforcer, we somehow had to improvise the whole thing; this entailed endless hassles about whether a ball was fair or foul, whether a runner was safe or out, or more generally, simply about what was fair. We gradually learned to understand the invisible boundary conditions of our relationships to each other. Don't be a poor sport or the other kids won't want you to play with them. Don't push your point so hard that the kid with the only catcher's mitt will quit the game. Pitch a bit more gently to the littler kids so they can have some fun, too; besides, you realize that you must keep them in the game because numbers are important. Learn how to get a game started and somehow keep it going, as long as the fun lasts. How to pace it. When to quit for a while to get a round of cokes or just to sit under a tree for a bit. How to recognize the subtle boundaries indicating that the game is really over—not an easy thing, since there are no innings, no winners or losers—and slide over into some other activity. "Let's play tag"—"Not it!" Perhaps after supper, a game of catch with your father, who might try to give you a few very non-professional pointers. Perhaps, for a few, excited accounts to the family of your success at bat that day and momentary dreams of later glory in the big leagues. But mostly on to the endless variety of other games, pastimes, and interests which could so engage a young boy on a summer afternoon or evening.

In terms of the learning models proposed by Roberts, Sutton-Smith, Moore, Piaget, Parsons, Kohlberg, and many others, it was all there. It was fun; the scale was small, and the risks were minimal; we felt free and relatively safe (at least psychologically); it was spontaneous, auto-telic, and agent responsive; it was self-pacing and the feedback was continuous and relevant. The game was so structured that it required us to use our utmost ingenuity to discover and understand the hidden rules behind the rules—the general principles which make games fair, fun, and interesting, and which had to govern our complex relationships with each other; the recognition of the subtle differences in skills, including social skills, which gave added respect and informal authority to some; the ability to handle poor sports, incompetents, cry-babies, little kids, and girls, when the easy out of excluding them from the game entirely was somehow impractical. How to handle it when your own anger or frustrations welled up dangerously close to the point of tears. Although the formal structure of the game was based on a model of competition and physical skill, many of its most important lessons were in the social-emotional sector—how to keep the group sufficiently cohesive to get on with the play, and how to handle the tensions which arose within and between us.

All these are things which were happening to the boys when left to themselves in this informal game situation. And it seems to me that they are far more important than what was happening to the ball. By now the ball is lost, anyway, somewhere in the bushes over by left field. Perhaps someone will find it tomorrow. And besides, it's too hot for baseball now, and the kids have all gone skinny-dipping in the little pond down the road.

How does Little League baseball stack up against this model? Rather badly, in my opinion. The scale is no longer miniature and safe, what with scoreboards, coaches, umpires, parents, and a grandstand full of spectators all looking at you and evaluating your every move with a single, myopic criterion: Perform! Win! The risks of failure are large and wounding, and in the pyramidal structure of League competition, only a few can be winners; everybody else must be some kind of loser.

In Little League ball, the spontaneity is largely killed by schedules, rules, and adult supervision—a fixed time and place for each game, a set number of innings, a commitment to a whole season's schedule at the expense of alternative activities. Self-pacing? Obviously not. Fun? Yes, in a hard sort of way; but please, no fooling around or goofing off out there in right field; keep your eyes on the ball! Instant feedback? Yes, loud and clear from all sides, if you make a mistake; but mostly from adults, in terms of their criteria of proper baseball performance.

The major problem with Little League baseball, as I see it, is that the whole structure of the game is rigidly fixed once and for all. It's all there in the rule books and in the organization of the League and the game itself. It is all handed to the children, ready-made, together with the diamonds, bats, and uniforms. It is all so carefully supervised by adults, who are the teachers, coaches, rule-enforcers, decision-makers, and principal rewarders and punishers, that there's almost nothing left for the children to do but play the game. Almost all the opportunities for incidental learning which occur in spontaneous self-organized and self-governed children's games have somehow been sacrificed on the altar of safety (physical only) and competence (in baseball only).

COMPETITION AND LITTLE LEAGUISM IN CONTEMPORARY AMERICA

No doubt there are some who will argue that ours is a tough, competitive society and that somehow, during the educational process, children must be readied for the rigorous competition of real life they will face later on. It is certainly true that competition has played a central role in American society, and for generations there were many, like Theodore Roosevelt, who thought of it as the backbone of American character and achievement. But at what cost to other values? More than thirty years ago the psychoanalyst Karen Horney, in her classic analysis of *The Neurotic Personality of Our Time* (1937), saw fit to devote an entire chapter to "neurotic competitiveness." But while Horney saw the problem clearly enough, most psychologists and educators of that generation did not. It is interesting to note that among the twenty-three experimental studies of competition reported by Murphy, Murphy, and Newcomb (1937), the focus is almost invariably upon the effects of competition on the performance of some task; not one of these studies dealt with any measures of the effects of competition upon the subjects themselves!

But there undoubtedly are effects, among them the apparent inability of American children, reared in a competitive style, to know when *not* to compete. This point was neatly demonstrated in an experiment by Madsen and Shapira (1970). An apparatus was so arranged that no child could get any reward without cooperating with the other children. Mexican children (and, in another study by Shapira and Madsen [1969], Israeli kibbutz children) were quick to fall into a cooperative plan, to everybody's mutual advantage, but the American children continued to compete even after it became quite obvious that no one could win anything.

The time has surely come to reassess the heavy stress we have placed on competition in our educational system, and in our culture generally. In this connection it is interesting to note that recent movements toward educational reform call for a drastic reduction in the role of competition. More generally, the new counterculture flourishing on our college campuses is strongly anticompetitive in basic orientation. Somehow a whole generation of fathers, still deeply involved in major sports and other facets of the old American dream, has managed to rear a generation of sons, a very substantial segment of whom will have no part of it.

What can be said, more specifically, of the effects of Little League competition on children? I shall not take space here to consider such measured physiological side-effects as the famous Little League elbow, or the evidences of measured galvanic skin responses of young boys before and after competition (Skubic 1955), or the reported losses of sleep and appetite before or following competition (Skubic 1956). I have no reason to doubt that first-rate child athletes, like the adult athletes studied by Ogilvie and Tutko (1971), really are better built, better coordinated, and have fairly well integrated, if somewhat aggressive, personalities, in comparison with less athletic peers. But the crucial question must be whether participation in Little League sports helps make them that way, or whether the reported differences are a result of the selection processes involved. In the adult study cited above, the authors believe that most observed differences result from the selection processes rather than from the character-molding experiences of athletic competition. Hale's (1956) finding that the Little League players who made it to the Williamsport national competition had more, darker, and curlier pubic hair than non-playing age mates almost certainly reflects a selective factor rather than a consequence of ball playing.

Similarly, in Seymour's (1956) study, it is clear that the major reported differences between the Little Leaguers and their class mates, documenting the superiority of the League players, all existed before the season began. On all the self-rating scales used in this study, moreover, the nonparticipants actually improved more than the participants, ending ahead of the participants in their post-season self-ratings of their feelings about "me and my school" and "me and my home." The nonparticipants also gained somewhat more than the participants in the teacher ratings on social consciousness, emotional adjustment, and responsibility. On the sociometric ratings, as expected, the athletes were the sociometric stars in their classrooms both before and after the season. The author does note, however, that on the post-season sociometric test, the Little League boys were somewhat less accepting of their peers, as measured by ratings they extended to others, than they had been before the season started. Perhaps these results represent a gentle forecast of the Ogilvie-Tutko description of adult athletes: "Most athletes indicate low interest in receiving support and concern from others, low need to take care of others and low need for affiliation. Such a personality seems necessary to achieve victory over others" (1971: 61–62).

If some processes of selection are at work in sifting out the children who get to play in League or interscholastic competition (as they quite obviously are), and if both the adult and peer cultures shower these children with special attention and kudos (as they surely do), then responsible educators must have some concern about all the other children who are losers or nonparticipants in this one-dimensional competition. How sure are we that the values and character traits selected and carefully reinforced in Little League sports are really the best for wholesome child development? In a culture as fanatically dedicated to excellence in competitive sports as we have become in modern America, are we needlessly and cruelly punishing the children who are physically smaller or less mature, or less well coordinated or aggressive, who can't compete successfully and perhaps don't even want to? Many will no doubt turn into fine and productive adults—but only after a childhood in which they were never able to live up to the myopic values of the peer culture, or to the expectations of their sport-addicted fathers.

Don't misunderstand me. I am certainly not coming out against baseball as such, though for the reasons indicated I believe that the informal, backyard variants have far more learning values for children than the formally organized, adult-supervised version. My most fundamental opposition to Little League baseball is based not so much on what it does by way of either harm or good to the players, as it is on what Little

Leagui*sm* is doing to the whole culture of childhood, to participants and nonparticipants alike, and to the schools, families, neighborhoods, and communities where Little Leaguism has taken root.

Look first at what has happened to organized sports in high schools, and the picture is perhaps clearer. In a high school of 2,000 students, only a relative handful get to participate even on the squads of any of the major teams. All the rest are consigned to the role of frenzied spectators at interscholastic meets, or, still worse, in many sport-minded communities, to being nonparticipant nonspectators, perceived by adults and peers alike as odd-balls or pariahs. As Coleman (1961) showed, this group may in fact include some of the best students, but they get precious little reward for their academic efforts. The kids who do go out in earnest for a high school sport find that, to compete at all effectively against our fanatic standards of excellence, they have to make it almost a full-time job both in season and out, at the expense of virtually all other extracurricular and leisure activities. In one way, you're damned if you don't participate; in another way, you're damned if you do.

In Little League and other variations of organized interscholastic sports, we now see clear indications of the invasion of this sports culture into the much more precious and vulnerable world of little children. Like the bad currency in Gresham's famous law, it is an inferior product which ends up driving out the good. Because of its peculiar fascination, more for the parents than for the children themselves, it nearly monopolizes the field and drives almost to bankruptcy the natural and spontaneous culture of play and games among American children.

Let me close with yet another quotation from the Opies' fascinating monograph:

> In the long run, nothing extinguishes self-organized play more effectively than does action to promote it. It is not only natural but beneficial that there should be a gulf between the generations in their choice of recreation. Those people are happiest who can most rely on their own resources; and it is to be wondered whether middle-class children in the United States will ever reach maturity "whose playtime has become almost as completely organized and supervised as their study" (Carl Withers). If children's games are tamed and made part of school curricula, if wastelands are turned into playing-fields for the benefit of those who conform and ape their elders, if children are given the idea that they cannot enjoy themselves without being provided with the "proper" equipment, we need blame only ourselves when we produce a generation who have lost their dignity, who are ever dis-

satisfied, and who descend for their sport to the easy excitement of rioting, or pilfering, or vandalism. (1969:16)

A final word to physical education professionals is in order. My rather limited contacts with physical education teachers have persuaded me that many (perhaps most) of you are really on my side on the matter of promoting competitive sports among young children. The problem, as I see it, stems not from the physical education programs in our elementary schools and from those who teach in these settings. It stems far more from the parents and from the common culture in our sports-ridden communities.

What can you do about it? Not too much, I'm afraid. But I can think of at least three things I would hope that you might try. First, in training students who will work with young children, urge them to keep in mind that "It's not what the boy is doing to the ball, but what the ball is doing to the boy!" Or, to reverse the old cliché: "Keep your eye on the boy!"

Second, physical education instructors, as experts in this area, are in a strategic position to influence public opinion on this important matter. I hope that you, in your contacts with parents, teachers, school administrators, and community leaders generally, will continually stress the important role of spontaneous play and of unsupervised, self-organized games for young children, and the very real costs involved when we push our children into competitive sports too early.

Finally, I hope that physical education instructors who work with children will do whatever they can to reintroduce some of the wonderful traditional games which earlier generations of children found so rewarding, and which, in my opinion, are far more appropriate for the elementary school ages. The instant success of capture the flag, introduced to one of our schools by a student volunteer, indicates that perhaps it can be done. The kids simply didn't know what they had been missing.

But once a game has been taught and is beginning to catch on with the children, I'm afraid the rest of my message really is: "Get lost!" Let the kids handle it themselves.

REFERENCES

Coleman, J.
    1961   *The Adolescent Society.* Glencoe, Ill.: Free Press.
Devereux, E. C.
    1970   "The Role of Peer Group Experience in Moral Development."
            In Hill, J. P., ed. *Minnesota Symposia on Child Psychology*
            4:94–140. Minneapolis: University of Minnesota Press.

1972 "Authority and Moral Development among American and West German Children." *Journal of Comparative Family Studies* 3:99–124.

Eifermann, Rivka R.
1971a "Social Play in Childhood." In Herron, R. E., and Sutton-Smith, B., eds. *Child's Play.* New York: John Wiley and Sons, Pp. 270–297.
1971b *Determinants of Children's Game Styles.* Jerusalem: Israel Academy of Sciences and Humanities.

Hale, C. J.
1956 "Physiological Maturity of Little League Baseball Players." *Research Quarterly* 27:276–282.

Herron, R. E., and Sutton-Smith, B., eds.
1971 *Child's Play.* New York: John Wiley and Sons.

Horney, Karen.
1937 *The Neurotic Personality of Our Time.* New York: W. W. Norton.

Kohlberg, L.
1964 "Development of Moral Character and Moral Ideology." In Hoffman, M. L., and Hoffman, L. W., eds. *Review of Child Development Research* 1:383–431. New York: Russell Sage Foundation.

Lewin, Kurt, et al.
1944 "Level of Aspiration." In Hunt, J. M., ed. *Personality and Behavior Disorders.* New York: Ronald Press.

Madsen, M. C., and Shapira, A.
1970 "Cooperative and Competitive Behavior of Urban Afro-American, Anglo-American, Mexican-American and Mexican Village Children." *Developmental Psychology* 3:16–20.

Menninger, K.
1942 *Love against Hate.* New York: Harcourt.

Moore, O. K., and Anderson, A. R.
1969 "Some Principles for the Design of Clarifying Educational Environments." In Goslin, D., ed. *Handbook of Socialization Theory and Research.* New York: Rand McNally. Pp. 571–613.

Murphy, G.; Murphy, L. B.; and Newcomb, R. M.
1937 *Experimental Social Psychology.* New York: Harper Bros.

Ogilvie, B. C., and Tutko, T. A.
1971 "If You Want to Build Character, Try Something Else." *Psychology Today* 5:60–63.

Opie, Iona, and Opie, Peter.
1969 *Children's Games in Street and Playground.* Oxford: Clarendon Press.

Parsons, R., and Bales, R. F.
1955 *Family, Socialization and Interaction Process.* Glencoe, Ill.: Free Press.

Piaget, Jean.
  1932   *The Moral Judgment of the Child*. New York: Harcourt.
Phillips, R. H.
  1960   "The Nature and Function of Children's Formal Games."
          Psychoanalytic Quarterly 29:200–207.
Roberts, J. M., and Sutton-Smith, B.
  1962   "Child Training and Game Involvement." *Ethnology* 1:166–
          185.
Seymour, E. W.
  1956   "Comparative Study of Certain Behavior Characteristics of
          Participants and Non-participants in Little League Base-
          ball." *Research Quarterly* 27:338–346.
Shapira, A., and Madsen, M. C.
  1969   "Cooperative and Competitive Behavior of Kibbutz and Urban
          Children in Israel." *Child Development* 40:609–617.
Skubic, E.
  1955   "Emotional Responses of Boys to Little League and Middle
          League Competitive Baseball." *Research Quarterly* 26:342–
          352.
  1956   "Studies of Little League and Middle League Baseball." *Re-
          search Quarterly* 27:97–110.
Sutton-Smith, B.
  1971   "A Syntax for Play and Games." In Herron, R. E., and Sutton-
          Smith, B., eds. *Child's Play*. New York: John Wiley and Sons.
          Pp. 298–307.
————, and Rosenberg, B. G.
  1971   "Sixty Years of Historical Change in the Game Preferences of
          American Children." In Herron, R. E., and Sutton-Smith, B.,
          eds. *Child's Play*. New York: John Wiley and Sons. Pp. 18–50.

Aspects of Deviance in Sport

Introduction

Having considered some of the debates over the social-psychological aspects of competition, we now turn to problems which may occur when the structure of competition changes from the play-like encounter to the highly institutionalized form of modern-day competitive sport. Loy (1968) describes some sport forms as institutionalized games characterized by "distinctive, enduring patterns of culture and social structure combined into a single complex, the elements of which include values, norms, sanctions, knowledge, and social positions (i.e., roles and statuses)." Here the institutionalization of a game implies a tradition which is more often evident in the most organized and structured form of the game. Even within the same sport (for example, baseball), the professional form of the game is a better illustration of its institutional nature than is a sandlot game. In the preceding section, Devereux outlines differences between these diverse forms of baseball in terms of models fostering greater learning in children. By contrast, the focus of the papers in the present section is on the types of behaviors that are thought to be deviant and that are nurtured by the structural changes which have occurred in highly institutionalized sport.

The transition of sport from occasional amusement to institutionalized game has received considerable scholarly attention. Huizinga (1950) notes that in modern life sport has been raised to such a high degree of technical organization and scientific thoroughness that the play element from which it derived is threatened with extinction. This increasing rationality of what was once play began in nineteenth-century England. Although Huizinga mentions some of the characteristics of English social life and topography that may have stimulated the rise of institutionalized sport, he notes that the specific Anglo-Saxon frame of mind that might be deemed as an efficient cause for such a development is much less clear. He stops short of speculating as to the possible psychological bent of the citizenry that may have spurred the historical development of institutionalized sport. However, a tentative explanation for the increase of sport during this time may reside in the occurrence of a commensurate rise in achievement motivation within the society. Recent findings bear this out; analysis of written documents in eighteenth- and nineteenth-century England showed that the achievement themes in English literature reached a peak during the decades immediately preceding the very rapid development of technology, industrialization, and institutionalization of games in England (McClelland 1961). A similar relationship of heightened achievement and the rise of institutionalized sport in America can be gleaned from analyses of American literature (DeCharms and Moeller 1962) and the beginning of organized sport in America (McIntosh 1963). In comparing these relationships one must guard against concluding that achievement is the causative factor. Whether the relationships are purely coincidental or in some way causal remains for future investigators to unravel.

Since the beginnings of organized sport, further changes have occurred as sport has become more commercialized. Tracing the structural changes that have taken place in institutionalized sport is an elusive undertaking. Structural forms of sport are multifaceted, with diverse roots which extend to play, work, drama, etc. For example, work has sometimes been transformed into sport, as in auto racing and tractor-pulling contests; sport has likewise been transformed into drama, as in professional wrestling and roller derby; individual sports have been restructured into ad hoc team sports, as in track and field and swimming; team sports have been redesigned into individual sports, such as one-on-one basketball and hockey contests. The reasons for these transformations are many, but one that is common throughout the writings of many investigators is the securing of what Durso (1971) calls "the All-American Dollar"; that is, a more lucrative consumer product. Here institutionalized sport becomes more like work, in that economic motives become of paramount concern. For the participant, it is argued that the increasing commercialization and professionalization of sport has altered the athletic role from that of a recreational pursuit to that of a service occupation; it is further argued that this change has elevated the saliency of extrinsic sources of motivation as a means of obtaining satisfaction in sport.

There is currently much concern regarding the content which highly institutionalized consumer sport conveys through the socialization process. Although consumer sport is a relatively recent phenomenon, previous investigators have alluded to problems which may be inherent in such extreme forms of sport. Caillois (1961) was one of the first to suggest that competition can become "corrupted," leading to harmful personality characteristics and behavior patterns, such as will to power, trickery, and violence. Today American sport has become increasingly appended to the complex of big business, entertainment, and instant media-produced superstardom. The socialization information that is transmitted via sport is neither inherently desirable nor undesirable; it simply reflects the values of the social environment of which it is a part. Although individuals learn and internalize values legitimating sport, and perhaps identify with idealized stereotypes exemplifying the necessary behavioral and attitudinal requirements for preferred role performance, there is competing ideational content, consisting of values and norms, underpinning the social structure of sport. Not only have the structural forms of sport changed over the years, but the ideational content of sport has changed as well. Sport has become increasingly like work, where much emphasis is placed on instrumental values. Expressive values, such as sociability and fun, have become subservient to ego demands and instrumental concerns (e.g., sport as an avenue to goals outside sport—character development, delinquency reduction, and economic profit). Too great an emphasis on instrumental values may render sport vulnerable to outside pressures and create tensions leading to instances of emotional self-indulgence and antisocial behavior on the part of athletes, physical educators, and coaches.

That socially undesirable behavior is elicited in sport is evident, but the reasons for such behavior are much less clear. One explanation resides in the degree to which the desire to participate is intrinsically or extrinsically motivated. Organized sport will to some extent involve extrinsic motivators, but the ratio of intrinsic to extrinsic motivation will depend on the level of participation. Emphasis on instrumental values may result in a greater concern with extrinsic rewards. The more sport is extrinsically rewarded (as in consumer sport), the more it tends to emphasize instrumental values and be work; the less it is extrinsically rewarded, the more it tends to elicit expressive values characteristic of play (Lueschen 1967). The differences in the official distinctions between amateurs and professionals indicate different kinds of player motivations. As Huizinga (1950) points out, the "spirit of the professional is no longer the true play spirit; it is lacking in spontaneity and carelessness." Supportive of Huizinga's statement are the comments of former professional athletes (Meggyessy 1970; Shaw 1972), who have indicated that the professional form of their sport ceased to be as much fun as the amateur form had been. The values of amateur competition have been advanced by many; these values include love of the game and a desire to win by one's merit in regulated competition. In this sense the adherence to norms, values, and expectations for both the ends and means of the contest are important to the "true amateur," or the "good sport" (Ingham and Loy 1973); not only is victory important, but the way in which the victory is achieved is also important. The extent to which this spirit is still a part of modern-day institutional sports is uncertain, for, as Webb (1969) has shown, age increases among adolescent boys are associated with a gradual increase in professionalization of attitudes; the importance which they attach to fairness decreases simultaneously.

The increasing trend toward consumer-oriented sport and associated instrumental values increases the likelihood that participants may opt to deviate from institutionalized expectations of desirable means and ends. In this sense the ends, and particularly the means by which they are to be achieved, may be circumvented and the institutionally accepted forms of sport corrupted for those primarily motivated by the attainment of extrinsic rewards.

Much of what is known about extrinsic and intrinsic motivation comes from educational psychology; there techniques have been developed for changing children's extrinsically motivated behavior to intrinsically motivated behavior. This research, however, may not be directly applicable to problems in sport, since the developmental process seems to be reversed. In sport participants are intrinsically motivated to participate (as in play), and then they increasingly create an externally motivated dependency for participation through the use of medals, prizes, money, etc. Extrinsic rewards may be detrimental to prolonged participation. As Deci (1972) has shown, the removal of extrinsic rewards curtails a desire to participate, whereas those not offered extrinsic rewards from the start justified their behavior as "doing it because they like it." Not only might the extreme use of extrinsic rewards negate prolonged enjoyment of sport, but an intense desire to achieve extrinsic rewards may also lead to an overemphasis on winning at the expense of fairness.

The essays in this section all deal with varying subjugations of legitimate means in favor of the instrumentalized goals of sport. At one extreme we find the good sport who accepts both the means and goals of sport. At the other we find the bad sport who adapts quite differently by rejecting both the ends and means prescribed by the rules of the contest. In the intermediate gray area we find the hustler, the cheat, and a host of other types who violate various institutionally expected forms of sport behavior. The cheat, according to Lueschen's analysis, adheres to the goals of the contest so as to appear to be playing the game as prescribed, but in fact he is intentionally violating or manipulating one or more of the means. By violating means, the cheat alters specific structural aspects of the game. According to Lueschen, the cheat is not as disruptive to the contest as the spoilsport, who is rather indifferent to the means and rejects the values and goals of sport. Society is more lenient with the cheat than with the more obtrusive spoilsport. Using a social system analysis, Lueschen further describes types of overt cheating and their consequences to the social system of sport. He attempts to analyze some previously undetected forms of cheating which have ultimately surfaced as sport scandals. It is noteworthy in terms of our previous discussion that the participation level most likely to exhibit predominantly extrinsic motivation—the professional level—is where Lueschen indicates that the greatest precautions are necessary in order to prevent cheating. At the professional level, cheating is particularly disruptive to the social (economic) system of sport. If the cheater is caught, spectator interest and revenue derived therefrom will probably be curtailed.

The essay by Mahigel and Stone and the essay by Steele both deal with another form of adaptation to the normatively prescribed sport role; namely, that of the hustler. Like the cheat, the hustler pretends to be something he isn't. But the similarity ends there. As Ingham and Loy (1973) indicate: "Whereas the cheat pretends to accept the form and ends up destroying it, the hustler pretends to accept the [ideational structure], but if his front is discredited [this structure] is negated." The hustler, therefore, is a con man who must have an edge in the game by an extraordinary manipulation of others' impressions that the contest is being entered on even, or favorable, terms. Mahigel and Stone describe the career of the hustler: the necessary skills and personal qualities, socialization into the career, and maintenance of the hustle. To obtain the payoff the hustler is forced to engage in a somewhat paradoxical situation: he must be known to get into the game, but his true skill must remain unknown so as not to frighten off the unsuspecting "fish." Further insight into the lifestyle of the hustler is provided in the essay by Steele. This essay begins by characterizing the part-time bowling hustler as a social underachiever who has few means for ego satisfaction in his dominant occupational role. To explain the seemingly strange fascination of the hustle, Steele employs the concept of the ephemeral role. It is suggested that the hustler utilizes the bowling hustle in order to satisfy ambitions that may have been frustrated in his dominant role activity. In this way the hustler substitutes bowling as a criterion for positive self-evaluation. Steele argues that, although monetary concerns are important, the most important satisfaction for the bowling hustler is ego satisfaction in knowing that the fish has been taken and that he has gained complete control of the situation.

The final paper in this section addresses itself to an analysis of violence in professional hockey. Violence, like cheating and hustling, can be attributed to strains between the expressive and instrumental nature of sport as an entertainment form. The expressive values inherent in sport become warped as the instrumental concerns of the business enterprise enter into sport. Sport begins to "pander to the vicissitudes of the consumer . . . for to be profit making, its form must conform to consumer taste" (Ingham and Loy 1973). Vaz (1972) has commented upon the spectator appeal of hockey to the working class, whose value system rewards those who never back down in a fight. Within the working class fighting and toughness are considered virtuous, and "fighting is often recognized as a moral and legitimate activity in settling disputes" (Vaz 1972:226). Violence in hockey has become an expected form of behavior and a fundamental part of the socialization and role expectations of players. The socialization of the young hockey player into violence is described by Vaz as follows:

> [The] implicit objective is to put the opposing star player out of action without doing him serious harm. Illegal tactics and "tricks" of the game are both encouraged and taught; rough play and physically aggressive performance are strongly encouraged, and sometimes players are taught the techniques of fighting. Minimal consideration is given the formal normative rules of the game, and the conceptions of sportsmanship and fair play are forgotten. Evaluation of individual performances (whether deviant or not) is according to their contribution to ultimate success of the team. . . . By the time boys reach the Midget and Junior professional levels, dominant role expectations of the hockey players include toughness, aggressiveness, physical strength and size, and ability to endure pain. Gradually the team is molded into a tough fighting unit prepared for violence whose primary objective is to win hockey games. (1972:230)

Under certain conditions failure to conform to expectations is variously sanctioned by coaches and players. In addition, players, coaches, and fans may legitimize and rationalize violence in sport. Consistent distortions of the expressive values in sport often become legitimated, for "if sport is aggressive to the point of being bellicose, then bellicosity can be legitimated as a healthy release of tension" (Ingham and Loy 1973:11).

Within this broader social system perspective of violence in hockey,

Faulkner takes the analysis one step further to examine the microsociology of the deviant act—that is, the interpretive process through which situations are defined and identities negotiated. He accomplishes this task through his discussions and observations of members of two teams in the American Hockey League. Managing others rather than being managed was important in our preceding discussion of the hustler, and it is likewise important in Faulkner's analysis of the professional hockey player. Whereas the hustler creates false impressions, the hockey player manages his identity in part through the use of violence. Faulkner stresses that the hockey player must show himself as a fighter in order to gain respect and a reputation as one who will not be pushed around. Faulkner demonstrates that through testing one's opponents and in turn being tested, social actors define each other and their environment. Within the environmental confines of rule-governed behavior and moral division of labor (e.g., the role of the team "policeman"), the social dynamics in hockey are described as involving both the creation of trouble and resolution of perceived violations of threats to self and colleagues.

REFERENCES

Caillois, R.
    1961   *Man, Play and Games*. New York: Free Press.
DeCharms, R., and Moeller, G. H.
    1962   "Values Expressed in American Children's Readers: 1800–1950." *Journal of Abnormal and Social Psychology* 64:136–142.
Deci, E.
    1972   "Work: Who Does Not Like It and Why." *Psychology Today* 6:57.
Durso, J.
    1971   *The All-American Dollar: The Big Business of Sports*. Boston: Houghton Mifflin.
Huizinga, J.
    1950   *Homo Ludens: A Study of the Play Element in Culture*. Boston: Beacon Press.
Ingham, A. G., and Loy, J. M.
    1973   "The Social System of Sport: A Humanistic Perspective." *Quest* 19:3–23.
Lueschen, G.
    1967   "The Interdependence of Sport and Culture." *International Review of Sport Sociology* 2:127–139.
Loy, J. M.
    1968   "The Nature of Sport: A Definitional Effort." *Quest* 10:1–15.

McClelland, D. C.
    1961   *The Achieving Society*. New York: Van Nostrand.
McIntosh, P. C.
    1963   *Sport in Society*. London: C. A. Watts.
Meggyessy, D.
    1970   *Out of Their League*. Berkeley: Ramparts.
Shaw, G.
    1972   *Meat on the Hoof*. New York: Dell.
Vaz, E. W.
    1972   "The Culture of Young Hockey Players: Some Initial Obser-
           vations." In A. W. Taylor, ed. *Training: Scientific Basis and
           Application*. Pp. 222–234.
Webb, H.
    1969   "Professionalization of Attitudes toward Play among Adoles-
           cents." In: G. S. Kenyon, ed. *Aspects of Contemporary Sport
           Sociology*. Pp. 161–178.

Cheating in Sport

GUENTHER LUESCHEN

Cheating in sport is the act through which the manifestly or latently agreed upon conditions for winning such a contest are changed in favor of one side. As a result, the principle of equality of chance beyond differences in skill and strategy is violated. Typically changes occur not on the level of goals, but on that of means. This pattern of behavior, therefore, would qualify in Merton's terms as *innovation* (1938), were it not for the fact that the cheater in sport agrees to the majority of the means as well. Since the participant strongly supports the goals of the contest, a contest may seem to be the same for the spectator and for the opponent as long as the act of cheating is not detected. Often only the cheater knows that the rules are being violated. Thus the undetected cheater in sport is less disruptive to the contest than the spoilsport, who by rejecting the values and goals inherent in the game disrupts the whole system of the contest; the disruption usually results in his eviction from the game by the referee. On the other hand, to avoid calling attention to himself, the cheater makes every effort to keep the system focused on the goal of the contest, and to keep the means for achieving those goals intact, so that the undetected cheater appears to be protected by the system.

Typically the hustler in billiards tries to reinforce the system of the contest in order to make it difficult for the opponent to quit and leave the scene (Polsky 1967). The cheater's seemingly conforming behavior may explain why fans so often support the cheater once he is detected. To them, cheating seems to be something private, of concern only to the individual involved, and something that does not affect the game system. Manifestly this may be true, since the "perfect" cheater does nothing to alter the course of the game; not even his opponent may know, and the latter may wholeheartedly congratulate him after being

Guenther Lueschen is a professor in the departments of sociology and physical education at the University of Illinois at Urbana-Champaign. He is currently president of the International Committee for the Sociology of Sport, which is affiliated with the International Sociological Association and the International Council of Sport and Physical Education.

cheated out of a win. Latently, however, the consequences are the same for the system. As soon as a cheat is detected, the system is disrupted strongly, despite support from the cheater's followers.

Cheating in sport does not have to be done in secret. The consequences for the system are usually not severe, since a referee may stop such acts of cheating, or the other party may protest or even quit the contest. Open cheating results in officials, players, and others responding through sanctions, so that the game system is restored to its former equilibrium. Or the other party may also respond with the same illegal means, thus creating a form of agreement which would make such acts part of strategy. It also appears (e.g., in basketball) that at the beginning of a contest the opponents and the referee will arrive at some kind of agreement concerning what will be considered legal and what will be considered cheating. Each party will attempt to extend the meaning of rules, as well as the general ideas and norms of a game, as far as the opponents and the referee will allow. Only after agreement has been established will any acts be clearly labeled as cheating. It may also appear that acts of open cheating are rather minor violations. Furthermore, it may appear that accidental violations of rules and norms, as a consequence of an individual's spontaneous response in a given situation, may not qualify as cheating since such acts are neither intended nor planned. Yet, in light of our definition at the outset, the consequences for the system would be the crucial determinant. A player must realize the repercussions of any of his acts. Moreover, seemingly minor violations may in fact be part of a planned strategy. The advice of the basketball coach to continuously touch the shooter's legs and lower body when the eyes of the referee and other observers typically are on the ball qualifies as cheating; its consequences can be drastic. Individual overt acts can also be wide-ranging. In soccer, for example, a defender may deflect or catch a ball above his head and thus prevent a pass into the free area that almost certainly would have resulted in a goal. In such cases the referee may be able to restore equilibrium by imposing a severe penalty. But the cheater counts on the fact that the referee may not do so, since he may overlook the violation or he may have no penalty at hand which is severe enough to restore equilibrium. In such instances, the system at large (in the form of a sport federation or its rule commission) may respond and penalize a cheater through special provisions that are not put into the rules. The proper conduct, therefore, is many times left to the consent of the opponents and to a supposedly built-in system quality that in the relations between opponents has been labeled *association* (Lueschen 1970). Of course, this leaves considerable space for open cheating, which is well known in such forms as foul play, wrong calls of the opponent's ball in tennis, interferences of all types with the opponent's action by players, coaches, or fans and spectators. Cheating is often used as part of strategy in order to put the opponent psychologically off balance.

It is much more difficult to describe forms of unobservable, undetected cheating. For one thing, data are scarce—necessarily, because most of such acts will remain unknown. Only scandals may later reveal what has happened in certain instances. Furthermore, quantification is difficult. We do not know how much undetected cheating goes on in sport. A number of cases that get publicity may let us conclude that the whole system is rotten—as illustrated by the series of scandals in German professional soccer. Yet scandals say little about the magnitude of a problem; rather, they may be an expression of tight moral controls and the singularity of such cases. The difficulty of arriving at quantitative conclusions is not at all unique for cheating in sport; it holds for other forms of deviance as well. Wallerstein and Wyle (1947) reported that 89 percent of all men and 83 percent of all women in their sample admitted to having committed larceny once in their lifetime—a higher figure than expected, a much higher figure than gets detected, and an even higher one than gets prosecuted. So our discussion of undetected cheating in sport will have to be one of quality only. Nevertheless such discussion may not only have theoretical implications, but may also be useful for policy decisions in sport. Sociologists who argue from a concept of totality of structure may be willing to draw conclusions from single instances, but in my opinion they are not justified in doing so. But to be perfectly clear, there is cheating in sport to a considerable degree, openly and secretly, and one can only hope that the amount of open cheating has no parallel in secret cheating.

Cheating can be performed by the individual athlete, by a whole team, by those who govern a team or club (coaches, managers, owners), or by judges. One would expect that cheating by judges would appear predominantly in sport events that are evaluated subjectively, such as gymnastics or figure skating. But cheating by judges may go as far as declaring the second finisher in a hundred-meter dash the winner. This happened in a meet between Nigeria and Ghana in 1969; the winner, Abdulai of Nigeria, was ruled to be second and put four yards behind.

While open cheating may occur predominantly in the above-mentioned forms of foul play and interference, the secret forms can only be guessed. Among them one would find competing below one's level of ability in order to let the other side win or retain its interest, as in hustling; competing above one's ability, predominantly through the use of stimulating drugs (whether such performance increases are possible physiologically is a different question); changing material conditions to the disadvantage of the opponent, as in lowering or raising the mound in baseball; making sure that the goal post will break down in soccer in case of an unfavorable outcome; dropping of the discus; or using harassment and fouls toward other players (although this will often be detected, at least by the player involved).

Why does cheating occur? How do we explain this phenomena? I am interested predominantly in the conditions that constitute the social structure of the sport contest. Personality characteristics, insofar as they are strictly individual, will not be considered, although I recognize that there are categories on the level of psycho-physiology that have figured rather predominantly in the history of criminology and may indeed have some explanatory power. Most of the following points are no more than hypothetical suggestions.

A contest of presumably well-matched opponents is an event with high uncertainty of outcome. Magic and ritual constitute one response to such a situation, and so does cheating. Cheating under uncertainty of outcome is less likely to be detected; nobody will be surprised by a win of cheating team A over team B if both are presumably equal. Too, cheating may make all the difference in winning; given equality, one need not even employ very rigorous means. Thus we can hypothesize that *the higher the level of uncertainty, the more likely that cheating will occur.* Sport events such as horse racing, cycling, and track often seem to confirm this hypothesis. The sip of champagne for the middle-distance runner right before the start of the race is a practice that long preceded recent stimulants in the form of drugs. The uncertainty hypothesis also seems to explain cheating in events where opponents are not necessarily well matched, but where specific conditions may result in uncertainty. Cheating in sailing, with many uncertainties ranging from wind currents to equipment, can be explained on this basis; so can fixes in boxing. In order to nourish a star and potential money-winner along, coaches and managers will make sure that chance, in the form of the lucky punch from the weaker opponent, is minimized. Boxing seems to lead to still another reason for cheating: *the rewards that are at stake in a contest will determine the amount and severity of cheating.* Predominantly because of the high odds at stake, two presidents of German soccer clubs felt compelled to bribe players of other clubs to lose or win against third clubs in order to let their own team survive in the professional league. Because the reputation of their country was at stake (a belief that they had reinforced through strong publicity), an East German team resorted to heating their sleds in order to slide faster in world bobsledding championships in France.

A contest is usually a zero-sum game; one side wins, and the other side loses. To put it differently, one side gets everything; the other, nothing. This of course is often determined by the perception and subjective evaluation of such an outcome. Both sides know from the beginning that it will be that way—unless a tie occurs. Yet inequity can result in strong cognitive dissonance. Dissonance may be resolved by playing down the meaning of the event through distortion of inputs and outcomes. One can leave the field rather than face the upcoming loss. One may alter the inputs and outcomes either for himself or for the other side, which shows the cheating potential of the sport contest as such (Adams 1965), particularly since it is zero-sum. On this account there should be differences between sport events that are strictly zero-sum and those that are not. Traditionally, German gymnastic events made almost every participant a winner, yet cheating still occurred. But there seems to be more cheating in contests that match one individual or team against another. In tennis one may consistently call one's opponents shots near the boundary lines incorrectly. In basketball, soccer, and football lesser forms of open cheating seem to go on almost all the time. The fencing bouts of earlier times allowed for considerable cheating. Today, with electrical recording of touches, it no longer pays off to fake a touch on an opponent by shouting loudly. By and large the characteristic of a contest as a zero-sum game seems to explain why cheating should go on at all levels—even where the odds at stake are not high. This impossibility of regulating every act and situation which results in the orientation of the cheat, accounts for a strong potential to cheat in sport at all levels.

The contest, teams, and personnel in sport are not a system in themselves. The sport system overlaps many other societal systems. The norms and values in sport are by and large those of the middle class. Members of the lower class may neither fully agree to the established means to reach a specific goal, nor understand a middle-class-bound social structure. Deviance in the form of cheating may thus occur more frequently among the lower class. Other theorists have accounted for deviance as a result of limited opportunities and resources. Again, this more likely would account for cheating by lower-class members. However, more careful considerations may result in quite different results from those hypothesized above. Indeed, the notion of white-collar crime and investigations that indicated equal rates of delinquency over all social classes should safeguard us against hasty generalizations. To account for social class differences at large, the theory of limited resources of the lower-class member holds in sport only to the extent that expensive equipment is a factor. Otherwise, the equality of chance in a contest, regardless of one's social background, may be a reason for a person with limited resources and opportunities in other societal areas not to cheat in sport.

Other factors to be introduced in dealing with causes of cheating may involve the family or other groups that have deviant standards as far as honesty in a contest is concerned. In certain subcultures of society, procedures in the employment of means to reach a goal may be considered perfectly honest, whereas in sport they are not.

The latter interpretation of norms also differs from one society to another. American society by and large interprets norms rather loosely, and the call of a referee in sport will not be easily accepted. In a different societal context certain actions may be considered violations of rules and norms and, because of their consequences, cheating. Europeans believe that South Americans cheat in their actions on the soccer field, while South Americans hold similar beliefs about European soccer referees. In the 1965 world soccer championships, the Germans felt that the Swedes had cheated them out of a win by the employment of very efficient cheerleading so familiar to the American scene. Not only do societies differ from one another in the interpretation of rules and acts, but there are also differences within societies over time. Normative standards and values can, at times, be in high conflict within societies and denote what Durkheim called anomie. Times of recession or high prosperity have been mentioned as relating to stages of high anomie. From this standpoint it is no surprise that at present, where norms and values have been questioned to such a high degree as in Western societies, one would also expect anomie to be high as exhibited in such forms as cheating in sport. Yet the questioning of values, including those of success in sport, may also result in a lower regard for winning in sport and thus, based on our earlier hypothesis, nullify these differences.

One should also be aware of the fact that a combination of such factors as discussed above will ultimately decide whether cheating occurs or not. With regard to Sutherland's theory of *differential association*, there must be a number of encouragements through association with others, different subcultures, and experiences that influence the behavior of a person or group concerning cheating (1955). According to other theories, a supporting cast and subculture is needed in order for cheating to occur; the individual cheater who is on his own will be the exception. Such supporting deviant subcultures need not consist of people from the same team or club. Third parties may become involved, such as gambling circles or other clubs that have a vested interest in the outcome of a sport contest. In such cases the groups usually try to cheat with as few players as possible—for reasons of detection and profit-making. Key players such as quarterbacks, pitchers, or goalies will more likely be involved in cheating. Big scandals have usually involved such figures.

Cheating requires competence. A good cheater will cheat with style, like the hustler who makes every effort to appear modest. In his attempts to slightly offset the differences in skill, the hustler consistently denies himself the brilliant plays (Polsky 1967). Cheating does not come easily and thus must be learned—another reason for the required presence of deviant subcultures. In the milder forms of open cheating and planned cheating as strategy, sport by and large composes such a subculture. In the severe forms of undetected, secret cheating, such subcultures seem to overlap with other sections of society, such as gambling circles.

At this point a side remark may be appropriate. Because of the high potential for deviance, sport may not necessarily be a good educational tool unless it is used responsibly; in such a case the deviant potentiality may even turn out to be a specific merit, since it will challenge the athlete to be honest. There is another potential for deviance in sport. Sport values success very highly; one may say that only in sport is one's rank typically determined by performance. Yet sport, with the exception of professional sport, does not provide the means to obtain such success in everyday life. Thus, with the ever stronger requests of athletes to devote themselves to sport only, the potential for later deviance in the pursuit of success in one's ordinary life becomes stronger. It would be very interesting to know how many former athletes have indeed become deviant and cheaters in everyday life.

After we have dealt with forms of cheating and their causes, let us see how cheating is controlled in sport. Controls in sport are farreaching and differentiated; patterns of deviance will normally be accounted for in the rules of a contest. Furthermore, rules and by-laws of sport associations and federations allow the control of cheating in their own contexts. Finally, sport as part of society at large has also to abide by the law which clearly defines and controls cheating. Thus Denny Kay, a cheater in British soccer, ended up in jail for two years.

The referee acts as the visible controlling agent of this structure of law enforcement in sport. He watches the proper conduct of a game and continuously deals out sanctions in order to secure equality of chance and a just outcome. Yet the referee's mandate does not go beyond the playing field and the control of visible acts and conditions. He may check for proper shoes and he may rule behavior to be foul, but he has no knowledge about a fix or about the deliberate bad plays of one athlete or whether players have been drugged or not. Of course, he may guess that something is wrong in the course of a game. Most likely he, like the other players and the spectators, will not know about an act of cheating. As far as drugs are concerned, doctors may be called in to detect their use. Most other acts and intentions to cheat outside of the arena will be difficult to control by rules and their enforcement, so cheating cannot be controlled in places where it is probably practiced in the more severe forms. Control of deviance and cheating is not a matter of rules and control agents only; indeed, such forms of *outer containment* cannot succeed unless *inner containment* works as well (Reckless 1961). As inner containment in the control of cheating in sport one could list two groups of factors. The first deals with the inner controls of the personnel involved in sport. Here we may account for learning experiences in one's family, neighborhood, and social class— the same factors that also could account for learning deviant acts. Recruitment in sport seems to be directed very much in favor of potentially less delinquent sections of society—with the notable exception of the so-called athletic clubs in gangs of big cities (Thrasher 1936). The other group of factors of inner containment has to do with the structure of the contest itself. Sport is to a certain degree unreal, an end in itself, as Huizinga put it (1950). Although the consequences are much more severe for one's status than Huizinga thought, there is ample evidence that consequences of bad performance in sport, for example, are not as severe as in occupational work. Even in professional sport one can easily rationalize that it is just a game which he can leave at any time. Structurally this accounts for much of the instability in a contest, most notably to be observed in the games of children. In order to keep such a system going, a high amount of mutual interdependence is essential— *association*, as I have called it elsewhere (Lueschen 1970). Association in a contest will serve as another mode of inner containment, as a control against cheating. Finally, a sport contest which is "all in the open," which implies high risk of detection in acts of cheating by one's opponent, the spectators, or one's own teammates, also serves as a deterrent to cheating.

Although after our earlier discussion one may expect that cheating is more likely at higher levels of competition, the professionalization in such an activity carries with it not only higher levels of competence and skill, but also a code of ethics that supports the system because of mutual interest between teammates and even opposing players. It would be a clear indication of incomplete professionalization in sport if such implications were not borne out. This seems actually to be the case in the recently developed German professional soccer clubs which are struggling with cheating that involves all but four of the first league's eighteen clubs (*Der Spiegel*, November 15, 1971). In general it would be self-defeating for such a system of sport to be involved with illegal procedures, since by definition only skill and strategy within the boundaries of rules and agreements should determine the outcome of a game. It is because of the interest in such outcomes, often reinforced by the fact that in normal life other factors determine one's status, that spectators directly or indirectly subsidize sport and thus make professionalization materially possible. Because of alleged acts of cheating, interest in soccer in Germany has fallen off strongly; so has the interest in boxing in the United States since the 1920's. Spectators also should thus be mentioned as factors of control; yet both belong more to the area of outer containment.

The net result of our discussion of open and secret cheating in sport has not yet led to a better understanding of this form of deviance. We definitely face problems of definition which are closely connected with researchability. I do not propose to solve such problems by defining cheating as merely those acts which are detected. For the undetected forms of cheating in sport, the study of scandals must suffice, although it is limited in that it cannot be quantified. I do not want to exclude the open forms from the definition, although the consequences are usually quickly remedied. Sport may indeed provide ample insights for the study of deviance and cheating in general. The usefulness of sport in providing information on deviance resides in the clarity of definitions of cheating in sport and the ease with which information can be obtained from cheaters in nonprofessional sports, who may be more willing to report such incidences since sport is considered to them to be "just a game."

At this point we are probably very dissatisfied with the hypothetical statements concerning the causes of cheating in sport. Do professionals cheat more or less than amateurs of much lower ability, where, besides the persons involved, very few care about the outcome? On one hand, the marked absence of controls on the lower level of performance may well account for similar rates of cheating among professionals. On the other, certain factors seem to favor the prediction that we would expect more cheating among professionals and in high-level amateur sport. Yet inner containment and social control in sport seem by all accounts to be so strong as to lead to the expectation that less deviance will be found in sport than in other sections of society (Schafer 1969). On the very lowest level of sport, in the competitive games of children, cheating (according to Piaget's subjects) is not possible for four reasons: it is naughty (forbidden, etc.); it is contrary to the rules of the game; it makes cooperation impossible ("You can't play anymore"); and it is contrary to equality (Piaget 1965). Cheating is notably absent from children's games. Of course, children often deliberate and argue so much following an incident of cheating that they never get on with the game. To pose yet another unresolved question: Does the swiftness of action in the highest echelons of sport conceal all the cheating that goes on there, or do the controls work so superbly?

REFERENCES

Adams, J. S.
    1965   "Inequity in Social Exchange." In Berkowitz, L., ed. *Advances in Experimental Social Psychology*. New York: Academic Press. Pp. 267–299.
Huizinga, J.
    1950   *Homo Ludens: A Study of the Play Element in Culture*. Boston: Beacon.
Lueschen, G.
    1970   "Cooperation, Association and Contest." *Journal of Conflict Resolution* 14 (1):21–37.
Merton, R. K.
    1938   "Social Structure and Anomie." *American Sociological Review* 3:672–682. October.
Piaget, J.
    1965   *The Moral Judgment of the Child*. New York: Free Press.
Polsky, N.
    1967   *Hustlers, Beats and Others*. Chicago: Aldine.
Reckless, W. C.
    1961   "A New Theory of Delinquency and Crime." *Federal Probation* 25:42–46. December.
Schafer, W. E.
    1969   "Some Social Sources and Consequences of Interscholastic Athletics: The Case of Participation and Delinquency." In Kenyon, G., ed. *Sociology of Sport*. Chicago: Athletic Institute. Pp. 29–44.
Sutherland, E. H.
    1955   *Principles of Criminology*. Philadelphia: Lippincott.

Thrasher, F. M.
　1936　"The Boys' Club and Juvenile Delinquency." *American Journal of Sociology* 42:66–80. July.
Wallerstein, J. S., and Wyle, C. J.
　1947　"Our Law-Abiding Law-Breakers." *Probation* 25:107–112, 118. March/April.

Hustling as a Career

E. LOUIS MAHIGEL AND GREGORY P. STONE

One—and only one—way of viewing social interaction or human life is from a "game" perspective or metaphor. Ordinarily, games are spacially bounded interactions between individuals or teams. They occur across boards, on tables, in courts, in stadia or pits, or on fields, tracks, streets, sandlots, or sidewalks. Although such games are extremely diverse in character, they have at least one thing in common—victories or pay-offs—someone or some group wins. Moreover, games are organized. Rules guarantee a regular, recurring pattern of interaction. George Herbert Mead apprehended this organized character of the game and likened the team to a community, while Eric Berne has recently extended the notion of the game to human interaction generally.

Where there's a game, there's a hustle. Just what is a hustle? Dictionaries tell us that to hustle is to shake, push, or shove roughly; jostle, often to force roughly or hurriedly as into, out of, or through a place. To be sure, that is what must be meant by the hustle in sports. Indeed, athletes are benched when they do not hustle. They are removed from the playing field and can only view the game from the sidelines. At the worst, this privileged view may also be denied them. They are sent to the showers or suspended from the team. But there is more to the hustle than the hustling of the jock. As we see it, the hustler can probably win—across boards, on tables, in stadia, pits, or sandlots, or on the streets. Especially on the streets. He can beat the community and win the game people play.

Hustlers always have an edge. Some may not have the same edge that others have honed; then a hustler is hustled. There is, in Kafka's sense, a metamorphosis; but instead of becoming a cockroach, the hustler becomes a fish, a sucker.

Competence is a prime requisite of the hustle; it is established as a matter of degree. All hustlers are competent, but some are more com-

E. Louis Mahigel is an assistant professor in speech communication at the University of Minnesota. Gregory P. Stone is a professor of sociology at the University of Minnesota.

petent than others, just like the pigs on the *Animal Farm* who came to dominate the farm. Why, then, do hustlers "hang in" when other hustlers are demonstrably more competent? They are involved. As the jocks would have it, they are "charged up," and they have character. They are dedicated to the victory or the payoff. They will employ almost any means available to realize that dedication. Dissimulation is one of the most frequently employed techniques. This is not so different from the hustle in sports. Every athlete worth his salt must dissemble— know how to feint or fake or dramatize fouls inflicted upon him. There are no penalties for faking, though, interestingly, there are penalties for faking injuries in American football. The hustler shakes, pushes, or jostles to force others roughly or hurriedly into, out of, or through a place. He accomplishes this in an extremely competent manner. The hustler is a dedicated con man who must have an edge in the game. His dedication may mean the end of his hustle, when he is taken by those who have a finer edge. But this takes us into matters of career. Where do hustlers come from? How do they maintain their hustle? How do they leave the hustle? In social-psychological terms, these are matters of socialization, socialized performance, and desocialization.

THE INCEPTION OF THE HUSTLE

Most hustlers begin their careers early, by twelve to fourteen years of age. In this sense, the inception of the hustling career is not unlike that of the concert pianist, the ballet dancer, the athlete, or, for that matter, any performer in the games adults play with one another. Most must have sponsors who are or were skilled participants in the game that will be hustled. Such sponsors are ordinarily intimate with their proteges. To cite only one case: a hustler of our acquaintance really began his hustle at the age of five. He started pitching pennies. He knew where the suckers were and when they would be there: Sunday after mass. They had their money for a collection they never offered. This lad practiced pitching pennies all week, but no longer than an hour and a half a day. With this practice, he honed an edge. Winning, he discovered his lust, and this lust was discovered by his brother, who was already well on his way to becoming an established pool and card hustler. The older brother took the younger one under his wing and taught him how to hustle cards. By this time, our incipient hustler had reached the grand old age of nine years. His brother was a competent hustler and schooled him in the tricks of the trade. By seventeen, this young man was operating his own gambling house and taking in about

$20,000 a year. Here we emphasize the competence of the sponsor.

There is also the matter of the transparent incompetence of the fish. To the person who is, for whatever reason, intelligent at an early age, the world is so clearly obvious that the possibilities of conning cannot be ignored. What stupid people! They are so manipulable. As Garfinkel would have it, the routine grounds of everyday activity are so transparent that the bright young one cannot afford to ignore the transparency. So he takes advantage. He hustles because he conceives the easy edge. Many parents are rank fish. Simply by being so, they may well encourage the hustle among their offspring. Compulsively, they play to lose. And while Gambler's Anonymous is not a society of losing parents, it is a society of compulsive losers.

LATTER-DAY-COMERS

These people are sometimes recruited. Usually they do not begin their hustle in preadolescence. There are many people who hang around gambling establishments, and some hustlers may take them into account. But there is a double bind—the hanger-on has a lust, and the hustler who perceives him perceives that lust and seeks to bring his incipient acts into the unreality of the game. A seventeen-year-old hung around a gambling establishment for a period of time. He ran errands for the players and kibitzed the games. His constant presence and willingness to do whatever the gamblers wanted him to do attracted the attention of an established card hustler. This hustler recruited our latter-day comer and taught him the nuances of gin rummy and poker. The comer eventually won third place in the international gin rummy tournament held in Las Vegas. One can become a hustler simply by hanging around the hustle. We are reminded of Sutherland's "differential association theory" of socialization into crime.

LATE-COMERS

There are those who are condemned to free choice, as Sartre would have it. Some of these have chosen, and must choose again. Skinner would remove these damning options from human games, but we would prefer not to. Take used car salesmen—these people must know how to make the game. Having failed at whatever previous games, they move into an easy game to make. They dissemble. In New York City there is a requirement that all used cars must be approved by a state licensing office. Licensing offices are provided by garages. A used car dealer can visit such an office and buy stickers certifying the reliability of a used car. Used car dealers may purchase these stickers by the dozen from state-approved dispensers, usually at neighborhood garages. Thus it is not unlikely that several such stickers will be delivered to a used car salesman, at his request, with a certain payoff of invisible remuneration. Those unfortunates who have failed in other legitimate lines of enterprise may well enter into this blatant kind of hustle. How many young used car salesmen are you acquainted with?

Frequently ministers fail to hustle their religion, so they look for another hustle. We may find them in used car lots, but more often they are peddling life insurance or real estate. What is the minister's real hustle if he is, in fact, a late-comer: Messiah, man, or money? All these hustles are interchangeable, and they are built for failures or for those who eschew the damnation of choice.

Some cannot avoid this sentence. We all know that those on the bottom—disadvantaged people—must make such choices; the street culture teaches them this. If the street culture fails, prison life teaches them. Of course, sociologists are beginning to find this out years after the process was initiated. Sociologists, however, have not even begun to understand that some of those who occupy high positions are coerced into a hustle. This is probably because many people in high positions, including sociologists in academia, ride out their careers. But there are those who still have a lust, a faith, integrity, or character. They continue to hustle their arguments, their ideas, and their publications. The world will not leave them alone. They are forced to maintain the hustle after it has been made. *Yeah !*

MAINTAINING THE HUSTLE

Once a hustle is begun it must be maintained. One way of doing this is to maintain anonymity by disguises, by moving around from one game to another, by hoping that there will be no continuity among the gaming circles, or by shifting masks within the same gaming circles. Usually this is not enough.

One must handle his side bets. Howard S. Becker considered side bets as the basis of commitment to a line of action. By this he meant that one's concerns with the world (other than his preoccupation with his hustle) objectively committed him to a line of action. Thus one becomes committed to whatever performance because he cannot escape the obligations that he owes to others who may not be involved in that performance, e.g., wives, children, households, or locations. This may be true for some people, but not for most hustlers. Some of the most committed have no side bets at all. Kate Coleman (*Ramparts*, December, 1971) writes about a whorehouse madam:

She has no friends outside her business, she claims, because she cannot "afford them." They could easily blow her scene. She speaks of her boredom with "the same old talks of prostitutes"—infections, money problems and pimps. The latter she calls "pimples" at every punning opportunity, for she considers them parasites. "I get tired of listening to it, honey," she intones. But, in the same breath she bounces back with gentle mockery, "But then, if you think about your family, it's just as boring. You've got to listen to all those squares talk to you."

So what Becker has said is not true for most hustles. In many hustles, one maintains his business by eliminating side bets.

CHARACTER

We think that Becker does not really understand the hustle at all. A hustler has character; that means he can turn side bets off and on. Hustlers may love their wives, but their wives should not approach them during the hustle. A hustler involved in a hustle at cards can tell his wife to leave him alone at the card table, but this does not necessarily mean that he does not have a side bet on the beauty of his relationship with his wife. Such side bets are not characteristic, but they build the character of the hustler. Side bets may mean commitments, but the hustler has the character to turn them off or on precisely because of his commitment. Perhaps this is what we are groping for when we employ that elusive term, "character."

Where does character come from? Only society establishes the perimeters of character. Howard S. Becker forgets about this; however, Anselm Strauss does not. He points out that encounters are thickly peopled and complexly imaged. The wonder of human interaction is that many different roles are played at the same time. One must decide which role will dominate the interaction. The hustler must decide, like anyone else, what role (or bankroll) he is betting on. The beginning of character may originate in this choice. How he can accomplish this choice remains a mystery, but he must accomplish it. Most of all, he must learn to say no. Perhaps there is a history of hurt or error somewhere along the line that predisposes the hustler to the development of character. Unlike the patients of Freud, he cannot repress the pain. He accepts it and learns from it. Max Weber has said the same thing about the political boss. The hustler must maintain his cool.

KNOWING WHERE THE GAMES ARE

Certainly one must have character and know how to maintain his cool in critical situations, but these virtues are meaningless unless he knows where the games are. Paradoxically, one must shed his disguises to gain this knowledge. He must become visible to those who sponsor or participate in the games, and this raises risks. Such visibility destroys his anonymity and might mean the end of his hustle. It is sometimes better for the hustler to move among many games than to concentrate his activity on any one. This gives the others a chance to forget his hustle but to remember his person. They will then accept him as a participant in their games.

Crucial games may exist among neighbors, friends at a distance from one another, in clubs, in Las Vegas, or Puerto Rico, or Gardena, California. The hustler is obliged to know about all these games and must become visible enough to be invited or accepted as a participant. The doors cannot be shut because of his very presence. He must have access to every game that he imagines he can hustle.

This implies a network of games, as well as a network of hustlers. Consequently, hustlers will often go to places where games are carried on merely to keep these networks alive. Such encounters do not necessarily impart established knowledge or games. They reassure the hustler; in the interaction (or the bullshit) the hustle is reaffirmed. His quest for knowledge of where the games are is validated. Such encounters or interaction maintain the lust of the hustler.

KEEPING THE GAMES GOING

To sustain this lust, games must continue, and the hustler sees to it that they do. An important part of this is knowing where the games are, but the very knowledge of where the games are perpetuates their existence. The hustler, by his act of knowing, continues the games. His knowledge takes him into a game, and, once he is there, the game continues. When he was talking about commitments established by side bets, Becker was really talking about suckers. The hustler knows this, although he quite probably has not read Howard S. Becker. He entertains the fish. He buys them drinks. He offers them cigars or cigarettes. He may even bring in some sexually appealing creature to distract the fish from his commitment. The hustler's commitment is established not by his own side bets, but by the side bets of the sucker.

This ploy may not always work. Some suckers are more interested in the game than they are in the side bets; the hustler knows this. Some fish may have a lot of money, and some may have less. He will often favor the player who has the lowest stake to catch the fat fish. When a poor poker player with a low stake in a game with other fatter fish misreads his hand, saying that he has a pair of fours in seven card stud, the hustler may accurately point out that he has a flush. The poor boy wins the pot, and the game is continued. The fat fish is still on the hook, nibbling at the bait.

To maintain a game there must be players. The hustler also knows this. He cannot ordinarily be concerned with recruiting players, so he must con other players to recruit new players. This is done in various ways. He joins organizations within which his game is carried on. He befriends the officers of such organizations (who are often rank fish), and he asks them to invite members into the game. The hustler, therefore, stands on top of the organizations that sponsor the games that he hustles. This is true of the neighborhood, friendships, and all the other organizations that the hustler cons. The hustler must be a good sociologist!

TERMINAL POINTS

Hustlers do not commit suicide. Even though they may be dying, and one eye may be closed, the other eye is looking for the sucker to turn the corner and come into view. The hustler dies a long death which he can never acknowledge. As Hemingway wrote, death comes in whispers that are not heard. The hustler can move his games from one place to another, but this becomes a futile effort, because he has become visible, and his hustle is known. And so we confront the paradox of the hustle— the hustler must be known to get into games, and unknown to make his hustle.

He may burn himself out when his hustle becomes obvious. We have seen this in sports; on November 27, 1971, the Florida defensive team offered no resistance to their opponents' touchdown drive so that their quarterback could surmount Plunkett's passing record in collegiate competition. This con was so visible to audiences that the quarterback can probably never win the honor Plunkett enjoys. The team hustle may well have been his death. If one is going to hustle, it cannot be obvious. One never announces his hustle, although he may have to announce his willingness to perform.

There may also be the matter of competition. A hustler can be outhustled, but he cannot accept this. If he does, he becomes a fish for other hustlers, because he maintains the lust—but not the competence —for hustling his game. Here was the death of Willy Loman in Arthur Miller's *Death of a Salesman*. His clientele had outrun his hustle, but Willy was committed to his old techniques.

A million things can call an end to hustles. Age, for one; arthritis in the hands can prevent the hustler from dealing the hand he wishes to deal. Or a hustler may be pricked in the heart by the arrows of respectability—somehow, and at some time, he comprehends the falsehood of his hustle. He may then surrender the hustle and move into religion or move his hustle into religion. We have in mind such people as John Phillip Quinn. For the true hustler, the death of the hustle means moving his hustle from one place to another. He looks for another corner around which another fish may be coming.

The Bowling Hustler:
A Study of Deviance in Sport

PAUL D. STEELE

Goffman (1959) suggests that a feature of institutionalized action is the development of a counterorganization "underlife."[1] This is true of organized game situations, where the formal rules, interaction patterns, and ends are altered by a small group of individuals to fit their own wishes and needs. This paper will explore and discuss bowling hustlers, a group of people who through their actions form the underlife of the game of bowling. My specific purpose is to identify this group and to analyze their attitudinal and behavioral relations to others within the bowling institution, and with the outside world as a whole. Their value structures as expressed in their participation in the institution and in society will be considered to give meaning to their hustling behavior. We will try to understand why these individuals have turned to anti-social and technically illegal behavior in their sporting world activity. Toward this end, the group of subjects under consideration will be identified, and the theoretical and methodological framework in which they will be evaluated will then be presented. The next section will explore the position of the hustler within the game of bowling, and in the outside world. Relationships between game and social status will be drawn and used to explain the hustler's behavior.

For our purposes, the hustler is an individual who manipulates game interaction with naive others; in this way he succeeds in winning money (or goods) in a bowling contest. Game situation manipulation is usually done through a false presentation of the hustler's true bowling ability to the opponent. Of crucial significance to the hustler is his ability to set up the match, to convince the "fish" (unsuspecting person being hustled) that he is entering the contest on even or favorable terms, and to

Paul D. Steele is assistant professor of sociology at the University of Wisconsin, Milwaukee.

1. This point is made by Goffman (1961) in his study of total institutions. It is evident in any type of institution that has a relatively explicit set of rules for performance, criteria of success, definitions of the situation, and models of the actors.

sustain the contest as long as possible to gain the maximum profit. In other words, the bowling hustler must be a master of the process of situation management.

Bowling hustlers can be differentiated as full-time and part-time hustlers. Full-time hustlers are involved for a living; Polsky points out that "some bowling hustlers do fairly well" (1967:68) in an economic sense. But full-time hustlers make up only a small part of the bowling hustler population. Far more common is the part-time hustler who has other means of financial support and does not participate in hustling as a dominant role activity.[2] Since these hustlers are more common, and since the techniques they use are the same as those employed by full-time hustlers, they will be the topic of study.

Because part-time hustlers are not engaged in hustling as a dominant role activity, Zurcher's (1968, 1970) concept of ephemeral role seems particularly applicable in analysis of their behavior.[3] "The ephemeral role can be seen to serve two primary functions for persons engaging in leisure sport: 1) temporary dissociation from dominant role obligations; 2) temporary fulfillment of needs not satisfied by dominant roles. These two functions are, of course, related." (Steele and Zurcher 1971)

In other words, we are interested in studying a group of persons who can be distinguished from others as spending their time outside dominant roles in socially deviant leisure pursuits. The conflict that arises in the hustler's attempts to operate in the dominant social world in a socially acceptable way, while at the same time pursuing deviance in leisure time, forms the basis of our inquiry.

Before proceeding, I should mention the empirical basis of the study. My familiarity with the activities of the bowling hustler is based on four years of interaction with the hustling situation. I participated as a hustler, was hustled by others, and formed close associations with many people actively involved in this activity. More formal participant-observer research was conducted primarily in Los Angeles. In addition, a number of formal interviews were conducted with hustlers to gain insight into attitudes toward the game and toward society. A study of the background, demographic, and attitudinal characteristics of nonhustler bowlers was conducted through systematic observation, interviews, and questionnaires.[4]

2. Dominant roles generally include primary social, familial, and occupational roles (Zurcher 1968).
3. The concept of ephemeral role is identified in Zurcher (1968), broadened in a later article (1970), and discussed and applied in Steele and Zurcher (1971).
4. The research was conducted partly for the preparation of my master's

The Hustler and the Game

The hustler's position within the bowling institution is unique. This is emphasized by the differences in his game behavior and attitudinal involvement. In general, the hustler spends a great amount of his free time in the bowling establishment; this is the source of his primary social relations. In addition, he bowls considerably more than the average nonhustler and has greater skill with the game. For example, male league bowlers as a whole average around 155 per game,[5] while the estimated average of most hustlers is 180–195 per game.[6] Those hustlers interviewed reported bowling twenty to sixty games per week on the average, while nonhustler league bowlers reported bowling four or five games per week.

Another aspect of game involvement is game attitude. Hustlers gain different sorts of gratification from bowling; as shown in Table 1, responses of the interviewed hustler group as to what satisfaction they derive from the game are significantly different from the responses of the nonhustler control group of regular league bowlers. While specific percentages cannot be considered conclusive because of the small subject population of hustlers, the extremely strong differences evident in the findings make for interesting contrasts. Particularly noticeable are the predominance of responses by hustlers in categories of identity generation, reinforcement, expression, status, and prestige. On the other hand, the category of affiliation, mentioned most often as pleasure derived from bowling by nonhustlers, was mentioned by only one hustler as characteristic of his game involvement. This seems to indicate that hustlers are more interested in generating a personal image and status than in gaining and maintaining friends through bowling.

It became obvious in my observations that, to the hustler, winning was more important than how he played the game. Hustlers performance and self-evaluation in the bowling situation can be considered of central importance to their self-concept, while of only peripheral interest to most bowlers. The bowling hustler places a great importance on his position in the bowling institution from a personal perspective, as witnessed by the great amount of time he spends in the game and the heavy emphasis he places on self-concept and status concerns generated by bowling performance relative to nonhustlers.

---

thesis. My thanks to the Graduate School of the University of Texas at Austin for the research funds supplied to collect much of the data presented here.

5. As reported in *Bowling News*.

6. The hustler's average skill is only estimated; hustlers are extremely reluctant to divulge this information to anyone.

TABLE 1.

Game function	Hustlers	Nonhustlers
Catharsis	20%	38%
Relaxation and recreation	10%	32%
Identity generation, reinforcement, and expression	70%	46%
Affiliation	10%	77%
Separation	10%	15%
Status and prestige	80%	5%
Number of subjects	10	241

THE HUSTLER AND SOCIETY

Since we are considering the part-time hustler, it is obvious that he has some interaction with and position in the outside world. The place of the hustler in society at large and its relation to his hustling activity and image may be of interest.

In determining the social position of hustlers, various indicators of social status and success can be used, including indicators of education, income, marital status, and type of dwelling. In this study hustlers are compared with nonhustler league bowlers and with national population averages.[7] The results are presented in Table 2.

TABLE 2.

Indicator	Hustlers	Nonhustlers	National average
Median annual income	$5800	$7925	$7653
Mean years of education	11.5	13.5	12.6
Type of dwelling			
House (own)	0%	77%	NA
House (rent)	10%	3%	NA
Apartment	80%	20%	NA
Other	10%	1%	NA
Marital status			
Single	50%	7%	22%
Married	20%	88%	67%
Separated or divorced	30%	5%	6%

Hustlers hold a social position in the outside world which is quite different from that of other bowlers and the general population. They

7. Nonhustler league bowler data is based on an Austin, Texas, sample. National data is reported from 1970 census statistics.

have a lower annual income and educational achievement level; they live in rented housing and generally live without a spouse. Those married hustlers interviewed had been married less than two years, and only one had a child. In general, the bowling hustler can be considered as a social underachiever. He has few if any accomplishments outside the bowling institution from which to derive positive status and a favorable self-evaluation.

APPLICABILITY OF THE EPHEMERAL ROLE CONCEPT

In reviewing the situation of the bowling hustler, some generalizations about his life condition can be made. First, the hustler seems to stand on the margin of the everyday world. He is more or less unsuccessful in academic, vocational, or social affairs, and he has few means of ego satisfaction in everyday life. In short, he holds the position of second-class citizen in our society. But he is different from other individuals in that status, because he has a concrete and direct outlet for his frustrations. The game-centered institution of bowling offers him a way to satisfy his needs for a positive self-evaluation and control over his life. Within the confines of the bowling establishment, the hustler can gain a sense of personal accomplishment and a high (albeit private) status. Because the positive self-opinion denied him in the outside world can be gained in the bowling institution, he places emphasis upon his performance and spends much time in the game situation.

The behavior and attitudinal involvement of the hustler closely follows the theoretical model of the ephemeral role. The hustler encounters frustrations in his attempts to sustain a positive self-image in his dominant role activity. Since the hustler can bowl well and can manage the hustling situation, he substitutes this activity as a criterion for positive self-evaluation. In this way he is able to fulfill needs for a favorable self-concept. Although this exploratory study cannot serve as a complete test of validation, this and other research employing the ephemeral role concept (Zurcher 1968, 1970; Steele and Zurcher 1971) suggest that the greater the drive state unsatisfied by dominant role activity and the greater the effectiveness of drive state resolution by an ephemeral role activity, the greater the relative emphasis upon and involvement in that particular ephemeral role activity.

A distinction must be made in our analysis. While intense involvement in the bowling institution is explainable in terms of the model presented, we are left with the question of why the particular individuals in question turn to hustling as their characteristic game behavior pattern. Intense involvement does not necessarily dictate hustling activity —it is also characteristic of professional bowling and heavy amateur participation. To resolve this question, we must examine the unique rewards that hustling makes available to the participant.

The most obvious reward is money. Hustlers can win money with less bowling skill than can professionals, since the competition is not as strong. However, this does not seem to be the prime reason for entering into this competitive bowling activity. The money cannot be counted on, since matches are not usually scheduled on a regular basis. The stakes often are so low, or matches are so infrequent, that no appreciable income can be gained from hustling. As one hustler put it, "As soon as you start thinking about the stake, you can forget about winning."

For the reason which bowling hustlers most commonly give for their participation, we must return to our earlier mention of situation management and control.[8] Again quoting the same hustler: "It's not the money that I bowl for. Of course it's nice to clean up once in a while, but you can't sit around waiting for the big fish. . . . The real kick I get [out of hustling] is 'taking' the fish. Real good ones [hustlers] are the guys who can get the fish on the hook and get 'em to bowl for all they got." As illustrated here, the important consideration is gaining mastery of the game situation. Monetary rewards are important, but merely as indicators of success in managing the situation, since the amount that the fish has with him varies in each case. The goal of the bowling hustler is to maximize his profits by gaining complete control of the hustling situation through accurate estimation of the fish's ability, impression management, favorable negotiation of the terms of the match, and sustaining the match as long as possible.

The characteristics of bowling hustling make situation management possible. In team league bowling, personal success is contingent upon the performance of teammates and opponents. In professional tournaments, it is dependent on the performance of other professionals. But in the hustling situation, personal management of the terms of the game can be so structured that the outcome is rarely in doubt. From the standpoint of the hustler, the game should be won before the first ball is bowled.

8. See Mahigel and Stone's (1971) discussion of impression management in card hustling, and Polsky's (1967) discussion of pool hustling. For a more general presentation, see Goffman (1959).

CONCLUSION

The bowling hustler is drawn to the bowling game due to his success as a bowler and his relative lack of success in the outside world. He comes to place great emphasis on bowling and defines his self-concept largely in terms of his activity in the bowling institution. The explanation has been posed in terms of the ephemeral role concept, and the data seem to be consistent with it. The reason for hustling as the particular form of bowling involvement appears to rest on a need for self-control and situation control offered in hustling activity but apparently absent from the hustler's dominant role involvement.

REFERENCES

Goffman, Erving
    1959 *The Presentation of Self in Everyday Life.* New York: Doubleday-Anchor.
    1961 *Asylums.* New York: Doubleday-Anchor.
Mahigel, E. Louis, and Stone, Gregory
    1971 "How Card Hustlers Make the Game." *Transaction* 8, 3: 40–45.
Polsky, Ned
    1967 *Hustlers, Beats and Others.* New York: Doubleday.
Steele, Paul, and Zurcher, Louis A.
    1973 "Leisure Sports as 'Ephemeral Roles': An Exploratory Study." *Pacific Sociological Review* 16:345–356.
Zurcher, Louis A.
    1968 "Social-Psychological Functions of Ephemeral Roles." *Human Organization* 27, 4:281–297.
    1970 "The 'Friendly' Poker Game: A Study of an Ephemeral Role." *Social Forces* 49:173–186.

Making Violence by Doing Work: Selves, Situations, and the World of Professional Hockey

ROBERT R. FAULKNER

This paper examines the social context in which violence occurs in professional hockey. I will look at the ways a player's adherence to the moral order of work shape his response to what he perceives as collective threat and personal insult. For the sociologist, whose concern is with describing and analyzing interpretive processes, not with promoting or appreciating professional sport as work, the question is, what does one learn about these processes from examining violence as concerted action?

My information comes from two sources: my own firsthand observations of violent incidents, and detailed interviews with thirty-eight players on two teams in the American Hockey League. I want in particular to show that members' definitions and interpretations involve generalizable qualities of their occupational culture. I am aware that causal explanation cannot be established on the basis of single instances, and, in fact, I have no interest in extrapolating from violence in professional hockey to force-threat practices (Goode 1973, 1972) and beliefs in general. My aim is at once more modest and more ambitious: in seeking an understanding of a particular work group, I am interested in the way players interpret violence. Viewed with respect to the procedures for making it happen, the interviews called for their profiling of incidents through their use of comparable and proverbial accounts of what it takes to do violence as a competent professional. Having observed many of the incidents "in motion" facilitated the concerns of this study. The integration of nonparticipant observation with detailed interrogation recommends the following proposals.

Reprinted from *Sociology of Work and Occupations* 1, 3 (August, 1974). © by permission of the publisher, Sage Publications, Inc., pp. 288–304.
Robert R. Faulkner is associate professor of sociology at the University of Massachusetts, Amherst.

INTERPRETING SITUATIONS

Although the concept of situation has been widely used in social psychology, it has yet to be given an adequate conceptual definition. Some theorists use the concept of situation as a "focused gathering" or, following Goffman (1964, 1961), as an encounter. Employed by Hymes (1964, 1962) and Ervin-Tripp (1964), it refers to the location of a gathering, its physical setting, point in time, occasioned work, the behavior patterns that accompany it, and the social relations of the individuals involved. Other theorists emphasize that situations and concerted action are understood in their course by the subjective meanings attached to them by members (Ball 1972; Stebbins 1967; Znaniecki 1952). In this framework situations can be viewed, to use Berger and Luckmann's terminology (1966), as "constructions of reality." Their formulations draw attention to the program of communicative work which furnishes a sum total of information which allows players to interpret the behavior of others, exert demands, infer motives, and align their action with the interests and actions of others.

In what follows, violence is viewed as a constitutent feature of this interpretive work. The meaning of violence in face-to-face encounters is not waiting there, available for any who would take it; it must be constructed in concert with like-situated others. As social action which takes account of and is oriented to the behavior of adversaries and team-colleagues, force-threat can be seen as meaningful work by which a player tests inferences about the role of others while making an implicit claim to be a person of a particular, occupationally approved character. In this communicative work players offer to themselves a folk version of Weber's adequate causal analysis. This is displayed by showing that the typical patterns of violence follow from a "correct" course of reasoning and decision-making. This wide-reaching scheme of interpretation is designed to show that responses to emotionally charged situations are reasonable, taken for granted, and recommended. The resolve to inflict physical injury is viewed by members as done under the auspices of membership and hence routinely sanctionable, i.e., institutionalized as a method of managing the task. Finally, interpreting situations in this way provided accounts of behavior in terms of one's status as a member of a special occupational world.

By calling this an occupational world, I wish to direct attention to the distinctive set of understandings and interpretations that arise in response to the organization of work and its contingencies. By contingencies I mean those enforced features of the setting upon which successful performance depends. The problematic features of doing work as a practical skill are seen by players as modifications of the outside world. More importantly, they involve interpreting interpersonal events on the ice as a series of self announcements and placements (Stone 1962; Goffman 1967). The emergent and open-ended nature of announcements and placements implies that occupational character is continually being defined, tested, and interpreted by others. A detailed analysis of the interpretive process (Blumer 1969; Mead 1934; Turner 1962; Wilson 1970) through which situations are defined and identities negotiated (McCall and Simmons 1966) provides a theoretical addition to what Albert Cohen (1965:9) has called the "microsociology of the deviant act." The substantive focus is to develop and document the hypothesis that if situations are rule governed, then occasions are to be found where the practice of provocation and force is the successfully constructed product of occupational control rather than its demise (Faulkner 1973).

WORK RELEVANCIES AND DEMANDS

Sociologists use the term "work relevancies" in three distinct but related ways: to delineate the ongoing practices in the work settings they describe; to specify what persons would like to see themselves entitled to as conditions of membership; and to refer to the focal concerns of members. This section is concerned mainly with the third meaning. In profiling the prevailing features of interpreting work, members insist that they merely use common sense when being attuned to the realities of the task. The realities of violence are observed to be matters of serious consequence. The practical concerns recommended below are not in the nature of options available to personnel as a matter of personal preference, although players do emphasize that some are more expert at handling and managing physical force. Each is recommended as a fact of life that a player comes to appreciate. The appreciation is contained in the course of dealing with actual situations. Members also suggest that coming to terms with work proceeds by way of handling the troubles generated by ignorance of, or inattention to, these demands.

RESPECT AND PRESENTATIONAL STRATEGIES: "SHOWING YOURSELF"

A prominent operational feature of this approach may be formulated as the player's concern for putting forth and preserving his status as a competent worker. A respectable showing is accomplished by managing others, rather than being managed. The concern centers around situations in which a player affirms for himself and others, in the language of gesture and deed, that he is to be treated as a certain kind of person. Like many occupational tasks organized around the theme of potential danger and crisis, a man's conduct on the ice is under the close scrutiny of other interactants, and he is expected to demonstrate essential qualities. In professional hockey, the adversarial idiom inevitably devolves on the integrity of one's physical being. Essential attributes are interpreted with an eye to physical deportment, courage, toughness, and skillful execution of one's performance under the pressure of physical injury (Goffman 1967:149–270). Honor revolves around a player's capacity to move into trouble and command deferential treatment from colleagues who are, in other respects, like himself. Sociologically, respect involves acting in terms of standardized expectancies so that others will impute to the actor the kind of identity he would want them to see him possess. Members learn, then, what identities are available to them, as well as the presentational resources at their disposal. The direct application of violence in the presence of colleagues and adversaries is a presentational resource for communicating or announcing, in terms of socially approved attributes, something about the self in the presence of others. It does not go unrecognized that one career contingency is, as the term "showing yourself" suggests, coming to the attention of others.

While not directly advocated as the only way of making a reputation, toughness and the taste for fisticuffs is viewed as part of a set of role enactments before colleague competitors, while at the same time serving as a line of behavior directed toward impressing coaches and management. Violence exhausts neither the complete repertoire of skills (skating, stick-handling, shooting, etc.) nor the political savvy needed to survive in pro hockey. Nevertheless, players are constantly attuned to the possibility of violence on the ice so that fighting well, for example, is advocated as a proactive means for cutting losses as well as enhancing "face," staking claims to a reputation of not being easily pushed around, and warding off prospective punishment or retribution through successful shows of toughness. Showing one's mettle suggests that open provocation of others is an occasion for putting forth one's essential courage—that is, demonstrating the capacity to move against adversaries in the face of recognized danger (see Goffman 1967:218). Players' estimates of colleagues and competitors occur dramatically under conditions of trouble or fateful play action in which there is physical, social, or psychological risk. It seems that appreciative evaluations are earned by those who skillfully manipulate and even seek out such encounters.

TESTING

Related to communicating definitions of the self and earning a reputation through fighting is the concern for "seeing what the opposition is made of." Players feel obliged to actively create trouble for others and employ tactics to engender anxiety, induce role discomfiture, and erode the confidence of their opposition. This emphasis appears to require, at minimum, a presumption that while playing does not necessarily cause all relations to be severely tested during game encounters, the possibility of being physically provoked and tested is not checked by the expectation that it will not occur.

In discussions about the level and form of belligerence, few players raised doubts about the importance of coercion and violence as means of defining focal participants and the game situation itself. Summed up by the imperative "you have to find out what they're made of," encounters become character contests, but more important, violence is used as a means for identifying an underlying pattern behind opponents' behaviors. In this way, testing is an interpretive process. Others' reactions to force are seen as expressions of, or as standing for, their more enduring social attributes. Documenting the motives and essential character of others involves socially sustained methods for making inferences about their intentions, motives, and purposes. If violence is geared to compel others to do as one wishes, then force as a testing strategy can be viewed as a means through which such role-related information and definitions of others evolve and change, and as a practical zero-sum strategy for controlling others against their will. Intimidation and insult in the form of the deft forearm or elbow, butt of the stick, and fist is a recommended procedure for finding out what others are about, what lines of action and interaction can be taken against them, and what troubles can be anticipated.

As for the informational clarity and quality of particular responses, there is a strong disposition to search out readily identifiable expressions, such as whether the opposing player continues his line of play but with imputed caution. Every defenseman interviewed noted that initial encounters are particularly important in defining other players. Here is a twenty-eight-year-old defenseman who emphasized the areas behind and around the net as places in which character contests took place.

> I know a lot of times a guy will go into the corner . . . that's where
> you find out if the guy is going to come back at you or challenge you
> or anything. You see what he can take.
> *Q: So the corners are important?*
> Sure, you go in and really rap him hard with the elbow and let him
> have it in the head maybe and the next time you won't have any prob-
> lems with the guy. Maybe he'll come in the corner but not as hard as
> he did the first time, he's taking a chance of getting another elbow in
> the mouth. Maybe you get a penalty, but you take him out of the play,
> that's a good penalty. . . . I'll give 'em an elbow and, you know, hit
> guys dirty. Now I wouldn't hit a guy in the head with a stick, but you
> get 'em solid with a good check. This is your job, and you watch, he
> won't come back into the corner too quick. You find out what he's
> made of.

The recommended maneuver for finding evidence of what an opponent
is "made of" involves what Goffman (1971:44) aptly describes as
incursions on the "personal territories of the self": "If territory-like
preserves are the central claims in the study of co-mingling, then the
central offense is an incursion, intrusion, encroachment, presumption,
defilement, besmearing, contamination—in short, a violation." Intrusion by force on another's personal space is viewed as a method for lo-
cating others. This involves the treatment of the other's reaction to
provocation as pointing to an underlying pattern. Asked about which
players demand deference, one player noted that what a person does in
the context of the ongoing game action is crucial. He stressed that the
appropriate means for testing others and resolving perceived threats
must be done with an eye to the application of rules by referees and
linesmen.[1]

> The guy you've got to worry about is the guy who turns around and
> really hits you back, bang, right in the nose, and the guy who keeps
> going into the corner to dig it out. The next time *you're* thinking, he's
> got *you* going. You've got to respect him because you know he'll take

1. Rather than outline the formally instituted rules and their application by
referees and linesmen, I shall consider what these mean to, and how they are
taken into account by, players on actual occasions of violence. The reason for
this emphasis is simple: formal rules of the game do not have a stable, determi-
nate meaning which is invariant despite the actual game situation. While I recognize the need to investigate the ongoing judgmental processes through which
officials bring rules to bear on relevant occasions, the definitions of the situations
described here are taken from the standpoint of players subject to these evaluations. Players recognize the open character of the relation between officials' definition of a rule violation and response to it. They also feel that in many cases
officials enforce rules in order to solve pressing practical problems in keeping
peace on the ice.

it and give it back. He doesn't back away . . . to intimidate a guy you've got to rap him, cheap penalties are no good really, a hooking penalty is a cheap penalty, tripping, holding is a cheap penalty. A good penalty is charging provided you hit the guy and he *knows* he's been hit. If you trip the guy, it won't hurt him, it doesn't even bother him, he won't care. Tripping is really stupid, the only time you'll trip a guy is if he gets behind you or if you miss the puck and hit his feet. These are stupid because you really haven't done *your* job. This means the guy's beaten you and you have to slow him down so you can hook him or hold him. If you can intimidate him he won't get in this position in the first place. I don't know in some ways you give the elbow, well, it's stupid, it doesn't even bother some guys, some guys are just unbelievable, you know, they just keep coming back.

Gameness is explicitly stressed as a rationale for according deference. As the player above notes, regard flows from a capacity to stick to a line of activity regardless of setbacks and pain, and this "not because of some brute insensitivity but because of inner will and determination." (Goffman 1967:218–219). As a practical organizational achievement, force-threat is conceptualized as a persuasive restraint which restricts another's chance of spontaneously carrying out his role. Success against an opponent defines the lines of action and interaction that can be taken with regard to him, as well as reflecting on his moral worth as a player. A player with a respectable record of penalties and a reputation for being a hard-nosed fighter moved easily from the use of body checks to fists as a way of increasing control over adversaries. As for defining the situation, ". . . you line up the opposition and you nail 'em, you let 'em know that this is the way it's going to be. These are the rules . . . you give 'em a warning about what's going to happen the rest of the season, you find out how different guys react. Now you pound someone really hard and even fight him if that's what it takes." As for the consequences of belligerence as a tactic in negotiating identities, "It's a known fact that there are certain guys on certain teams that if you nail 'em once or twice, if you show 'em you're going to take charge, well, they can't take the hitting and so they've got to respect you. They'll be looking, so you can kill their game."

The strength and directness of these statements indicate that the respondents are not embarrassed by the topic of violence and are not disposed to vague platitudes about its proper use. I would also argue that they are not inclined to exaggerate the notion of physical toughness. As the brute realities of competition are faced, more prosaic and craftsmanlike definitions of force emerge. The use of coercive intervention is seen as totally unremarkable by all players; the presumption of assault is a most obvious and commonplace assumption. Not only do they approach their competition in this manner, and hold their colleagues to do likewise, but they also expect to be treated this way by their adversaries. And they are. This in itself serves to modify or soften exaggerated invidious claims. Not surprisingly, this player, like his colleagues, sees intimidation and interpersonal testing as normal responses to focused encounters where one maximizes a power position at the expense of others. As he says, these are the "rules." By these standards players continually stake claims for their own character, evaluate others and their essential gameness, and witness the hard checking and occasional decking of colleagues and competitors with the critical eye of a professional.

As outcomes of these game-embedded character contests, imputed lack of gameness is a sign of weakness. This has two important implications. First, lack of character means that one can be easily intimidated, and hence subject to the induced control of other players. Killing another's game is like defiling his identity. Second, the above player's closing theme implies that the inability to withstand dangers and threats means that the opponent will be unable to take full advantage of future opportunities. There is a presumptive belief that once a player has given in, interpersonal domination over him can be continuously applied. A player's reactive moves are viewed as having strategic informational value; namely, they determine prospective courses of action that can be taken with regard to him as an adversary.

> You have to show yourself. You have to play tough, no doubt about it, because if you don't take some of these guys into the boards, they'll just dance around you. You've go to hit 'em and let 'em know you're there. You don't want to get a dumb penalty out of it, like just go in and hit him and draw two minutes. But you've got to hit clean and play the body and if you get a chance put them into the boards so that next time, they'll decide to shoot it instead of trying to go around you. If you don't do this they're going to get around you and make a fool of you. If you have to drop your gloves to establish yourself with these guys then that's what you do.

Players' estimates of colleagues' and competitors' worth occurs most dramatically under conditions of fateful play action where there is physical, social, or psychological risk. A player shows his smartness by moving in and handling trouble. Appreciative evaluations of colleagues are earned by those who skillfully manipulate and even seek out such encounters.

BEING TESTED

Directly related to the character of control exercised over others is the concern for violence directed against the self, and its consequences for the subsequent course of activity. If testing and moving into trouble is a means for making respect and earning the grudging deference of competitors, then giving in or backing down is a sure way of losing it. Just as a loss of face is much more obvious and observable than the gaining of respect, so those behaviors which appear when one is subject to another, or *not* being a smart player, are more obvious to colleagues.

It must be emphasized that in these matters every player is not on his own, for conceptions of respect and character influence modes of interaction as men recognize and seek recognition from others. A player's courage and toughness are viewed in this work culture as his immediate protection against aggression. A player is expected (indeed, morally required) to fight if he wants respect. "It doesn't matter if you lose a fight, there's respect in losing but there's no respect in just doing nothing." There is honor in being obstinate; moreover, a man cannot give way to another without loss of manhood and dignity. And fighting or challenging the person who has wronged him suggests to teammates that the individual can be depended upon to behave in a manner which will not bring disgrace to the team, that he can be relied upon to sustain the projected definition of the situation. Refusal to fight or reluctance to even the score against an opposing team is viewed as cowardly and disruptive of collective efforts. Several players interviewed suggested that those who backed down, or allowed their game to be compromised by the violence of others, earned the label of "chicken" and the disrespect of the colleagues.

> I know we've got a couple of guys on our team, well you know . . . he's [*sic*] scared. He's just scared. You can tell him not to worry that if anything happens don't worry about it, the guys will back you up. But this guy is just scared, you'll make a pass to him and he'll let the pass go off his stick, he'll make a stupid play, he'll move away from trouble. Last week we got the puck out to him across the blue line and their defensemen came in to take him out of the play and our guy just let the puck go off his stick. So this guy on the other team got it and went in to make a shot on net. Now damn, that's really bad. My defense partner and myself were on the bench and he said, "Look at the goddamned chicken." And you just look at that type of thing and it makes you mad. This guy better change his attitude or everybody will tell him. I don't think there's nothing worse than being a chicken.

Two aspects of this respondent's comments are particularly interesting. First, his disgusted and bitter account sounds a common theme running throughout the interviews. Backing away from trouble, especially when the player is in possession of the puck, is unquestionably a sign of weak character and personal failure. That the team member in question does have the skill but allows others to control his game in such an obvious way is a demonstration of disregard for the obligations he owes to others. Second, this respondent says implicitly that his demand that colleagues should stand up and take punishment is based on the shared and self-evident fact that he works hard, is willing to take on the opposition, and in fact encourages trouble. Out of these expectations and the angry response called forth when they are violated, this player fashioned a general view of hockey. He said, "It's a tough game, if you can't take the hitting then you should get out; you can tell in the first two years. Some guys aren't made for it."

While all players admit that some of their colleagues are more adept at moving into and quickly controlling trouble, to a man they recognize that if one is on the receiving end, he is obliged to react. There is a strong presumption that once a player has demonstrated weakness, he becomes essentially different. He becomes fair game for everyone in the league. The reconstruction of a player's reputation under these conditions can be particularly grim. "If you want to get kicked around, high-sticked and have the league running at you, all you have to do is get a reputation as someone who'll back down."

Players are very much aware of their moral identity in the eyes of others. And as this player suggests, regularly perceived fatefulness and risk to self and identity are induced by career concerns where demonstrated gameness and courage are closely tied to and involved in securing the proper respect of others. Once others find evidence for the appropriate attributions of character, the player is accorded a measure of relief from the dirty bodycheck, the deft elbow in the head, and the blade end of the hockey stick in the face. While those granted this deference are not totally immune to the standardized expectations concerning belligerence, they are privileged to be on the receiving end of their more judicious applications. Players see a measure of justice in this. Established pros not only expect to be the recipients of ritual regard, but they also find themselves obliged to coerce it from others at times. The closing and rather grim remark above reminds us that a sense of security and fear permeates relations between adversaries. The player is attuned to invidious dominance; he continually assesses how far opponents intrude into "territories of the self."

TRUST

Several basic uses of force have been considered: those which deal with the aggressive and defensive substance of violence. If an individual's outlook mobilizes defenses to perceive threats, then the awareness of similar events to his colleagues serves to legitimate and discipline the use of protective strategies. As Evans-Pritchard (1969) reminds us, tribal rights are often concerned with the moral and physical welfare of group members; a colleague under attack becomes something of a ceremonious occasion for unhesitating support, for discharging one's duties by keeping adversaries out of the action, and by coercive intervention if a teammate is being defeated. "You've got to trust one another, you back the guys up, you just can't leave your teammate to get his head beat in, you go in and get the other guy off, it's automatic."

As a way through which a player is obliged to express his commitment to collective efforts of those around him, protective reaction is a display of the fundamentally important capacity to be courageous and skillfully assertive. Players note it as a sign of trustworthiness. As in the work of miners, firemen, ironworkers, and bomber crews, the importance of trust derives in no small measure from the need to come to terms with a work environment harboring threats to the self, as well as threats of physical injury. Just as players see what the opposition is made of, so they assess what their colleagues are all about. One problem involves determining whether a player can be relied upon to back others up. Demonstrated reluctance to fight, or to restrain an opponent from moving into a brawl being won by a colleague, raises doubts about another's character. These situations dramatize the worth of his relationships with colleagues.

... your teammates back you up if you get into trouble because all it takes is some guy to pull your skates out from underneath you with his stick and you get hit with a shot. I've seen it happen, I experienced this once. I was in a scuffle and one of the guys tripped me with his stick, I lost my balance and went down. Now by that time everybody was in and there was no damage done, but the idea was he was *allowed* to do it. I was really disappointed.
Q: That he could get in there and get away with it?
Sure, now I'm not blaming anybody but when a fight starts everybody should be there either keeping a guy out of it or holding onto a guy or backing your guy up if he is getting in. I think its something that should be thought of 125 percent. If somebody jumps you from behind you end up saying what the hell, I'm not going to risk my neck

if nobody else's going to help me, so the hell with 'em. Your team
morale can split like that.

The reciprocity and advantages to be gained from these protective relations furnish incentives for collective effort. It is clear that, at these
highly consequential junctures in games, players assess just who some
of their colleagues are playing for, themselves or the team. The bitter-
ness and indignation felt by the above player indicates that failure to
react to and control opponents entering a scuffle is interpreted not only
as a breach of the moral order but also as an insult to one's honor. In
short, colleagues are honor bound to exact vengeance if attacked or, at
least, to provide the appropriate conditions so that others can freely
move against their adversaries; each is thereby forcefully reminded of
how indispensable he is in protecting others from getting hurt and in
preserving a sense of social solidarity.

The potentially explosive consequences of intervention when a colleague is in trouble are recognized by the league rules. The person labeled by the referee as the third man in a fight shall receive a fine and a
game misconduct, which means he is removed from the game. (The
player is therefore faced with the dilemma of either watching a colleague lose a fight with the knowledge that others are watching him, or
interceding and having the team lose his services for the remainder of
the game.) In response to the eagerness of others to protectively react,
another rule levels harsh penalties against any player leaving the bench
during an altercation. That benches empty on occasion and colleagues
still intervene means that the formal rules and their application by officials are to be observed rather than obeyed. Moreover, respondents
note the difficulty linesmen and referees face in deciding just who inter-
vened at what stage of an unfolding brawl. They also point to the ease
with which they can abuse this edict if it is not properly enforced, as well
as to the indignation they feel when discretion is used unfairly or un-
realistically by the referee. Most respondents appear to support these
rules, with the understanding that they *should* be designed to keep
escalation and retaliation under control and within bounds, rather than
to preclude them entirely. Like craftsmen everywhere, they jealously
guard their available work resources.

Players also recognize that giving protection to colleagues and receiving it from them is essential if a projected definition of the team is
to be transmitted and maintained. That players ought to be held by a
collective bond, and that violence is unavoidable, frequent, and, most

important, a *clearly manageable domain*, is recognized in an embarrassingly trite but important phrase: "The team that fights together plays together." There are important anxiety-allaying functions in this, as a twenty-nine-year-old centerman put it:

> If the other team knows that when one of your players is in trouble the whole team will back him up, then we *all* have confidence. This is why some teams are feared, like with S., everyone is there. Someone will put a stick in to stop a punch, if a guy is trying to throw a sucker punch from behind. As a team they're tougher because they back each other up all the way. You never let your teammates get beat because it can swing a whole game around. A guy works your teammate over pretty bad, that gives the rest of them a lift and if we don't go out and challenge him and straighten him out we're *dead*.

There is a strong presumption that one's occupational colleagues have mastered important parts of their work role to the extent that they provide the conditions for personal autonomy and expertise. Each is obliged to offer his colleagues the spectacle of his own character and virility in protection of their collective honor. As this player notes, letting the opposition freely use force without a measure of retribution weakens the uniting bonds of collective strength and reduces the sense of control which members have over these encounters and their work on such occasions. Like the firemen studied by Killian and Griffin, hockey players acquire a perspective which does not regard these battle-like situations as fear-provoking or dangerous, as long as the member knows "with what he must cope or what actions he can take to protect himself" (Turner and Killian 1957:42). Situational uncertainty is thus augmented by the perceived lack of support and help which he gets from his co-workers: "The worst thing about some of these guys is you never know what they're going to do, that's where your buddies have to back you up." As in the fighting military unit and other fateful lines of work, rationales of protection such as these enhance a player's courage, remind him that these risks are spread throughout the work group, and promote shared confidence in one's own role performance.

The belief that one can depend on colleagues for help when in difficulty decreases the anxiety, as a signal of danger, engendered in the demands of contention by force. But more than this, the experience of being called upon by others to protect them appears to increase a player's sense of confidence in his own skills. Retaliation thus serves others as a diagnostic index of his essential attributes, his character, while at the same time being a strategy for carrying out obligations in the interest of receiving ritual regard.

The orientation to force is rudimentary. In theory, imputed derogation of a team member affects the collective honor. All should respond in kind to the perceived insult. In practice, players pursue an offense to colleagues less vigorously when a peripheral rather than core player (such as a high-scoring centerman, or goalie) is the recipient of an open threat. Moreover, not everyone on the team responds in the same degree. There is a division of labor for handling provocation, threats, and the problem of intimidation of key colleagues. As one player put it, "You've got to take care of your small guys, you can't let the other team move in and push your wingers around. My job is to make sure they're not intimidated. Sure they can take care of themselves, but not if a defenseman is giving it to 'em. You got to settle the score, fast." It becomes the task of some to relieve core players from the pressure of force while raising the cost of open belligerence for an opponent.

Power accrues and respect is accorded to skillful practitioners who can control this area of uncertainty and trouble. Like the men in charge of propping up the roof in the mine studied by Gouldner (1964:120–123), these men ward off trouble and prop up their colleagues' courage. These players regard themselves, and are regarded by others, as the enforcers. In the division of team labor they are viewed as having demonstrated inclination for moving into danger, for controlling the intimidation of their colleagues by others, and for bringing justice to the action. These players are called policemen. Most teams have (or would like to have) one or two of them. Their activities are reflected in the disproportionate number of penalties they typically accumulate during the season. Thus the scope of violent activity appears to be structurally narrowed by specialization because it is delegated to certain players. Their availability at the moment an incident unfolds signals formidable opponents, in effect, to back up their claims and threats with action. They are a strategic work resource for controlling the symbolic assailants on the other team.

> This is one of the problems we have on our team right now. We have no policemen. We have no guy who'll go out there and who has the personal makeup that he can just knock somebody's head off. Y. is not really what you'd call a good policeman, he was with us a few years ago, and he just didn't have the smarts. He'd just go out and hit anybody, you just don't do that, it takes brains to play this game and if you're going to draw a penalty, you should do the team some good. So if you get a misconduct or a dumb penalty it's not smart at all.

It would be a mistake to conclude from observations such as this that other players are unconcerned about their own use of aggression. Rather, they engage in a style of play which, in their own eyes, puts the best possible emphasis on skating and scoring. They view the differential distribution of types of skill on the ice, and particularly the role of the policeman, with the outlook of a craftsman. While they do not react indifferently either to challenges or to brawls, they are convinced that they should be allowed to do what they do best, and to do this requires freedom and some relief from the pressures of provocation. In a sense, their specialization is geared toward the presence of positive outcomes for the team. What preoccupies them is scoring. By way of contrast, the policeman is typically associated with the absence of negative outcomes. His job is to contribute to the smooth operation of his colleagues; his task is construed as one of forestalling trouble and deflecting threats to his team. By these role prescriptions he can offend players by the failure to satisfy what they see as the basic requirements of smart playing. To the extent that he is seen as a goon—that is, as interfering with these arrangements—teammates will respond negatively to him.

In effect, in carrying out a team's violent work the policeman is given considerable discretion while constrained by the following work relevancies. First, intervention can only be carried out when a colleague is losing; to do otherwise is to take the fight out of a teammate's hands, thereby showing a lack of respect for his autonomy. Second, under certain game conditions a disproportionate amount of violence can bring about a penalty and thereby hurt the entire team. Finally, and related to the above, generally the obligation to back up a teammate must be carefully weighted against the possibility of drawing penalties. By this shared outlook, players who are imputed to be not tough enough, whose playing ability is seriously compromised and affected by adversaries, or whose use of violence falls appreciably below that of colleagues, are judged as essentially unskilled craftsmen. They earn the disapprobation of others and are labeled chickens. Correspondingly, colleagues whose use of force is indiscriminate, who draw many cheap penalties, and whose action is dictated by giving free rein to aggressive impulses are viewed as undisciplined. Construed over-involvement in the use of assault, as well as getting oneself into situations where others are continually called upon to protect the player for no good reason, earns the disrespect of others and the title goon or animal. Both types are recognized as harmful for attaining collective ends. The use of "chicken" and "goon" also point out the importance of moral evaluations which are central to the control and skillful application of violence.

Conclusion

Interactionist theories of the social organization of work, like interactionist theories generally, pay attention to how social actors define each other and their environments. Following the urgings of Hughes (1971) I have paid particular attention to the rule-governed nature of the moral division of labor in professional hockey. I have focused on members' conception of the work relevancies that should govern the selection of the appropriate means for creating trouble for opponents, and for resolving perceived violations of threats to self and colleagues. It has been argued that, from the moment a player steps on the ice and goes to work, a special world is in the process of being constructed in which force and violence have meaning and significance. I have tried to show that a moral drama is involved in this work. In that individual and collective honor are at stake, the interpersonal tactics for making, taking, and avoiding "status bloodbaths," to borrow a phrase from Erving Goffman (1961:78) are a fundamental feature of the micro-organization of work encounters in professional hockey. Portending threat to self and others, physical force on the ice draws to it special activities and core beliefs of this occupational world.

In this study I have not analyzed the entire organization of this line of work, but have concentrated on some central definitions which violence highlights. These work relevancies and interpretations make up an important reality of professional hockey, for while the act of violence stands distinct from the meanings imputed to it, the beliefs and meanings which members construct around these acts are their reality.

At one level these considerations suggest that the intent and meaning of violence are provided by members' interpretive practices for dealing with the practicalities of action in this setting. It was noted that there are strategies which are primarily aggressive, or proactive, in the sense that they involve the initiation of force, as distinguished from those that are reactive or involve response to opponent-initiated measures. There is, to be sure, considerable blending of these reactive strategies. Still, players distinguish those which are defensive, in that a player seeks to resist perceived threats to himself, from those which are primarily protective. In the latter, a player seeks to prevent opponent-initiated coercion or force from threatening his colleagues. Priority is assigned to the task of "taking charge," if only to define the situation by the creation of an atmosphere in which each is attuned to some threat and thus prepares himself for interaction under such auspices.

At a second level such findings have a number of implications for studying the social organization of violence. Since I am investigating a special type of work setting, it would be possible to argue that what is found in combative contest games might not be found in other settings. Yet the findings presented here are remarkably similar to those of Westley (1970, 1953), who observed that in police organizations members look upon interpersonal threat and violence as an occupational as well as personal resource for coercing respect and deference. As a form of communication about the self and others, coercive encounters become a means for announcing selves, ratifying identities, and testing the prospective future of collective action. In a different substantive context, studies of gang violence have repeatedly pointed out that fighting often serves to demonstrate the unity of the group, to display honor and personal integrity, and to enhance the status of core members (Horowitz and Schwartz 1974; Keiser 1969; Miller 1966, 1958; Rosenberg and Silverstein 1969; Short and Strodtbeck 1965; Thrasher 1927; Werthman 1967). Although violent acts in focused gatherings may be depicted as unproblematic happenings, the above considerations demonstrate that the application of force is appraised and, therefore, subject to redefinition and variation within these role relations. From members' perspectives, violence is not incidental to, but a constituent feature of, collective action. It can be seen as a factor contributing to stability of expectations, as well as to the solidarity of members (Radcliffe-Brown 1952; Evans-Pritchard 1969; Skolnick 1966). Violence is more than an extension of the politics of identity by other means. In many lines of work it is a display of organization, rather than its demise (Blake 1970), and it thereby becomes one of members' principal sources of information about what others are up to, as well as the normative boundaries of their subculture. In professional hockey, fisticuffs, for example, serve to demonstrate the unity of the fighting group, mark it off from others, and reaffirm customary roles. In that violence is a means of domination, it can strengthen existing bonds and establish new ones among players as they deal with their adversaries.

To follow out the implications of these observations, it may be noted that a critical factor in an actor's decision whether or not to employ physical coercion and strength as a means of interpersonal domination is the structure of his relationships with his colleagues and identified adversaries. The social organization of violence in professional hockey suggests that similarities may exist between the ways in which members go about doing their work and the problematic character of honor, revenge, and retaliation. If this impression is confirmed by further research, it will lend obvious comparative support to the argument advanced above. Regardless of the final outcome, the situational determinates of violence seem eminently deserving of further study, for the analysis of gesture, task, motive, and work draws attention to the ways in which the factual reality of an occupational world impresses its hold on the person, while revealing the taken-for-granted props on which the self relies in its obsessive concern with the basic questions of identity, regard, and relation.

REFERENCES

Ball, D. W.
   1972 "The 'Definition of the Situation:' Some Theoretical and Methodological Consequences of Taking W. I. Thomas Seriously." *Journal of the Theory of Social Behavior* 2, 1:61–82.
Berger, Peter and Luckmann, Thomas
   1966 *The Social Construction of Reality.* New York: Doubleday.
Blake, J. A.
   1970 "The Organization as Instrument of Violence: The Military Case." *Sociological Quarterly* 2 (Summer):331–350.
Blumer, Herbert
   1969 *Symbolic Interactionism: Perspective and Method.* Englewood Cliffs, N.J.: Prentice-Hall.
Cohen, Albert
   1965 "The Sociology of the Deviant Act." *American Sociological Review* 30 (February):5–14.
Ervin-Tripp, S.
   1964 "An Analysis of the Interaction of Language, Topic and Listener." In J. J. Gumperz and D. Hymes, eds. *The Ethnography of Communication.* Pp. 86–102. Also in *American Anthropologist*, Special Publication, 66, 6, Part 2.
Evans-Pritchard, E. E.
   1969 *The Nuer.* New York: Oxford University Press.
Faulkner, R. R.
   1973 "On Respect and Retribution: Toward an Ethnography of Violence." *Sociological Symposium* 9 (Spring):17–35.
Goffman, Erving
   1961 *Encounters: Two Studies in the Sociology of Interaction.* Indianapolis: Bobbs-Merrill.
   1964 "The Neglected Situation." In J. J. Gumperz and D. Hymes, eds. *The Ethnography of Communication.* Pp. 133–136. Also in *American Anthropologist*, Special Publication, 66, 6, Part 2.

1967 *Interaction Ritual.* Chicago: Aldine.
1971 *Relations in Public.* New York: Harper and Row.
Goode, W. J.
1972 "The Place of Force in Human Society." *American Sociological Review* 37 (October):507–519.
1973 "Violence between Intimates." In *Explorations in Social Theory.* Pp. 145–197. New York: Oxford University Press.
Gouldner, Alvin W.
1964 *Patterns of Industrial Bureaucracy.* New York: Free Press.
Horowitz, R., and Schwartz, G.
1974 "Honor, Normative Ambiguity and Gang Violence." *American Sociological Review* 39 (April):238–251.
Hughes, Everett C.
1971 *The Sociological Eye.* Chicago: Aldine-Atherton.
Hymes, Dell
1962 "The Ethnography of Speaking." In T. Gladwin and W. C. Sturtevant, eds. *Anthropology and Human Behavior.* Pp. 13–53. Washington, D.C.: Anthropological Society of Washington.
1964 "Introduction: Toward Ethnographies of Communication." In J. J. Gumperz and D. Hymes, eds. *The Ethnography of Communication.* Pp. 1–34. Also in *American Anthropologist,* Special Publication, 66, 6, Part 2.
Keiser, R. L.
1969 *The Vice Lords: Warriors of the Streets.* New York: Holt, Rinehart and Winston.
McCall, G. J., and Simmons, J. L.
1966 *Identities and Interactions.* New York: Free Press.
Mead, G. H.
1934 *Mind, Self, and Society.* Chicago: University of Chicago Press.
Miller, W. B.
1958 "Lower-Class Culture as a Generating Milieu of Gang Delinquency." *Journal of Social Issues* 14 (Summer): 5–19.
1966 "Violent Crimes in City Gangs." *Annals of the American Academy of Political and Social Science* 354:96–112.
Radcliffe-Brown, A. R.
1952 *Structure and Function in Primitive Society.* New York: Free Press.
Rosenberg, B., and Silverstein, H.
1969 *The Varieties of Delinquent Experience.* Massachusetts: Blaisdell.
Skolnick, J.
1966 *Justice without Trial.* New York: Wiley.
Short, J., and Strodtbeck, F.
1965 *Group Process and Gang Delinquency.* Chicago: University of Chicago Press.
Stebbins, R.
1967 "A Theory of the Definition of the Situation." *Canadian Review of Sociology and Anthropology* 4 (August): 148–164.

Stone, G. P.
1962 "Appearance and the Self." In A. H. Rose, ed. *Human Behavior and Social Processes*. Boston: Houghton-Mifflin. Pp. 86–118.

Thrasher, F. M.
1927 *The Gang*. Chicago: University of Chicago Press.

Turner, R.
1962 "Role-taking: Process versus Conformity." In A. H. Rose, ed. *Human Behavior and Social Processes*. Boston, Houghton-Mifflin. Pp. 86–118.

————, and Killian, L. M.
1957 *Collective Behavior*. Englewood Cliffs: Prentice-Hall.

Werthman, Carl
1967 "The Function of Social Definitions in the Development of Delinquent Careers." In *Task Force Report: Juvenile Delinquency*. Appendix J, pp. 155–170. Washington: U.S. Government Printing Office.

Westley, William A.
1953 "Violence and the Police." *American Journal of Sociology* 69 (July):34–41.

1970 *Violence and the Police*. Cambridge: Massachusetts Institute of Technology Press.

Wilson, T. P.
1970 "Conceptions of Interaction and Forms of Sociological Explanation." *American Sociological Review* 35 (August):697–710.

Znaniecki, F.
1952 *The Cultural Sciences*. Urbana: University of Illinois Press.

Racial Discrimination in Sport

Introduction

The third section of this volume addresses itself to racial discrimination in sport. Discrimination, which is defined as unequal treatment of a particular group based upon task-irrelevant criteria, has been present for some time in American society for certain racial and ethnic minorities, as well as for women. Rather than presenting a somewhat cursory analysis of discrimination against many different minority groups, essays in the present section deal exclusively with discrimination against black athletes. The first essay by McPherson presents an extensive review of the popular and scientific literature on the black athlete. As McPherson notes, "At times sport has been praised for its role in integrating blacks into the mainstream of the dominant society," but at other times the integration value of sport has been labeled as a myth which shields the racial prejudice, discrimination, and segregation existent in sport. Many of the incidences of overt discrimination against blacks (as indicated in the historical accounts given by McPherson, and particularly in the essay by Loy) have since disappeared. This does not mean that incidences of discrimination are no longer evident; in fact, many investigators argue that discrimination has merely been relegated to more subtle forms that are sometimes difficult to identify. For example, we have moved from very obtrusive forms of discrimination and racism in which blacks were denied opportunity to participate on college and professional teams to a period where participation was permitted. This participation, however, was accompanied by many severe social restrictions on dating, sleeping, and eating arrangements while on the road. Although these forms of discrimination are for the most part behind us, they provide an important backdrop for understanding the current areas in which discrimination is said to occur; that is, there appears to be a disparity in the number of blacks in sports leadership positions (i.e., team captains, quarterbacks, coaches, and managers), as well as obvious discrepancies between blacks and whites in specific performance measures.

Performance differences between blacks and whites have evoked a number of explanations, many of which have postulated physical differences between the races. A popular example of this type of research has been Worthy and Markel's (1970) finding that blacks perform better in reactive skills and whites better in self-paced skills. Their explanation for these differences eventually led Worthy (1971) to postulate that genetic variation in perceptual ability occurs between blue-eyed and brown-eyed people. This line of research has not been overly convincing, however. There is virtually no evidence linking pigmentation of the eye with variation in motor performance, and several of the basketball and baseball performance findings used initially by Worthy and Markel to support their thesis have not been replicated in more recent investigations (Jones and Hochner 1973). Other explanations attributing performance abilities to physical and anthropometric differences between black and whites have also been unproductive. As Malina's (1969) review suggests, some physical differences are evident between the races, but these have not been related to the more numerous interracial performance disparities. It is important to recognize the present limitations of physical explanations, as well as their potential dangers. These explanations have many times served as the foundations for social stereotypes (e.g., "the paucity of blacks in hockey is due to their intolerance to cold"), and as a result have deterred the ready acceptance of many of the social explanations contained in the following essays.

Both the McPherson and the Loy essays emphasize many areas of discrimination, prejudice, and racism that have yet to be investigated. They suggest that more needs to be understood about black spectators and the integration of blacks via sport. In the latter area some pioneering work is available. For example, concerning racial integration through sport, Blalock (1962) proposed several propositions to account for the relatively rapid advances made in recent years concerning the integration of blacks into baseball. Blalock specifies many inherent characteristics of competitive games which, other things being equal, will tend to nullify the competitive disadvantage in gaining access to the labor force that is often evident in individuals who have an initially low occupational status, but who are in a highly visible minority. The following characteristics inherent in competitive professional sports, but not in many other occupational roles, are suggested by Blalock as factors which tend to reduce discrimination: competition among employers for players of high performance levels—that is, a specific kind of performance that can be accurately evaluated and obtained without expensive training; lesser degree of intragroup competition among specialists who must interact as a team; the difficulty for players, already under contract, to change jobs so as to avoid minority players; and finally, performance level in sport, unlike that in the business world, is relatively independent of skill in interpersonal relations. Supplementing Blalock's propositions are valuable case studies of the process involved in such integration. These accounts add substance to the structural factors postulated by Blalock and illuminate additional factors which have been important in the past for fostering integration of minorities into sport. As mentioned by Brown in the final essay of this section, the planning strategy formulated in the 1940's by Dan W. Dodson (1954) and his associates in the Mayor's Committee on Unity of New York City was instrumental in assisting Jackie Robinson's entry into major league baseball. After presenting some of the techniques used to promote racial integration, the Brown essay goes further to present a discussion of other contemporary strategies for bringing about greater racial equality in sport-related areas yet to be entered by blacks (e.g., professional coaching, managerial, and other administrative positions).

Perhaps the area that has received the greatest attention from researchers is the unequal distribution of blacks in specific playing positions, otherwise known as the "stacking phenomenon." Grusky's (1963) theory of formal organizational structure has had an important theoretical application in accounting for the underrepresentation of blacks in central positions in football and baseball. According to Grusky's theory, high interactors would be those individuals occupying relatively central positions in an organization and performing tasks whose completion is dependent upon others' assistance. Borrowing from the analyses by Grusky and others (e.g., Ball 1973), sport sociologists have inferred the rate of interaction among teammates in sport strictly on the basis of the field position and the type of task performed.[1] Since Loy and McElvogue (1970) first exposed the magnitude of the disparity between blacks and whites in central positions, the situation has changed very little (see *Sports Illustrated* 1972). The essay by Madison and Landers provides some additional data to show that blacks more than whites switch from central positions as college football players to peripheral positions as professional football players. Such a reversal could be due to subtle forms of discrimination on the

1. A better approach to making inferences as to probable interaction rates in sport would be field studies designed to actually quantify the degree of average interaction (e.g., throw of the ball) among players occupying different field positions. However, such an approach has not been undertaken and is long overdue.

part of coaches, or to practical considerations of ability and/or other parameters. To determine which of these is more important requires, as Loy suggests in his essay, "a more definitive analysis . . . involving field work wherein observers examine who tries out for central and non-central positions during training camp and exhibition games, and then compare who plays where during the course of the regular season." The Madison and Landers finding, however, does not lend much support for McPherson's (1970) hypothesis that the positions played by blacks are a function of prior role models. This role-modeling hypothesis does not offer a definitive explanation for the occurrence of shifts from central positions among blacks as they move from the college to professional level. In addition, as Castine and Roberts (1974) have shown, blacks only play the same position as their "idol" sportsmen prior to entrance into high school. After entry into high school it appears that other factors (ability, discrimination, etc.) may become more influential determinants of playing position.

The ideas, hypotheses, and facts discussed in this section represent the primary avenues of research on race and sport. Although many other studies (e.g., Yetman and Eitzen 1972) could be mentioned, these merely exemplify additional cases of previously investigated hypotheses. Recently, however, a few novel approaches have begun to appear in this area. Due to the newness of studies using these approaches, investigators have yet to accumulate sufficient hard data to support or reject predictions. Nevertheless, these approaches appear useful for integrating many of the discrete findings that for so long have lacked a coherent framework for analyses of a more theoretical nature.

The first approach is a social-psychological examination of the consequences of socialization influences which stem from cultural background and lead to personal and behavioral expressions. Jones (1972) has proposed that, because of variants in cultural background, black and white athletes are socialized differently along three orthogonal aspects of personality; achievement, power, and affiliation. Pilot work demonstrated that most performance correlates between blacks and whites were best accounted for by the achievement dimension, consisting of polarities of success on the one hand and style on the other. Success was the personality disposition characteristic of whites and was seen "as the traditional successful achievement described in terms of the Protestant Ethic. That is, under the auspices of delayed gratification for future rewards, practice and the pursuit of technical competence is a prerequisite for this form of achievement" (Jones 1972:5). In contrast, achievement for blacks was postulated to emphasize style in the way the performance is executed; here the emphasis is on the means in which the goal is attained. The pilot findings indicated that success-type athletes played organized sports longer and were more frequent starters than style types. Thus far this research appears fruitful, but much more information is needed to differentiate the processes operating in black and white cultures that might produce such individualized expression. Perhaps research along these lines may lead to an explanation for many performance differences between blacks and whites in team sports (e.g., foul shooting in basketball), and also to the detection of problems in interpersonal relations that may exist between a coach and athlete having different conceptions of achievement expression. This line of research may also aid in explaining the absence of blacks in many sports not involving expensive equipment or facilities (e.g., throwing events in track and field).

Most approaches to race and sport have been at a social-psychological level of analysis. Although approaches at this level have been relatively successful in unraveling some of the racial disparities evident in modern day sport, these approaches are often criticized for lack of a historical framework explaining how and why specific differences have come about. A definitive analysis at a social system level is needed in this area. One social system approach that has been suggested[2] is a historical examination of economic rationality; that is, the directing of all activity toward the making of money. As with American society in general, the management of sport has become increasingly oriented to rationally assessing the economic problems of resource acquisition and allocation. Sport has tended to mirror the "formalized, hierarchical, rule-laden, and efficiency seeking type of social organization, the principal prototypes of which are big government, modern business enterprise, and the military establishment" (Page 1973:32).

Up until now economic rationality has been encroaching on sport, but in terms of profit and the minimization of financial risks, it has not spread far enough for it to be functionally rational for blacks to be managers, administrators, or otherwise in the public eye of sport. It can be argued, however, that we are rapidly approaching the extreme form of rationality where performance based upon merit is of paramount importance, rather than racial factors that are unrelated to the task at hand. With increasing rationality, discrimination cannot be legitimated because greater individual abilities and knowledges are

2. This hypothesis and the reasoning behind it were suggested in a conversation with Alan G. Ingham. He has since elaborated upon this hypothesis in papers presented at professional meetings.

required to maintain an efficient and viable organization. To test this hypothesis, it would be useful to examine other instances of minority breakthroughs by ascertaining if they have historically occurred in sport organizations having higher levels of economic rationality (e.g., professional sports). As the next section shows, there has been considerable concern in recent years about the ways in which traditional American cultural values (including rationality) are mirrored in sport.

REFERENCES

Ball, D. W.
   1973   "Ascription and Position: A Comparative Analysis of Stacking in Professional Football." *Canadian Review of Sociology and Anthropology* 10:97–113.
Blalock, H. M.
   1962   "Occupational Discrimination: Some Theoretical Propositions." *Social Problems* 9:240–247.
Castine, S. G., and Roberts, G. C.
   1974   "Modeling and the Socialization Process of the Black Athlete." *International Review of Sport Sociology* 9(3–4):59–74.
Dodson, Dan W.
   1954   "The Integration of Negroes in Baseball." *Journal of Educational Sociology* 18:73–82.
Grusky, O.
   1963   "The Effects of Formal Structure on Managerial Recruitment: A Study of Baseball Organization." *Sociometry* 26:345–353.
Jones, J. M.
   1972   "Psychological Contours of Black Athletic Performance and Expression." Paper presented at the Symposium on Race and Sport, Slippery Rock State College, June 19–23.
————, and Hochner, A. R.
   1973   "Racial Differences in Sports Activities: A Look at the Self-paced versus Reactive Hypothesis." *Journal of Personality and Social Psychology* 27:86–95.
Loy, J. W., and McElvogue, J.
   1970   "Racial Segregation in American sport." *International Review of Sport Sociology* 5:5–24.
McPherson, B.
   1970   "Minority Group Socialization: An Alternative Explanation for the Segregation of Playing Position Hypothesis." Paper presented at the Third International Symposium on Sociology of Sport, Waterloo, Ontario.
Malina, R. M.
   1969   "Growth and Physical Performance of American Negro and White Children." *Clinical Pediatrics* 8:476–483.
Page, C. H.
   1973   "The World of Sport and Its Study." In Talamini, J. T., and

Page, C. H. *Sport and Society: An Anthology.* Boston: Little, Brown.

Worthy, M.
    1971   "Eye Darkness, Race, and Self-paced Athletic Performance." Paper presented at the Southeastern Psychological Association Meeting, Miami, April.

————, and Markle, A.
    1970   "Racial Differences in Reactive versus Self-paced Sport Activities." *Journal of Personality and Social Psychology* 16: 439–443.

Yetman, N. R., and Eitzen, D. S.
    1972   "Black Americans in Sports: Unequal Opportunity for Equal Ability." *Civil Rights Digest* 5:21–34.

The Black Athlete: An Overview and Analysis

BARRY D. MCPHERSON

INTRODUCTION

Although the involvement of blacks in many social institutions is severely restricted, the color of an athlete is frequently overlooked when success in sport is highly valued by members of the dominant society. Participation by blacks is differentially encouraged and sanctioned by those who control and support teams associated with particular institutions, cities, or nations. Yet, within the same sport milieu, even though a black is encouraged and permitted to play the role of athlete, he often experiences subtle or overt acts of segregation, discrimination, or racism, similar to those he encounters in other social institutions. This differential interaction between members of the dominant and minority group has been noted by both black and white authors in recent years. As a result, at various times sport has been praised for its role in integrating blacks into the mainstream of the dominant society, and at other times it has been vilified for fostering prejudice, discrimination, and segregation. Unfortunately, most of the literature has been descriptive, factual, and anecdotal, with little empirical work at the causal or explanatory level. Working within this limitation, then, the present paper provides a structured overview of the popular and scientific literature which has appeared prior to December, 1971, and proposes some avenues for future inquiry in the area.

ORIGIN OF BLACK INVOLVEMENT IN SPORT

Although a social historian would find it difficult to document the first time a black competed in institutionalized sport, Henderson (1968)

Barry D. McPherson is an associate professor in the department of kinesiology, University of Waterloo. A revised version of this chapter appeared in J. Wilmore, ed., *Exercise and Sport Science Reviews* II (New York: Academic Press, 1974).

reported that boxing was a common activity for slaves on the southern plantations.[1] Not only were there intraplantation matches to determine the most proficient boxer, but also matches (promoted by the plantation owners) with champions from other plantations. If a black was successful in these competitions, he often gained preferential treatment and a special status from the plantation owner. This suggests that the relationship between sport and social mobility may not be a recent phenomenon.

Prior to 1900 blacks were active and successful participants in a variety of sports. For example, in 1805 a black won an American boxing championship for the first time; by the 1860's blacks participated in organized baseball (Boyle 1963; Voigt 1966); on May 15, 1876, a black jockey rode in the second Kentucky Derby (Clement 1954); in the 1880's a black jockey rode three Kentucky Derby winners (Quarles 1964:247); and by 1890 black boxers were recognized as world champions in most weight divisions (Clement 1954). Thus, throughout the 1800s blacks were quite active in organized sport. However, by the late 1800s the first evidence of overt discrimination towards blacks in a sport setting was instigated by white politicians in the South. Because their antipathy toward blacks filtered throughout the country, black athletes were driven from baseball, horse racing, and most other sports—with the exception of boxing, where they frequently had to consent to lose before they could obtain a match (Boyle 1963: 103). Barred from organized baseball, they formed their own leagues which, although poverty-stricken, remained in existence until after the color bar was again broken in 1947. During this period a number of blacks did pass into organized baseball; however, they participated only until their own people, through celebration of their participation, caused them to be removed (Boyle 1963:106; Voigt 1966:278).

Until 1947, then, the colorline was prevalent in organized sport, just as it was in most other social institutions. Blacks were not permitted to participate, and they were discouraged from attending sport events as spectators. Thus, although the integration[2] of Jackie Robinson into professional baseball was considered to be an initial step in the eventual total integration of blacks into all white institutions, these expectations have not been realized in many instances.

1. For a detailed history of black involvement in sport, see Boulding (1957), Davie (1949), and Henderson (1968).
2. For a detailed discussion of how this integration was achieved, see Dodson (1954).

Degree and Type of Involvement

Kenyon (1969) has suggested that an individual can play many roles in a sport system. Although both blacks and whites usually have the cognitive and motor capacity to play either participant, consumer, or producer roles, whether the roles are played depends upon a number of factors. The following would appear to be relevant: the availability of role models and significant others so that behavioral patterns associated with the roles might be learned; an opportunity set conducive to learning and enacting the roles; positive sanctions for attempting and playing the roles; and a value climate which encourages interest and participation in a particular role. In many instances these social factors have not been functionally present for most blacks.

The extent to which blacks are involved in sport as active participants has been investigated almost annually since the color line was broken in 1947. In most cases, these descriptive studies have been interested in the number of blacks involved in professional sport. Since the number involved changes annually, rather than to redundantly cite statistics from the plethora of reports (Dodson 1954; Davie 1949; Baltimore 1951; Abrahams 1952; Boulding 1957; Boyle 1963; Davis 1966; Blalock 1967; Henderson 1968; Maher 1968; Olsen 1968; Pascal and Rapping 1969; Greendorfer 1970; Loy and McElvogue 1970; Smith and Grindstaff 1970), a brief overview will be presented.

Boulding (1957:115) reported that the percentage of blacks participating in professional baseball, basketball, and football grew from zero in 1935 to 10.9 in 1955. During this same period, the total black population only increased from 9.7 percent to 10.5 percent. In the spring of 1970, Cummings (*Wisconsin State Journal*, April 9, 1970) reported that 30 percent of the players on the AFL and NFL football teams were black, and that 56 percent of all players in both professional basketball leagues were black. In addition, it was noted that in professional basketball blacks accounted for 65 percent of the scoring, 75 percent of the rebounding, and 77 percent of the credit for assists. Thus not only is basketball the only sport with a black majority; it is a sport which is statistically dominated by blacks. Greendorfer (1970), after examining the *Baseball Register; 1970*, found 15 percent of the active major league baseball players were black, with another 11 percent being foreign born (including Latin Americans).

It has also been noted (*Time Magazine*, April 6, 1970, p. 79) that a black has won the National Baseball League's Most Valuable Player award sixteen times in the past twenty years; that the Most Valuable

Player award in professional basketball has been won by a black twelve times in the preceding fifteen years; and that all four rookie of the year awards in professional football in 1970 were won by blacks. The only other major professional sport dominated by blacks is boxing. For example, before Marciano won the heavyweight title in 1952, blacks had dominated this event for fifteen years. Similarly, after Marciano's defeat they continued to dominate this and most other weight divisions. Not only are they involved to a great extent; they are also highly successful.[3]

Although there is no direct indication of the extent to which blacks are involved in college sport, a survey conducted in 1968 (*Sports Illustrated*, February 19, 1969) showed that for the 59 schools that were surveyed, 10,698 grants-in-aid were awarded, of which only 634 (6 percent) went to black athletes. The survey also indicated that the number of scholarships given to blacks varied not only from conference to conference, but also from school to school within a conference. For example, in the Southeastern Conference, only 11 of the 2,236 scholarships were awarded to blacks. This was well below the average, despite the fact that 1.4 per cent of their student body was black. This suggests that there may be some selective discriminatory policies in the recruitment of black college athletes.

Although blacks are now well represented in the major professional sports (baseball, basketball, football and boxing), in the minor or so-called social sports (tennis, golf, swimming) they tend to be under-represented, although the situation is improving as more facilities and opportunities are opened to them, and as more blacks attain success in these areas.

The involvement of black youth in amateur sport has been studied indirectly by Short and Tennyson (1963) and directly by Kraus (1969). In an analysis of the behavior of black and white gangs, Short and Tennyson reported that sport was a favorite type of activity for both groups. However, there were sport differences for each race. Black gangs were more involved in basketball, boxing, wrestling, and track and field, whereas white gangs were more involved in bowling and football. These differences may be related to the socializing situation and to the availability of visible role models and facilities. Kraus (1969) also found that blacks tended to participate both in activities and in age groupings that varied widely from those of white residents. The sports in which blacks were most involved included boxing, judo, karate, track and field, basketball, weight training, and wrestling.

---

3. Henderson (1968) has documented the success of blacks in all sports for the past fifty years.

As noted above, an individual can also play the role of sport consumer. Although it has been suggested that sport is a major topic of conversation among blacks (Frazier 1957), we do not as yet have empirical data indicating to what extent males and females think about, read about, attend, watch, listen to, or talk about sports. For example, for economic reasons, very few blacks are season ticket subscribers to professional sport events; on the basis of their educational background and attainment, very few attend college sport events. Furthermore, we do not have empirical data to support the hypothesis that sport is one of the most highly valued domains in the black community. Nevertheless, it is suggested that sport is salient for the black, partly because of societal and subcultural expectations that he excel in and be interested in sport; partly because of early socializing experiences wherein he observes significant others enacting similar behavior; and partly because of a lack of opportunity to experience and internalize alternative activities. Because of these and other possible factors, future studies should be directed toward determining the degree and types of consumption experienced by nonwhites; determining how these characteristic ways of behaving in a sport system compare with the behavioral patterns of members of the dominant society and those belonging to other ethnic, racial, or religious subcultures; determining how blacks become socialized into the role of sport consumer; and determining to what extent members of a minority group identify with professional sport teams, and what effect this relationship has on various forms of collective behavior (e.g., the "jubilant celebration" in Pittsburgh following the Pirates' victory in the 1971 World Series).

Finally, in addition to playing the role of athlete or consumer, the black could occupy the role of sport producer if given the opportunity. With few exceptions, the opportunity to occupy this role at all levels has been severely restricted. There have been no head football coaches, few executives, and few black play-by-play announcers or commentators identified with any network or team.

In summary, it can be seen that blacks are somewhat overrepresented in professional sport compared to society at large; that they have achieved a high level and degree of success in baseball, basketball, boxing, football, and track and field; that they are becoming more involved and more successful in other sports (e.g., tennis, golf); and that they are underrepresented at the management and executive levels. At the descriptive level, then, it would appear that athletics may be a social equalizer and that ability, not race or class, determines opportunity, success, and mobility in sport. However, while this may be true for some blacks on the playing field, it may not be a viable statement for all blacks, and it may be untenable when one considers the nonperformance facets of the various sport roles.

INTEGRATION VIA SPORT

John Betts, as cited by Boyle (1963:100), noted: "Nowhere is the process of Americanization more in evidence than in sport. . . . It is significant that the greatest fighter of recent decades was a Negro (Joe Louis), the most spectacular ball player a German (Babe Ruth), the most respected football coach a Norwegian (Knute Rockne), the most successful baseball manager an Irishman (Joe McCarthy), and the most highly paid jockey an Italian (Eddie Arcaro)." The validity of this generalization as it applies to blacks will be investigated in this section.

Since 1947 it has been frequently intimated that the integration of blacks into institutionalized sport has served as an example and model of that which can be attained in other social institutions. For example, in 1951 the secretary of the National Association for the Advancement of Colored People (Simon and Carey 1966) stated that the most visible sign of change in race relations was the removal of the color line in professional sport (White 1951). Dodson (1954), based on his experience as an advisor to Branch Rickey during Jackie Robinson's entrance into professional baseball, proposed twelve principles which could be utilized to achieve integration in other social institutions. Similarly, Clement (1954) praised sport for its integration policy, while Quarles (1964:248) reported that "the participation of the Negro in sport has been a significant development in bringing him into the mainstream of American life and thereby promoting American democracy." Young (1963), after describing the agonizing problems which the black has had to contend with in his rise for equality in sport, concluded that the world of sport is an undeniable force in moving the United States toward total integration. Finally, Olsen (1968) quoted a grateful black leader as saying, "If only we could achieve in housing, in education, and in economic opportunity all the things we have achieved in sport, the race problem in the United States would disappear." Thus, from the point of view of many who are outside sport, it would appear that the black athlete has been totally integrated into American society. In reality, however, although the black athlete has been partially integrated into a sport system, he has not always been integrated into white society.

One of the frequent complaints of black athletes on college campuses and in professional sport is that once they leave the locker room they are subjected to the same prejudices and discrimination as a Harlem resident who ventures out into white society. Black collegiate and professional athletes report that they are dehumanized, exploited, and discarded, and some even report that they were happier back in the ghetto (Olsen 1968). Frequently this prejudice is demonstrated by their teammates. This is not surprising, in view of the finding (Charnofsky 1967; Ibrahim 1968) that there are no differences between athletes and nonathletes in their attitudes toward minority group members (Jews and Negroes). Similarly, Brown (1969) suggested that the biggest disappointments experienced by the black athlete are those which occur off the field, rather than on the field. They may be cheered as athletes on the field, but when their uniforms are removed, their interactions with white society in nonsport situations are frequently similar to those experienced by other blacks who interact within the dominant group (Carter 1970). Boyle (1963), after examining black-white relations away from the sport environment, noted that blacks tend to segregate themselves from whites. For example, he found that they declined invitations to parties, had their own hangouts in each city, had an argot which they guarded closely, and had leaders in each club to socialize newcomers into the major leagues with respect to acceptable social behavior. It has also been suggested that other factors in this self-imposed segregation are related to interactions with women and to feelings of tension and insecurity. Black athletes reported that they were required to ignore white women because "players who have played with fire have been sent down"; they also reported that they experienced tension to the point that they felt better among their own people (Boyle, 1963:126). Fitzgerald (1960), and Charnofsky (1968), also reported that much of the apparent segregation is self-imposed. For example, Charnofsky (1968), in a study of 58 major league baseball players, concluded that racial and ethnic equality is far from being the democratic ideal that the popular literature would lead us to believe. He reported that nearly all players (57 of 58) preferred to spend their leisure time with others of the same ethnic or racial background. Finally, Calvin Hill, in an interview with *Time Magazine* (April 6, 1970, p. 79), stated: "There is not very much after-hours socializing between black and white players. The main reason, I think, is because they date white and we date black. In addition, there are certain cultural differences." This awareness of cultural differences in intergroup and intragroup interactions is extremely relevant in the

1970's now that blacks, athletes as well as non-athletes, are beginning to identify with a unique black culture.

Davis (1966:808) also noted that integration did not extend beyond the locker room and suggested that one reason why blacks have not been readily accepted in tennis and golf is that these sports involve social intercourse with the opponent after the contest. While many more opinions could be recorded, especially the multitude of grievances reported by Olsen (1968) and other journalists, it appears that sport as a social institution has not made as great a contribution to race relations as we are often led to believe.

Although most interest has been centered upon the elite athlete in collegiate or professional sport, a recent study (Kraus 1969) sought to determine whether recreational sport programs were fostering integration and improving race relations. The investigator found that community recreation programs were doing little to achieve integrated participation; recreation leaders reported that when blacks entered community recreation programs, whites tended to withdraw. In analyzing the composition of teams in recreational leagues, he also found that most teams were segregated across all sports, and that this trend increased with the age of the participants; although most teams in the childhood and early adolescent age groups were integrated, most (if not all) teams in the adult bracket were segregated. This report indicates further that blacks have not been integrated into the mainstream of American society, or into the total sport environment. Thus, while sport may facilitate integration for the elite athlete, it may not serve the same purpose for the masses who participate in recreational sport. At the same time, Kraus reported that the frequency of participation by black adults in public recreational programs tended to be low. He attributed this trend to the fact that the activities which they actively pursued in adolescence were no longer appropriate later in life, and that they had had little opportunity to develop interests and skills in new activities in the intervening years.

In summary, then, it appears that while the elite black athlete has been integrated into college and professional sport as a functioning member of a team, he has not been totally integrated into the dominant group with respect to his nonsport roles. There may be exceptions to this conclusion (the "star" performer), but the subjective and objective evidence suggests that participation in sport does not guarantee integration for the masses. Thus the athlete, whether interacting in a recreational, collegiate, or professional sport environment, finds himself in a position similar to that of an assembly line worker who, although integrated into a large corporation for his work role, faces segregation in his nonwork roles.

THE RELATIONSHIP BETWEEN SPORT AND EDUCATION FOR BLACK STUDENTS

In addition to claims that involvement in sport facilitates integration, it has also been suggested that participation in sport improves the opportunity for blacks to receive an education. A closer analysis reveals that while athletic prowess may permit a black to receive an athletic scholarship and thereby move into an institution of higher education, it in no way insures that he will receive an education. For example, Harry Edwards, as cited by Olsen (1968), claimed: "Black students are not given athletic scholarships for the purpose of education, they are brought in to perform and any education they get is incidental to their main job, which is playing sports. In most cases their college lives are educational blanks." Olsen further noted that many black athletes who receive grants-in-aid fail to graduate, either because they lack financial support once their athletic eligibility expires, because they lack credits, or because they do not have a required concentrated area of study. At one institution only 7 of 20 black football players graduated in a ten-year period; at another only one of 46 received a degree in the normal four-year period, and only 11 others eventually received a degree; at another less than 20 percent of the black athletes graduated; and finally, at another only 4 of 9 black athletes graduated in a two-year period (Olsen 1968).

Although these statistics suggest that racial exploitation may be an explanation, it may not be the major determinant. Since the evidence is based on small samples in isolated cases, generalizations should not be made at this time. Second, it is not known how many of the athletes who failed to graduate were drafted and subsequently experienced successful careers in professional sport, thereby perhaps lacking the time, interest, or present need to complete the educational requirements. Third, comparable data on black non-athletes is not presented. In other words, is the failure to graduate unique to athletes, or is it related to early socialization experiences, or to the place of education in the value hierarchy of all blacks? Finally, since very little information is presently available concerning the extent to which white athletes are similarly exploited and fail to graduate, a racial basis for the explanation is inadequate. Of 56 members of a Big Ten football team who were to graduate in June, 1970, only two were successful—one black and one white. Similarly, Webb (1969), in an empirical analysis of the relationship between sport and mobility, reported that 56 percent of the white athletes and 38 percent of the black athletes received degrees. Finally, Pascal and Rapping (1969) found that while comparable proportions (48 percent of blacks, 47 percent of whites) of professional black and white baseball players have attended college, only 5 percent of the black and 14 percent of the white players eventually graduate. In addition to considering exploitation as a possible explanation of the high failure rate, investigators must also consider the deprived educational background of both the black and the lower-class white athlete. For example, the black athlete who arrives on the white middle-class campus from a segregated ghetto school will experience cultural shock, both academically and socially. In this respect, having some identity with a team may facilitate the adaptation of black student athletes. Some tentative support for this statement can be found in the study by Simon and Carey (1966). They found that black athletes did not share the same sense of alienation as other campus blacks, since they were better integrated into the structure of the university because of their involvement in athletics. In future studies the academic ability and educational background of an individual and the admissions requirements of a particular institution should be considered prior to citing failure rates as an indication of exploitation and discrimination. Finally, Brown (1969) suggested that the overemphasis on sport in some schools may be deleterious to the educational progress of blacks, especially at a segregated school. He cites the strike in 1968 at a predominantly black college by athletes who demanded a greater emphasis on education and less emphasis on sport. This suggests that future studies should be concerned with the quality of education which athletes, especially blacks, are receiving at both the high school and college level.

SPORT AND MOBILITY

Closely associated with the relationship between educational attainment and sport participation is the question of whether participation in sport facilitates social mobility. In recent years there have been a number of studies directed toward this question. Schafer (1968) suggests that there are at least four ways in which successful participation in athletics might bring later rewards that might not otherwise be attained. For example, he suggested that participation in high school and college athletics may enhance educational attainment, which in turn increases the chances for later rewards in money, power, and prestige. Recent studies by Eggleston (1965), Loy (1969) and Webb (1969) suggest that it is difficult to make the case that members of a lower class will move upward because of participation in sport. The key question concerns whether it is participation in sport or a college degree which facilitates upward mobility. Since many black and white athletes do not receive college degrees, it may be possible to control for this variable in future longitudinal studies. Schafer also suggested that professional sport often serves as a direct channel to money and prestige, without going through the usual educational or early occupational route. Again there is little empirical support for this suggestion as it applies to black athletes. The extent to which this is true likely varies for different sports, both in terms of prestige and income. Weinberg and Arond (1952) in their study of black professional boxers found that even if upward mobility occurred, it was usually not sustained once the career was terminated. However, now that athletes are organizing player associations and gaining pension plans, an improvement in social position attained during the active career may be retained later in life. Nevertheless, the number who actually achieve success in professional sport and hence attain permanent wealth and prestige is minimal, especially among black athletes. In addition, since most athletes receive a high salary and experience fame for only a few years, their opportunities to maximize economic gains and achieve prestige are somewhat limited.

The third proposal suggested by Schafer indicated that "occupational sponsorship" may occur for athletes whereby they are sought out or given special consideration in hiring, and perhaps even in promotion. Again it was unlikely, until very recently, that a black would be recruited for commercial endorsements or be given an executive position in a corporation. However, with the increasing trend toward hiring blacks to promote a product, this source of revenue will be more accessible in the immediate future—but only for the so-called stars. Similarly, there is little likelihood that a black athlete will use his popularity and prestige to establish dating patterns with well-to-do coeds and thereby perhaps marry into wealth and prestige (cf. Annarino 1953). The fourth way in which athletics may facilitate upward mobility is by developing or reinforcing values, skills, or attitudes that enhance one's attractiveness to an employer or improve one's job performance. Schafer suggested that cooperation, high level of aspiration, high achievement motivation, and persistence are characteristics desired by employers. Although it has often been suggested that these characteristics are developed in sport, we unfortunately do not really know to what extent, if at all, sport develops these traits.

The contention that athletes from lower-class or minority backgrounds are able to turn successful careers in athletics into subsequent upward mobility has been based on the study of a few elite athletes. For example, Blalock (1962) analyzed the situation of the black in baseball and concluded that a high level of performance could enable an individual to raise his status. Blalock attributed this potential mobility to the following specific situational factors found within baseball: there is no direct competition among teammates; there is no control over teammates; there are no educational requirements necessary for success; there is only a slight dependence on others in the performance of the task; and there is no interaction on the job with the opposite sex. Loy (1969), after an extensive review, concluded that not much is really known about the extent to which athletic participation facilitates upward mobility, if in fact it does.

[For the black athlete, then, the opportunity to move upward on the social scale may be restricted for the following reasons: there are relatively few positions open in the major professional leagues; he frequently does not have a meaningful college education and degree to fall back on when his athletic career is finished; as with the white athlete, he must become a star before he can maximize economic rewards;[no black athlete to date has developed the charisma which would be beneficial to a producer; and none has been able to gain access to positions of authority and power, either within or outside sport.]

It appears that only a minority of blacks may experience upward mobility as a result of participation in college or professional sport. For most blacks, upward movement on the social scale may be of short duration and may vary directly with the success of their athletic careers. For those who attain the star category and the associated income, upward mobility may be more permanent. Although they may lose the prestige and the occupational component of social status when their career is completed, they may retain their social position due to wise economic investments in their most productive years. For others in the journeyman category, upward movement may be followed by regression toward their original social positions. Again, however, investigators must ask whether this phenomenon is unique to the black athlete, or whether it holds for all athletes. In addition, future studies should consider relationships between mobility and such variables as college attended, years of schooling completed, academic program pursued, professional sport played, and the number of years as a professional.

DISCRIMINATION AGAINST THE BLACK ATHLETE

Discrimination against the black athlete began as early as the late 1800's at a time when Senator Tillman of South Carolina advocated the slaughter of 30,000 Negroes in his home state, and when a book entitled *The Negro, a Beast* was a best seller (Boyle 1963:103). This prevailing attitude in society was reflected in sport as illustrated by a story, in an 1891 issue of *Sporting Life*, which reported that the feet-first slide into second base was innovated as an attack on a black second baseman (Boyle 1963:103–105). Similarly, Charles Dana, a journalist for the *New York Sun*, voiced the opinion of many who felt that it was humiliating to have a black dominate a fight division. In an editorial entitled "The Negro Domination in the Field of Fistic Sport," he warned the public of the growing threat of black supremacy in athletics, particularly in boxing (Fleischer 1938:6). The most overt discrimination was evidenced in the 1936 Olympics, when Hitler labeled American Negro athletes "black auxiliaries" and refused to present four gold medals to Jesse Owen.

Discrimination, according to the definition utilized by Pascal and Rapping (1969:3), is the discrepancy in treatment between candidates who are identical in all relevant characteristics. One of the irrelevant characteristics which promote unequal treatment in sport is race. Pascal and Rapping report that discrepancies may be manifested in unequal compensation to persons with the same relevant characteristics, or through unequal opportunity in entry, promotion, or assignment. Discrimination may take many forms, but a major mode is that of segregation whereby individuals are totally excluded from social organizations, or from specific positions within organizations. This section analyzes the extent to which segregation and discrimination are present in the following social environments associated with sport: first, the educational and social environment associated with college and professional sport; and second, the sport milieu wherein elite black athletes interact with members of the dominant group.

Although many charges of discrimination against black collegiate athletes are based on isolated cases, problems can be identified when incidents begin to evolve around central themes. For example, Simon and Carey (1966), Olsen (1968), and Alcindor (1969) all reported that the social lives of black athletes were regulated by coaches. More specifically, black athletes have reported that they have been overtly or covertly discouraged from dating white girls on college campuses. For example, Alcindor (1969) cites a personal experience in which both he and a white girl were harassed to the point that they had to stop dating. At another institution, three black fooball players were asked by a member of the football staff to stop dating or being seen with white girls. This was the precipitating incident in the search for what Simon and Carey (1966) called the "phantom racist," wherein the specific charges of discrimination were never proven, and the issues raised were never resolved. As a result of a post mortem analysis of the crisis, Simon and Carey found that most athletes reported that they had suffered discrimination from coaches and fellow students; that the athletic association and the department of physical education gave them lower grades than they deserved; that they were prevented from gaining recognition in certain sports; and that they were policed in their social activities. Finally, Olsen (1968) cited a number of incidents relating to the campus and off-campus social life of blacks. These included: players being benched for dating white girls at one university; white athletes failing to speak to black teammates away from the practice field at another; and the segregated assignment of roommates on road trips by a third. Although these were isolated incidents, they represented different geographical regions and athletic conferences. However, it must be noted that these incidents were reported in the mid-1960's. Thus, in view of the increasing acceptance of interracial dating, and the assignment of roommates regardless of race, in most regions of the country it is likely that this problem will not be a source of grievance in the future.

A second type of discrimination is related to the right of athletes to select a program of studies. Olsen (1968) reported that this is one major grievance of contemporary black college athletes. For example, they are almost seduced or forced into becoming physical education majors, regardless of interest or intellectual abilities. Second, it has been reported that classes for many athletes are scheduled by a coach in order to avoid conflicts with team practices. This scheduling is often completed with little regard for institutional regulations concerning required courses or the necessity of a major. Again it must be considered whether these acts are experienced by just the black athletes, or whether it is a problem encountered by all athletes. This type of discrimination is also disappearing on most campuses due to recent black and white demands for impartial and competent academic counseling.

Within the professional sport milieu the most frequent charges of discrimination and segregation include discrepancies between white and black salaries for those of comparable ability; unequal distribution of blacks by team and by playing position; and unequal opportunities for blacks in leader, official, and entrepreneurial roles. Blalock (1962) generated thirteen propositions as to why discrimination against minority groups was relatively low in professional baseball. He suggested that blacks possessed a positive skill advantage over white players; hence, once the racial barrier was broken, there was a rush to tap the reservoir of skilled manpower. Thus he stated that the integration of blacks into baseball was a legitimate act, not merely a token attempt to dispel charges of discrimination.

It has been alleged that salaries paid to professional athletes are a function not only of ability, but also of race. An empirical study by Pascal and Rapping (1969) fails to support this hypothesis. They found that, contrary to popular belief, there was no salary discrimination (1968–69), regardless of position, against black baseball players who had achieved major league status. This conclusion was based on a linear regression model in which the player's salary for the coming season was regressed on his expected ability (based on lifetime batting average, batting average for the previous year, and number of years of experience in the major leagues) and the alternative salary that the player could earn outside baseball. In addition, they reported that, on the average, black salaries were higher than white salaries in the major leagues. They suggested two reasons for this: major league executives tend to pay players as a function of their demonstrated ability, and baseball appears to restrict major league opportunities to those blacks who are superior to their white counterparts. Thus they noted "that there seems to occur equal pay for equal work but unequal opportunity for equal ability" (Pascal and Rapping 1969:41). An article in *Time* (April 6, 1970, p. 79) supported the finding that black athletes, at least for the very elite, do not lag behind in salary. They noted that for the 1970 season four of the six baseball players in the $125,000 bracket were black. Unfortunately, in both of these reports, baseball players comprised the sample. The Pascal and Rapping study should be replicated for basketball and football if we are to determine to what extent the salaries received by blacks are based on ability and race. Finally, as a further extension of the Pascal and Rapping study, a model could be constructed in which total income (salary, endorsements, off-season earnings) is considered as the dependent variable. This would provide a better understanding as to whether and where black athletes experience discrimination in the financial domain of professional sport.

As noted by Pascal and Rapping, a second type of discrimination involves unequal opportunity for equal ability. They found that, position by position, the average lifetime batting averages of American-born blacks exceeded that of the white athletes. They concluded that on the average a black player must be better than a white player if he is to have an equal chance of being promoted into the major leagues. They further suggested that this major league entry barrier results in salary discrimination against blacks, since those who are retained in the minor leagues receive a salary lower than their abilities warrant. Many black athletes have contended that being as proficient as a white player does not suffice in the professional leagues (Boyle 1963:129; Boulding 1957; Olsen 1968; *Time*, April 6, 1970, p. 79). An article in *Time* suggested that the number of blacks selected for recent all star games (baseball, 20 of 56; football 27 of 61; basketball, 30 of 48) is quite low, considering the number of individual awards that have been won by black athletes in recent years. Although blacks have dominated batting championships, scoring and rushing records, and Most Valuable Player awards, they have not attained similar rewards in the visible forms of collective recognition, such as all star teams. It has been suggested that there is discrimination in situations where the presence of "too many" blacks constitutes a threat to the status of a "white game." For example, prior to the 1971 all star baseball game, it was predicted by some black athletes that two black pitchers would not be allowed to start the game despite the apparent right of the two pitchers to play this role.

Rosenblatt (1967) also supported the unequal opportunity for equal ability hypothesis. He studied the distribution of blacks in proportion to whites throughout the game to see if blacks were as well represented among the journeyman players as among the stars. He found that the higher the batting average, the greater the proportion of blacks in that performance category; as the batting average declined, fewer blacks were represented at each level. In a critique of Rosenblatt's work, Whitehead (1967) claimed that other facets of the game must also be considered before drawing the conclusion that blacks must be superior to be treated equally. He noted that managers weigh the key baseball skills differently; therefore only if some of these other variables (e.g., speed, defensive skills, bunting ability) were considered could one conclude that racial discrimination does or does not occur at the substar level. Finally, a recent study by Yetman and Eitzen (1971) investigated the extent to which black college basketball players are overrepresented in the star category, and underrepresented in the average or journeyman category (cf. Rosenblatt 1967). They found that two-thirds of all black players were members of the starting five, as opposed to 44 percent for the white athletes. This relationship held for each region of the country and for schools of varying size and type (private, denominational, public). The investigators suggested that this finding might be explained in two ways. First, there may be discrimination in recruitment practices (cf. Edwards 1969:9–10); second, as an alternative explanation, they cited the following quote by Al McGuire: "The ghetto environment of the black demands that he be a star if he is to participate at all. He could never justify an understudy's role to himself or to the brothers he left behind . . . there is no point recruiting blacks who will not start" (*New York Times*, March 1, 1971, p. 37). This latter statement suggests that blacks may have different expectations concerning their role in sport. These expectations may be learned as a result of differential socialization experiences early in life (cf. McPherson 1975).

Another form of discrimination was first reported by Rosenblatt (1967). He noticed that the distribution of positions on a team was different for blacks and whites. Despite the fact that there are twice as many pitchers on a team as there are outfielders, he found that there were three times as many black outfielders as there were black pitchers. He hypothesized that it is difficult for a black to be a pitcher, since it is a decision-making position and it also places him in a face-to-face confrontation (in which he has control) which may stimulate racial tension. On the other hand, when a black plays in the outfield, he is not involved in direct interaction with teammates or opposing white players. Rosenblatt concluded that blacks appear to be more readily accepted in follower roles than in leadership roles. A number of recent studies have investigated whether segregation by playing position is a myth or reality.

Pascal and Rapping (1969) surveyed the *Baseball Register* for 1968 and found that a high percentage of blacks played in the outfield (53%) and at first base (40%), while a low percentage were pitchers (9%) and catchers (12%). The investigators offered two explanations and a prediction based upon these observations. First, they attributed this segregation by playing position to the fact that blacks are excluded from the key positions of pitcher and catcher because they are important decision-making positions and blacks are not to be trusted with this responsibility. This appears to be a questionable argument, in view of the many outstanding pitchers (e.g., Ferguson Jenkins, Bob Gibson, Vida Blue) and catchers (e.g., Elston Howard, Elrod Hendricks, Manny Sanguillen) who have been instrumental in their team's success. A second explanation proposed that pitchers and catchers required more coaching and minor league experience, and therefore if white managers and coaches preferred not to interact with blacks, players attempting to play these positions would be disadvantaged. This latter suggestion may be plausible; however, it cannot be validated until statistics are available which indicate the percentage of black pitchers and catchers who play these roles in the youth and minor leagues. Finally, recognizing the importance of role models, they suggested that segregation by position is reinforced as black youths concentrate on positions in which black stars are most visible. Thus they predicted that blacks will continue to be concentrated in the outfield and at first base, "positions in which the primary quality demanded is hitting ability, that is, a more 'natural' talent" (Pascal and Rapping 1969:39). Similarly, McPherson (1975) suggested that involvement in sport by members of minority groups may be accounted for by differential socialization experiences in early life. He hypothesized that the learning and subsequent occupation of specific sport roles by members of a minority group may result from self-induced imitative learning, rather than from overt or subtle discrimination by members of the majority group in the sport system.

An alternative explanation for the frequent occupation of specific positions by blacks was offered by Worthy and Markle (1970). They hypothesized that blacks tend to perform better in reactive activities (i.e., the individual must respond appropriately to changes in the stimulus situation) than in self-paced activities (i.e., the individual responds when he chooses to react to a relatively static or unchanging stimulus). More specifically, they hypothesized that more blacks than whites would excel as hitters than as pitchers in baseball, and as field goal scorers than as foul shooters in basketball. The hypothesis was supported; that is, black athletes performed better in reactive than in self-paced activities. The investigators also suggested that such social factors as father deprivation, experiences with coaches, racial differences in preferred activities, and ability to delay gratification (e.g., practicing self-paced activities by oneself) may be related to the type of activity selected for specialization.

In one of the few studies having a theoretical frame of reference, Loy and McElvogue (1970) examined racial segregation in professional baseball and football. Drawing upon Grusky's (1963) theory of the formal structure of organizations, they investigated the relationship between segregation and spatial location in a sport group. In their examination of baseball they defined outfield positions as being noncentral and found that blacks did occupy these positions to a greater extent. Similar results were obtained when the offensive and defensive positions in the National Football League were dichotomized into central (e.g., center, two guards, and quarterback) and noncentral roles. Hence the hypothesis that racial segregation in professional sport is related to centrality was confirmed. However, since it is unlikely that this hypothesis would be tenable for professional basketball, the segregation by playing position hypothesis may be sport-specific. Furthermore, it can be argued that while there may be clusters of positions which are structurally central, these same positions may not be functionally central with respect to the purpose of the game—namely, success. Some baseball managers would argue that the key to a team's success is the level of ability "down the middle," that is, in the role of catcher, pitcher, second baseman, and center fielder. It might be worthwhile to reanalyze the data in terms of functionally central roles; those which are functionally central to a specific play in football (e.g., an end run) might be compared with those which are functionally noncentral. Finally, in a related study of the Canadian Football League, Smith and Grindstaff (1970) found that in the preceding fifteen years only 11 percent of the black athletes occupied central positions on the offensive teams. However, on defense, they found that the black players were not over or underrepresented at any position. This difference between the offensive and defensive teams was accounted for by the fact that each team is allowed fourteen imports (non-Canadians) and most teams employ their imports, black and white, on offense. Thus, although it appears that blacks are overrepresented in certain sport roles, a definitive explanation for this phenomenon has yet to be presented.

In concluding the section on segregation by playing positions, two additional charges of discrimination should be noted. Interviews with black athletes and white coaches (Charnofsky 1968:45; Olsen 1968; Smith and Grindstaff 1970) have indicated that a quota system restricts the number of blacks on any one college or professional team. A second charge, related to the "be better" theme, argues that through the process of "stacking" (blacks are forced to change positions so that they will be placed in competition with another black for one position) only one black gains a position. This policy, if it exists, insures that a white player will not have to compete with a black to win a position on a team; thereby racial conflict within a team will be avoided. It should also be noted that this practice would relieve the coach of making a decision which could be interpreted as racist if a white player of equal or inferior ability was selected for a position. To date very little empirical evidence is available to substantiate these charges. Perhaps the best approach has been the study by Smith and Grindstaff (1970), wherein they interviewed five black and eleven white players in the Canadian Football

League. They reported that the five black players felt that there definitely was a quota system whereby each team limited the number of black players to four or five, especially in the Western League. Similarly, six of the eleven white players felt there was a quota system, four felt there was not, and one said there was, but only on certain teams. With respect to stacking, the perceptions of the black and white players also differed. Whereas most black players reported that there definitely was stacking, especially at offensive back or receiver, only three of the eleven white players felt that this was a problem for black athletes. Rather, they reported that this practice was more prevalent for American (import) players, whether they were white or black. That is, a large number of American players are brought in to compete for the fourteen "import" positions. Finally, it should be noted that charges of discrimination may be related to feelings of antagonism and insecurity aroused when athletes are suddenly faced with the fact that they have failed in sport. Simon and Carey (1966) reported that they received the continuous impression that an athlete senses discrimination to the degree that he is unsuccessful in athletics. Again, however, no empirical evidence is available to support this impression. Thus it appears that many players perceive both a quota system and the practice of stacking. However, the evidence is based on limited samples and on a few sports. Future studies should be concerned with other sports and should elicit responses from both successful and unsuccessful black and white college and professional athletes; coaches and general managers should also be interviewed, and samples should account for regional differences.

Discrimination has also occurred with respect to the desire of blacks to pursue leader, official, and entrepreneurial roles. A number of articles (Fitzgerald 1960; Boyle 1963; Rosenblatt 1967; Olsen 1968; Brown 1969) have cited statistics which indicate the relative absence of blacks at the managerial or executive level in college and professional sport. In high schools, however, the situation may be improving, especially in the larger urban centers where an increasing number of blacks are occupying the role of head coach for the first time (Jordan 1971).

Similar to contemporary white athletes, the black athlete seeks to pursue entrepreneurial gains while he is an active player and can capitalize on his achieved prestige as a professional athlete. Two additional sources of income include a bonus for signing the initial contract with a team, and remuneration received for endorsing or promoting commercial products. Again it has been claimed that access to these benefits is highly dependent on the race of the athlete. Boyle (1963:129–130) reported that black major league baseball players complained about the lack of commercial endorsements, and about receiving lower bonuses than whites when they signed their initial contract. It has been suggested that only the few black athletes who are potential stars, and are therefore highly visible, will receive a bonus comparable to that which a white player might receive. Similarly, it is argued that only a minority of black athletes are associated with a commercial product, and that those offers which the black player does receive are less lucrative than those received by his white teammate. Pascal and Rapping (1969:40), citing the Equal Employment Opportunity Commission report of 1968, reported that black athletes appeared in only 5 percent of 351 television commercials associated with New York sports events in the fall of 1966. This situation has changed considerably in recent years, as noted by the increasing number of blacks who are appearing in television commercials (especially those related to drug prevention).

In view of the brevity of an athletic career, athletes must obtain post-retirement employment. Although a frequent source of employment for many exathletes is within the sport itself (e.g., coaches, managers, or general managers), Pascal and Rapping (1969:40) reported that successful black baseball players are not yet considered qualified for major supervisory positions. This finding is in agreement with the results of a study by Baron (1968), in which it was demonstrated that blacks in nonsport institutions are underrepresented in policy-making positions. He also noted that, when they do get representation, their power is restricted. Similarly, Kraus (1969) found that while substantial numbers of blacks were employed in leadership positions in public recreation and park programs, few of them held supervisory or administrative positions. To date, only a few blacks have held executive positions in professional sport.

Thus there is evidence of segregation and discrimination in sport, both on and off the field. At the present time, however, it is impossible to identify to what extent this is attributable to: a conscious or unconscious act by the white sporting establishment; self-inflicted segregation by the black himself through the process of minority group socialization experiences in the early years; or a combination of both of these factors.

ROLE CONFLICT FOR THE BLACK ATHLETE: RADICAL OR TOM; STUDENT OR ATHLETE

The contemporary black athlete faces role conflict engendered by the demand for rapid social changes in society. On one side he is bound to the traditional ultraconservative and apolitical sport establishment; on the other, he is faced with the demands of black radicals to become actively involved in the social movement for black freedom and equality. This section analyzes how and why the black athlete is faced with these conflicts, and how he is resolving them.

From 1947 until the late 1960's white and black society proclaimed that sport was the exemplar of integration and brotherhood, and the model for race relations. For example, it has been stated:

> Sport has often served minority groups as the first rung on the social ladder. As such, it has helped further their assimilation into American life. It would not be too far-fetched to say that it has done more in this regard than any other agency, including church and school. (Boyle 1963:100)

> Sport is one of the most responsive of many integrating mechanisms now active in the great social movement. (Tobin 1967:32)

> Every morning the world of sport wakes up and congratulates itself on its contributions to race relations. The litany has been repeated so many times that it is believed almost universally. It goes: Look what sport has done for the Negro. (Olsen 1968:7)

In reality, the black athlete has been faced with overt or covert forms of segregation and discrimination in both amateur and professional sport. Because he has been so dependent (economically, socially, educationally) on the white sport establishment, the black athlete has been reluctant to speak out or to take action when confronted with discrimination. At the same time, with the increasing rise of black dissent and activism, the black athlete has seen other visible blacks (e.g., entertainers) become active in the overall movement for equality and the attainment of civil rights guaranteed by legislative enactments. Because of his failure to take an active part, the black athlete has been criticized and accused of being a Tom by other blacks. Therefore, despite the claim that sport has been a great equalizer, it has been infected by the same racism that is found in other social institutions, and, as Brown (1970) noted, sport has "tommed out" in too many instances. That is, sport has not taken the opportunity to be innovative in fostering social change in intergroup relations. That the black athlete has the potential to be a social and political leader was evident in the 1968 presidential campaign, when both parties actively sought the endorsement and support of both amateur and professional black athletes.

Turning to the question of why the black athlete has increasingly left the locker room to lend his support to social issues, three reasons are suggested. First, whereas in the past these athletes had expediently spoken out on their own behalf, an increasing empathy with their race has led them to regard the black struggle as their struggle. Second, blacks have realized how salient sport is in the American way of life and that athletics is a source of power—"power which could be gained from exploiting the white man's economic and almost religious involvement in athletics" (Edwards 1969:47). Finally, the emergence of more articulate leaders, combined with an improved quality of education, has led black athletes to realize that not everyone can "make it" in professional sport, and thus they should no longer be totally dependent on the sports establishment for mobility and security.

Similarly, they are resolving the conflict between their role as students and as athletes. This conflict has been engendered in the past by some of the following factors. First, many, if not most, blacks arrive on college campuses with a disadvantaged educational background, and as a result they have little or no conception of themselves as students. Since they are recruited to attend college on the basis of their performance in the role of athlete, they are expected and encouraged to play this role, with only minimal expectations and few, if any, sanctions received from coaches, alumni, professors, and peers for performing in the role of student. Since they are constantly reminded that success in college sport guarantees financial rewards and a position in professional sport, the athlete role tends to be preemptive. Since they, like most individuals, prefer to perform in tasks in which they are successful and can achieve prestige and recognition, they prefer the athlete role. Yet, conflict occurs because they know they must achieve in the student role to remain eligible. Because of all of these factors they tend to believe that the athlete role is the only one they can or should play.

This conflict is being resolved by the presence of an increasing number of "athletes-turned-scholars" who are functioning as role models. These individuals, by example, are demonstrating that since not everyone is able or desires to "make it" in professional sport, a college degree can enable a black to achieve long-range goals similar to those which might be realized by a career in professional sport.

Black athletes are increasingly resolving role conflicts, with the result that they are playing a more active role in protests against exploitation, dehumanization, and discrimination within both sport and society. In addition, a small but increasing number are achieving success in the role of student.

SUMMARY AND CONCLUSIONS

In summary, this overview of many journalistic sources and few empirical studies has indicated: that sport is salient for blacks, both as participants and as spectators; that participation in sport does not guarantee permanent membership in the higher strata of the dominant society; that sport as a social institution is not devoid of prejudice, discrimination and racism; that black athletes are resolving role conflicts and thereby playing the role of student and activist, in addition to the role of athlete; and that sport has been utilized, at least for a minority of blacks, to bring about social, economic and academic gains that have not been available in other social institutions.

Finally, it has been indirectly demonstrated that, except for a few empirical studies, much of the literature relating to the black athlete consists of anecdotal, impressionistic case studies of isolated incidents, most of which occurred in the 1960's. Therefore, if we are serious about advancing our knowledge concerning race relations within a sport context, scholarly endeavors must be initiated by those interested in the black athlete as a social phenomenon.

The following section represents some suggestions as to what approaches might be taken in order to justify this phenomenon as a viable research area. First, in view of the fact that very little concerning the black athlete has appeared since 1971 in either the popular press or the scientific literature, a decision must be made as to whether the phenomenon is a viable research area for social scientists, and, if so, which issues and hypotheses should be examined. For example: has the social situation for black athletes, both within and outside sport, improved to the extent that it is no longer a social problem? Was the interest in this area in the late 1960's merely a passing fad as an area of study and concern for sport sociologists?

If the phenomenon is worthy of further study, frames of references or perspectives should be established. For example, the phenomenon of the black athlete in a basically white institution could be examined: as a social problem associated with a culturally and economically disadvantaged minority group interacting in a dominant culture; as a study of intergroup relations (white "hope" vs. black "hope") or intragroup relations (black-white role relationships in a small group); as a study of social change (the integration of "white" institutions); as a study of social conflict (double standard, opposing interests and values); as a study of the socialization process of minority groups in their early years, and the desocialization and resocialization process in the later years (the adaptive patterns of retired black athletes); as a study of the role of blacks within a social institution (varying expectations concerning the enactment of sport roles by blacks and whites); as a study of social disorganization (society's inability to cope with social change); or as a study of the inequality of economic or educational opportunity (cf. Pascal and Rapping 1969).

Regardless of the frame of reference, since theory, methodology, and empirical data are inevitably intertwined in any adequate scientific explanation, future efforts should be based on models and theories, should be empirical rather than impressionistic in nature, and should include the construction and testing of theories. With respect to methodology, longitudinal and cross-sectional studies rather than isolated case studies should be initiated, and the multivariate approach should be used. For example, in order to examine the extent to which the early life and present experiences of black athletes, white athletes, and coaches contribute to discriminatory or racist acts in a sport context, the path analysis technique (using a multistage, multivariate approach) might be employed. Furthermore, in addition to the problem areas discussed in this chapter, future efforts should be directed toward the consideration of related, but hitherto neglected problems such as: the black woman athlete (cf. Hart 1971:64); the participation in and consumption of sport by blacks who are not elite athletes; and the relationship between sport involvement and community identification by blacks (especially the question as to whether identification varies with the success achieved by community teams).

There is a need to move beyond the descriptive and impressionistic level if the complex causal relationships involved in producing and perpetuating the present racial interactions are to be identified and understood. If the problem is worthy of study, then empirical data and theoretically based analytic attempts are needed to substantiate or refute the present myths and impressions.

REFERENCES

Abrahams, A.
    1952   "Race and Athletics." *Eugenics Review* 44 (October):143–145.
Alcindor, L.
    1969   "My Story." *Sports Illustrated*. October, 27, pp. 82–98.
Annarino, A. A.
    1953   "The Contributions of Athletics to Social Mobility." *56th An-*

nual Proceedings of the College Physical Education Association. New York.

Baltimore, C. H.
1951   "Negro in Basketball." *Negro Historical Bulletin* 25:49–50.

Baron, H. M.
1968   "Black Powerlessness in Chicago." *Transaction.* 6 (November):27–33.

Blalock, H. M.
1962   "Occupational Discrimination: Some Empirical Propositions." *Social Problems* 9:240–247.
1967   *Toward a Theory of Minority Group Relations.* New York: John Wiley & Sons.

Boulding, D. C.
1957   "Participation of the Negro in Selected Amateur and Professional Athletics, 1935–1955." Master's thesis, University of Wisconsin. P. 174.

Boyle, R. H.
1963   "A Minority Group—the Negro Baseball Player." In Boyle, R. H., ed. *Sport: Mirror of American Life.* Pp. 100–134. Boston: Little, Brown.

Brown, R. C.
1969   "The Black Athlete in Perspective." Paper presented at the Annual Meeting of the American College of Sports Medicine, Atlanta.
1970   "Is Sport Tomming Out?" Paper presented at the AAHPER Annual Meetings, Seattle.

Carter, M. S.
1970   "Black Fullback." *Christian Century* 87 (January):69.

Charnofsky, H.
1967   "The Major League Professional Baseball Player: Self-Conception versus Popular Image." Paper presented at the annual meeting of the American Sociological Association, San Francisco.
1968   "The Major League Baseball Player: Self-Conception versus the Popular Image." *International Review of Sport Sociology* 3:39–55.

Clement, R. E.
1954   "Racial Integration in the Field of Sports." *Journal of Negro Education* 23:222–230.

Davie, M. R.
1949   *Negroes in American Society.* New York: McGraw-Hill.

Davis, J. P.
1966   "The Negro in American Sports." In Davis, J. P., ed. *The American Negro Reference Book.* Pp. 775–825. Englewood Cliffs, N.J.: Prentice-Hall.

Dodson, D. W.
1954   "The Integration of Negroes in Baseball." *Journal of Educational Sociology* 28 (October):73–82.

Edwards, H.
    1969   *The Revolt of the Black Athlete.* New York: Free Press.
Eggleston, J.
    1965   "Secondary Schools and Oxbridge Blues." *British Journal of Sociology* 16:232–242.
Fitzgerald, E.
    1960   "The Negro in American Sport." *Negro History Bulletin* 24:27–31.
Fleischer, N.
    1938   *Black Dynamite—the Story of the Negro in the Prize Ring from 1782–1938.* New York: C. J. O'Brien.
Frazier, E. F.
    1957   *Black Bourgeoisie.* Glencoe, Ill.: Free Press.
Grusky, O.
    1963   "The Effects of Formal Structure on Managerial Recruitment: A Study of Baseball Organization." *Sociometry* 26:345–353.
Greendorfer, S.
    1970   "Birthplace of Baseball Players: City Size, State and Region." Unpublished paper, University of Wisconsin.
Hart, M.
    1971   "Sport: Women Sit in the Back of the Bus." *Psychology Today* 5 (October):64, 66.
Henderson, E. B.
    1968   *The Black Athlete—Emergence and Arrival.* New York: Publishers Company.
Ibrahim, H.
    1968   "Prejudice among College Athletes." *Research Quarterly* (October):556–559.
Jordan, P.
    1971   *Black Coach.* New York: Dodd, Mead.
Kenyon, G. S.
    1969   "Sport Involvement: A Conceptual Go and Some Consequences Thereof." In Kenyon, G. S., ed. *Aspects of Contemporary Sport Sociology.* Pp. 77–84. Chicago: Athletic Institute.
Kraus, R.
    1969   "Race and Sports: The Challenge to Recreation." *Journal of Health, Physical Education and Recreation* 40 (April): 32–34.
Loy, J. W.
    1969   "The Study of Sport and Social Mobility." In Kenyon, G. S., ed. *Aspects of Contemporary Sport Sociology.* Pp. 101–119. Chicago: Athletic Institute.
Loy, J. W., and McElvogue, J. F.
    1970   "Racial Segregation in American Sport." *International Review of Sport Sociology* 5:5–23.
Maher, C.
    1968   "The Negro Athlete in America." *Los Angeles Times*, Part 3, March 24, 26, 27, 28, 29.

McPherson, B. D.
1975 "The Segregation by Playing Position Hypothesis in Sport: An Alternative Explanation." *Social Science Quarterly* 55:960–966.

Olsen, J.
1968 *The Black Athlete—a Shameful Story.* New York: Time.

Pascal, A. H., and Rapping, L. A.
1969 "Racial Discrimination in Organized Baseball." Mimeographed. Pp. 44.

Quarles, B.
1964 *The Negro in the Making of America.* New York: Collier.

Rosenblatt, A.
1967 "Negroes in Baseball: The Failure of Success." *Transaction.* 5 (September):51–53.

Schafer, W. E.
1968 "Athletic success and social mobility." Paper presented at the AAHPER Annual Meeting, St. Louis.

Short, J. F., and Tennyson, R. A.
1963 "Behavior Dimensions of Gang Delinquency." *American Sociological Review* 28:411–428.

Simon, R. J., and Carey, J. W.
1966 "The Phantom Racist." *Transaction,* November, pp. 5–11.

Smith, G., and Grindstaff, C. F.
1970 "Race and Sport in Canada." Paper presented at the Canadian Association of Sport Sciences Meeting, Quebec.

Sports Illustrated
1968 "In Black and White." February 19, p. 10.

Time
1970 "Black America, 1970." April 6.

Tobin, R. L.
1967 "Sports as an Integrator." *Saturday Review,* January 21, p. 32.

Voigt, D. Q.
1966 *American Baseball: From Gentleman's Sport to the Commissioner System.* Norman, Okla.: University of Oklahoma Press.

Webb, H.
1969 "Reaction to Loy Presentation." In Kenyon, G. S., ed. *Aspects of Contemporary Sport Sociology.* Pp. 120–131. Chicago: Athletic Institute.

Weinberg, S. K., and Arond, H.
1952 "The Occupational Culture of the Boxer." *American Journal of Sociology* 57:460–469.

White, W.
1951 "Time for a Progress Report." *Saturday Review,* September 22, pp. 9–10, 38–41.

Whitehead, P. C.
1967 "Letter on Rosenblatt's Article: Negroes in Baseball." *Transaction.* 5 (October):63–64.

Worthy, M., and Markle, A.
    1970   "Racial Differences in Reactive versus Self-Paced Sports Activities." *Journal of Personality and Social Psychology* 16:439–443.
Yetman, N. R., and Eitzen, D. S.
    1971   "Black Athletes on Intercollegiate Basketball Teams: An Empirical Test of Discrimination." In Yetman, N. R., ed. *Majority and Minority: The Dynamics of Racial and Ethnic Relations.* Boston: Allyn and Bacon.
Young, A. S.
    1963   *Negro Firsts in Sports.* Chicago: Johnson Publishing.

Racial Discrimination in Football: A Test of the "Stacking" of Playing Positions Hypothesis

DONNA R. MADISON AND DANIEL M. LANDERS

It is often maintained that professional sport, music, and entertainment, more than other occupations, have been areas in which minority groups could have equal opportunity with whites. It is generally acknowledged, however, that initially blacks entering white-dominated sports underwent the severest type of racial discrimination. For example, Boyle (1963:104) cites the experiences of Ed Williamson, a great white shortstop who played in the 1880's in the Eastern League for a team known as the Buffaloes. Williamson describes his own and his teammates' tactics in using the slide at second base to rid the Buffalo team of a black second baseman by the name of Frank Grant, nicknamed "Black Dunlap".

> "The Buffaloes—I think it was the Buffalo team—had a negro for second base. He was a few lines blacker than a raven, but he was one of the best players in the old Eastern League. The haughty Caucasians of the association were willing to permit darkies to carry water to them or guard the bat bag, but it made them sore to have the name of one on the batting list. They made a cabal against this man and incidentally introduced a new feature into the game. The players of the opposing teams made it their special business to live to 'spite' this brunette Buffalo. They would tarry at second when they might easily have made third, just to toy with the sensitive shins of the second baseman. The poor man played in two games out of five perhaps; the rest of the time he was on crutches. To give the frequent spiking of the darky an appearance of accident the 'feet first' slide was practiced. The negro got wooden armor for his legs and went into the field with the appearance of a man wearing nail kegs for stockings. The enthusiasm of opposition players would not let them take a bluff. They filed their spikes and the first man at second generally split the wooden half

At the time of this investigation, Donna Madison was a senior in physical education at State University College at Brockport, New York. Daniel M. Landers is an associate professor of physical education, Pennsylvania State University. Appreciation is extended to Shirley Finnegan, Deborah Jayne, Janet Richardson, and Becky Willis for their assistance in this study.

cylinders. The colored man seldom lasted beyond the fifth inning, as the base-runners became more expert. The practice survived long after the second baseman made his last trip to the hospital. And that's how Kelly learned to slide, concluded the reminiscent Williamson."

Although Williamson's account is undoubtedly exaggerated, his attitudes reflected the temper of the times.

Today, of course, we hope that such overt examples of racial discrimination in sport are a thing of the past. More subtle forms of discrimination are still evident in recruitment practices for blacks (Edwards 1969) and their opportunities for social interaction both on and off the field (Meggesy 1970). An even more subtle form of discrimination is suggested by Olsen (1968) and Edwards (1969), who point out the differential stacking of blacks in certain playing positions.

In a recent study, Loy and McElvogue (1971), using Grusky's theory (1963) of organizational structure, have shown the extent to which blacks are found in spatially peripheral field positions and whites in more central positions on professional football and baseball teams. During the 1968 season Loy and McElvogue found that only four blacks played in central offensive positions in football (quarterbacks, centers, and guards), whereas blacks were overrepresented in peripheral positions such as tackles, ends, and backs. Results were similar for both of the professional baseball leagues, with many blacks playing outfield positions but few playing infield positions.

Many explanations have been advanced to account for these differences between black and white athletes in the playing positions. Everyday observations of national and international sprinting championships as well as research evidence (McIntyre, 1971; Kane, 1971) indicates that blacks run faster on the average than whites. Although the sprinting speeds of blacks may explain their overrepresentation in peripheral positions, their absence in central positions necessitates further explanation. McPherson (1971) suggests a role-modeling explanation, where blacks select playing positions in which their highly salient black heroes have excelled. This explanation, however, does not explain the presence of blacks in central positions in collegiate and interscholastic teams or blacks desiring to play central positions.

The explanation favored by Loy and McElvogue (1971), Olsen (1968) and Edwards (1969) is that blacks who have played or wish to play central positions are encouraged by coaches to play peripheral positions. If this explanation is correct, then this switch should be evident in changes in playing central and peripheral positions from one competitive level to the next. The purpose of this study is to examine changes in playing positions (central and peripheral) from college-level competition to professional football. In accord with the explanations of Loy and McElvogue (1971), Edwards (1969), and Olsen (1968), it was hypothesized that blacks will (more often than whites) change from central positions in college to peripheral positions in professional football.

METHOD

The procedure to test this hypothesis consisted of contacting the directors of public relations of the twenty-four professional football teams. In this letter the name, playing position, race, college attended, and college playing position for each of the players on the roster was requested. Eighteen replies, with information about 563 players, were received for a return of 75 percent.

The directors of sports information at 141 colleges were then contacted in an attempt to obtain vital missing information. From this request, 98 replies from colleges were received for a 70 percent return. Twenty-seven athletes played more than one position either in college or at the professional level; these athletes had to be excluded from the study since they could not be categorized properly. Two of the professional players did not go out for football in college, and two did not go to college. These athletes also had to be excluded from the study because there was no chance for change to occur from the college to the professional level. One college contacted about a player did not have a football team; this was due to incorrect information from one of the professional teams, and this player also had to be excluded.

Gerald D'Agostino, former coach of the Brockport football team, suggested changes in Loy and McElvogue's categories of central and peripheral football positions. To Loy and McElvogue's central positions on offense—that is, quarterback, center, and the right and left guard—the investigators added the right and left tackles and the fullback. The fullback was classified as central because of the direction he takes when in motion. On defense the two tackles were added by the present investigators as central positions to the three linebackers originally used by Loy and McElvogue.

Both the colleges and the professional teams did not distinguish between the middle linebacker and the right and left linebackers. The middle linebacker is a central position, and the right and left linebacker positions are peripheral. All linebackers in the present study, therefore, had to be categorized as central positions.

Players were categorized as same if they occupied the same position in college and at the professional level. The categories of central-central and peripheral-peripheral were used for those who changed, but continued to occupy a position in the same category. (For example, if they played a central position in college and changed to another central position as a professional.) Finally, the categories of central-peripheral and peripheral-central were used if they changed from one position in college to a different category of positions as a professional. (For example, a change from a peripheral position in college to a central position at the professional level.) A 2 X 5 chi square analysis was applied to the number of black and white players who remained in the same playing position or changed from one position to another position. The frequencies of these changes are summarized in Table 1.

TABLE 1. Change in Playing Position from College to Professional Football

Race		*Type of Change*				
	Same	Central-Central	Peripheral-Peripheral	Central-Peripheral	Peripheral-Central	Total
Blacks	95	10	32	24	6	167
Whites	199	68	39	29	29	364
Total	294	78	71	53	35	531

$X^2 = 40.58$, df $= 4$, p $< .01$.

The resultant chi square was significant at the .01 level, indicating that there were significant changes in the positioning from college level to the professional level of both black and white players. Inspection of the discrepancies between observed and expected frequencies indicated that, in support of the hypothesis of this study, blacks as compared to whites were overrepresented in changes from central to peripheral positions and underrepresented in changes from central to central positions.

The significant results found in this study offer support for the notion that pressures, probably from the coach, are applied to encourage black athletes to play peripheral positions. The alternative notion that blacks make an uncoerced choice to play peripheral positions seems less plausible, since highly salient models (for example, a black occupying a specific playing position) are not likely to change from the college to the professional level. In addition, the highly developed skills obtained by football players who have played a specific position for four years at the college level make it unlikely that they would suddenly desire to change positions after being recruited by the professional teams.

If blacks are pressured to change positions more than whites, the nature of this change is of central importance. The competition for starting positions on professional teams often necessitates changes in playing positions for those who are not given starting positions. Why these changes occur more often for blacks than whites, however, is still the central point at issue.

Due to existing stereotypes which suggest that blacks are better in peripheral positions and whites better in central positions, many coaches knowingly or unknowingly have a predisposition to encourage players to play selected positions. If asked, coaches may use vague reasons for these expectancies ("Blacks are not suited for central positions"; "Blacks may choke under pressure"; "They cannot be trusted in a leadership position like quarterback"). Whether these changes in position are due to coaches' expectancies, developed through their social learning experiences in sport, or to the latter discriminatory reasons remains to be determined. More in-depth analyses of specific coaches' and players' reasons for these changes are indicated before concrete statements can be made concerning team playing positions as an indicator of racial discrimination.

REFERENCES

Boyle, R.
  1963 *Sport: A Mirror of American Life.* Boston: Little, Brown.
Edwards, H.
  1969 *The Revolt of the Black Athlete.* New York: Free Press.
Grusky, O.
  1963 "The Effects of Formal Structure on Managerial Recruitment: A Study of Baseball Organization." *Sociometry* 26:345–363.
Kane, M.
  1971 "An Assessment of Black Is Best." *Sports Illustrated*, January 18, pp. 72–83.
Loy, J., and McElvogue, J.
  1971 "Racial Segregation in American Sport." *International Review of Sport Sociology* 5:5–24.
McIntyre, T.
  1971 "A Field Experimental Study of Cohesiveness, Status and Attitude Change in Four Biracial Small Sport Groups." Ph.D. dissertation, Pennsylvania State University.
McPherson, B.
  1971 "Minority Group Socialization: An Alternative Explanation for the Segregation by Playing Position Hypothesis." Paper presented at the Third International Symposium on the Sociology of Sport, Waterloo, Ontario, Canada.

Meggesy, D.
1970 *Out of Their League.* Berkeley, Calif.: Ramparts.
Olsen, J.
1968 *The Black Athlete: A Shameful Story of the Myth of Integration in American Sport.* New York: Time-Life Books.

Race and Sport: A Reaction to the McPherson and Madison and Landers Papers

JOHN W. LOY

THE BLACK ATHLETE: AN OVERVIEW AND ANALYSIS

McPherson is to be highly commended for his very thorough and thoughtful overview and analysis of the popular and scientific literature dealing with the black athlete. He has treated several substantial issues in his paper. In examining each issue he has cited current research and theory associated with a particular topic, raised critical questions regarding present theoretical and empirical work related to specific issues, clearly spelled out lines of needed investigation, and offered helpful guidelines as to how one might best pursue future studies bearing upon the relations between race and sport.

I have no major criticisms to make concerning his many insightful observations. I wish, however, to briefly expand upon his treatment of certain subjects and to touch upon selected problems not directly discussed by him.

ORIGIN OF BLACK INVOLVEMENT IN SPORT

As most of the substantive issues examined by McPherson are essentially problems of social change, I would like to emphasize the importance of giving greater scholarly attention to the origin of black involvement in sport. A major reason for this emphasis is that a full understanding of the problems associated with the present plight of the black athlete cannot be acquired without some awareness of its historical antecedents.

It is indeed true that a social historian would find it difficult to document the first time a black competed in an institutionalized sport. Nevertheless, case studies of early black athletes afford keen insights into the manifold interrelationships among race, sport, and society. The earliest account of a black American athlete that I have encountered is contained in a British set of volumes entitled *Boxiana* written by Pierce Egan between 1812 and 1829. He reports that during the

---

John W. Loy is professor of sport studies and sociology at the University of Massachusetts, Amherst.

course of the Revolutionary War General Percy of the British forces captured the town of Richmond near New York and befriended a slave whom he named Bill Richmond. Percy provided Richmond with various forms of sponsorship, including a tour of Europe and educational support in England. Richmond became involved in boxing as the result of a victorious bout against a white Englishman whom Richmond had challenged to a fight following the former's issue of rude remarks to Richmond while the latter was escorting a white woman. Notwithstanding certain marked forms of racial discrimination, Richmond experienced a long and successful boxing career in England. Moreover, he was influential in furthering the career of Tom Molyneux, the first black to win an American boxing title (1805). Richmond was Molyneux's second at ringside when he fought Tom Crib, the English heavyweight champion during the first decade of the nineteenth century. As an aside I note that Richmond is reported to have been an excellent cricket player; thus we may assume that he was the first black American to engage in that genteel game.

My reading of the pugilistic exploits of early black athletes in Egan's *Boxiana* whetted my historical appetite. In collaboration with Jack Berryman and Guy Lewis, I recently delved into the matter of the beginnings of black involvement in sport in my local area, Amherst. We discovered that several black students had achieved both athletic and academic success at Amherst College and at Massachusetts Agricultural College (now the University of Massachusetts) between 1890 and 1910. As this period marks the height of racism in America, I am especially interested in ascertaining why there was an apparent lack of racial discrimination in collegiate athletics in Amherst during this period. Another problem which interests me is trying to discover what underground railroad was at work to bring black youth to western Massachusetts from small communities in the Deep South. Finally, I am most interested in determining the effects of this early educational sponsorship of black athletes upon their post-college careers.

Apart from the largely intrinsic interests just expressed, I believe that historical analysis of the black athlete can provide much knowledge about the evolution of racial myths. In view of the great outcrop of writing concerning racial stereotypes, it is somewhat surprising that more efforts have not been made to account for the rise and fall of various racial stereotypes within the realm of sport in American society.

Another neglected aspect of historical scholarship has to do with the lack of attention given to the study of sport involvement within various sectors of the black community. Since the turn of the century blacks have been actively involved in sport via their own country clubs, athletic associations, and professional sport leagues (see, e.g., Peterson 1970), but the social significance of such sport involvement has been virtually ignored by black and white scholars alike.

DEGREE AND TYPE OF INVOLVEMENT

McPherson's discussion of the degree and type of sport involvement on the part of blacks clearly indicates the limited research that is available on the subject. For example, there are almost no data concerning black spectators, yet it seems apparent that black fans have had some degree of influence on the development of modern sport. Blalock (1962, 1967), for instance, suggests that pressure from the growing number of black spectators in franchise cities following World War II may partially account for the acceptance of black athletes into professional baseball during the late 1940's.

One would think that the major corporations who pay for most of the television advertising for professional sport programs would direct some of their market research to determining the social parameters of the black clientele for different sports, but such does not seem to be the case. For example, although many ice rinks are located in or near black ghettos, the potential black spectators living in these areas have been all but ignored by professional hockey clubs.

I note in passing that three graduate students majoring in sport administration at Massachusetts are currently conducting market research for an expansion hockey team in Boston. They are paying special attention to the matter of the black spectator. As regards socialization into hockey spectatorship, one interesting fact which emerged from one of their early pilot surveys was the finding that several blacks were led to view games at rinkside as a result of their earlier involvement in "street hockey." Some of their more dismaying findings to date bear upon the matter of racial stereotypes. For instance, when spectators were asked to explain the scarcity of black athletes in professional hockey, many fans gave as standard replies the "facts" that blacks typically have "weak ankles," are "warm-blooded," "lack balance," etc.

My own particular concern related to the degree and type of sport involvement has to do with the fluctuating differential admission rates of blacks into various sports and their assignment to specific social roles and positions within given sport organizations at different points in time. I am especially intrigued as to why there seems to be a more or less constant ratio of blacks to whites in any given sport for any given year. How do norms develop as to what sort of percentage is going to be set? What are the individual and social consequences of the notion that for any particular sport a team can only put so many black athletes on a field or court at a given time? What has happened to those teams who haven't abided by these implicit norms? These considerations lead us to the third topic treated by McPherson.

INTEGRATION VIA SPORT

Most analyses of integration via sport have been highly superficial in nature. Most observers have been content to cite the relatively large percentages of blacks who have been accepted in sport situations, as compared with other situations in society. Moreover, with the exception of Blalock's theoretical work, even the matter of structural assimilation has not been adequately analyzed. Why are so few blacks found in sports involving a high degree of social interaction? Why do black athletes in team sports typically occupy positions requiring independent tasks rather than dependent tasks? Why haven't blacks been given "power positions" in the world of sport? Why do blacks generally occupy those positions that can be most readily evaluated?

Perhaps it is time for researchers interested in the area of race and sport to begin giving attention to the many kinds of integration and assimilation on and off the field. Greater attention might be given to each of the seven stages outlined by Milton Gordon (1964:71) as follows:

1. Cultural assimilation—"change of cultural patterns to those of host society";
2. Structural assimilation—"large-scale entrance into cliques, clubs, and institutions of host society on primary group level";
3. Marital assimilation—"large-scale intermarriage";
4. Identificational assimilation—"development of people-hood based exclusively on host society";
5. Attitude receptional assimilation—"absence of prejudice";
6. Behavior receptional assimilation—"absence of discrimination";
7. Civic assimilation—"absence of value and power conflict."

To varying degrees each of these types of assimilation is worthy of examination with respect to the black athlete in both his sport and non-sport roles.

THE RELATIONSHIP BETWEEN SPORT AND EDUCATION FOR BLACK STUDENTS

A relevant context for the analysis of assimilation is higher education. Do black youth experience greater assimilation at each of the levels mentioned as a result of attending a college or university? More particularly, do black collegiate athletes, as a result of their special college experiences, undergo greater assimilation at each stage than their non-athletic counterparts; Are black athletes, because of their special student status, more likely than non-athletic black students to accept the dominant cultural patterns of a university, to gain admission to fraternities, to be elected to student body positions, to date across racial lines? Or are black athletes because of their marked visibility more likely to experience prejudice, discrimination, and role conflicts?

If I had to suggest one primary area of study as concerns the problem of sport and education for black students, I would likely suggest a focus on counseling. *What* advice from *whom, when* and *where* does a black athlete receive at each educational level? What is the importance of such advice on the quality of education he receives, and on his consequent social mobility?

SPORT AND SOCIAL MOBILITY

A worthy investigation would be a comparison of the career mobility patterns of black vs. white athletes vs. black and white non-athletes at contrasting institutions of higher education. Relatively speaking, does the black athlete outdistance the non-athletic student in terms of post-college career success? Or does the black student on a scholastic scholarship experience greater social success than the black student on an athletic scholarship? Or how about the black Rhodes Scholar who combines the classic Greek ideal of student-athlete? Is an Ivy League education of more relative value for black athletes than white athletes?

Another important and related matter has to do with the opposite end of the continuum—students who fail. What are the relative long-run consequences for black and white students who fail athletically and/or academically? What specific opportunity structures are available for each to plug back into society?

DISCRIMINATION AGAINST THE BLACK ATHLETE

As McPherson has presented a detailed description of discrimination against the black athlete, I would like to shift the emphasis somewhat and suggest a need for renewed attention to race relations. Just what role can sport play in furthering race relations? With the exception of one or two studies (such as the excellent field experiment recently conducted by Thomas McIntyre), we have relatively little knowledge regarding the consequence of sport involvement for race relations. Moreover, the recent rise of the black power movement, minority quests for ethnic identity, etc., have seemingly made obsolete the standard text-book guidelines on how best to further interracial harmony. I believe that black social scientists and sportsmen can be of great assistance in providing sound advice on the subject, and I hope that the recent trend of hiring a substantial number of black coaches for collegiate teams will enhance the development of better race relations in American sport.

ROLE CONFLICT FOR THE BLACK ATHLETE

If nothing else, black coaches employed by our colleges and universities could be instrumental in helping black students on their teams to resolve the many role conflicts outlined by McPherson. The extent to which they fulfill this function, however, depends upon the degree to which they themselves are free from similar role conflicts. For example, are black coaches, by virtue of their typically subordinate positions in the coaching ranks, indirectly forced to "Tom out"?

Let me close on a rather dismal note by expressing a major fear; namely, that notwithstanding the inherent scientific and humanistic significance of the study of the black athlete in particular, and race and sport in general, I am afraid that serious study of these subjects will not be intensely and extensively pursued. I fear that the study of race and sport is only a passing fancy of white sport sociologists; that black scholars will increasingly devote their attention to what they consider to be more substantial issues; that radical observers of the sport scene will soon tire of the issue and find another problem to attack; and that one and all will forego the search for hard facts, sound theory, and adequate application of relevant knowledge.

RACIAL DISCRIMINATION IN FOOTBALL: A TEST OF THE STACKING OF PLAYING POSITIONS HYPOTHESIS

Madison and Landers have gone to a good deal of trouble to test an interesting hypothesis, and they are to be complimented for their effort. I will comment briefly on two dimensions of the investigation; namely, its empirical and theoretical aspects.

EMPIRICAL CONSIDERATIONS

The title and underlying rationale of the investigation implies that the phenomenon of racial "stacking" in professional football denotes a form of discrimination. An implicit but apparent assumption is the notion that white members of the professional football establishment directly or indirectly induce black athletes to switch from central to peripheral positions. While "stacking" may indeed represent discrimination, data of the present investigation cannot confirm the matter. Knowledge of where black athletes played in college and where they now play on professional teams only depicts a change in status; it does little to indicate whether the change in playing position is a function of ability, racial stereotyping, or some other parameter.

A more definitive analysis of the stacking hypothesis requires field work wherein observers examine who tries out for central and noncentral positions during training camp and exhibition games, and then compare who plays where during the course of the regular season. Observers would, of course, have to be keenly attuned to individuals' perceptions of the situation. A white coach, for example, might be only too willing for a black athlete to try out for a central position, but a black athlete may nevertheless believe that he doesn't have a hope of making it at a central position and thus opt out early on for a peripheral position. How one ascertains and deals with such self-fulfilling beliefs (if indeed they exist) is a moot question.

Although this investigation and similar studies have placed primary emphasis on socio-psychological characteristics and conditions, one mustn't rule out the consideration of physical attributes. A complete analysis of "switching and stacking" should take into account the physical and bodily requirements associated with particular playing positions in both collegiate and professional football. Perhaps stacking is due in part to the fact that an athlete of moderate size can successfully play at certain positions at the college level but not at the professional level. Thus a 210-pound black linebacker is not going to move from collegiate circles to professional ranks unless he greatly increases in girth.

Other explanations are also available which may account for the differential distribution of white and black athletes by playing position in professional football. These include the role-modeling hypothesis offered by McPherson, or the simple factor of the reward structure of professional sports. That is to say, one often finds in professional sports that high prestige and income are associated with peripheral playing positions—for example, flankers, wide receivers, and outfielders. The availability of different alternative explanations for stacking leads us to several theoretical considerations.

THEORETICAL CONSIDERATIONS

First I would like to comment on the categorization of central and peripheral football positions employed by Madison and Landers. The conceptualization of centrality in the present study seems to be based more upon the fundamental direction of movement of players in particular positions than upon the primary spatial location of given positions. It is certainly the prerogative of the investigators to conceptualize centrality in any manner they want, but since past studies have typically considered centrality in terms of spatial location, and since the investigators in large measure were drawing upon the Loy-McElvogue study, I suggest that a comparison of the two models of centrality are in order as concerns the major hypothesis of the investigation. In short, which model of centrality illustrates the most marked change in playing position from college to professional football? What are the theoretical and empirical implications of the differences found for each model? Are there other models which might be more heuristically useful in accounting for stacking?

McElvogue and I (1970) drew upon the work of Grusky (1963) when we first examined racial segregation in professional sports for several reasons. Grusky was on the faculty of UCLA, and we were familiar with his work; his work dealt with baseball, which was the first sport we examined; and it seemed to be related to Blalock's analysis of discrimination in professional sports, which also focused on baseball. For exploratory purposes we accepted Grusky's model as given, but we were aware that the assumptions underlying his model had not been confirmed in sport situations; namely, that all things being equal, the more central an individual's spatial location, the greater the likelihood that an individual will interact to a high degree with teammates, and perform basically dependent tasks.

The formal structure of professional baseball organizations permits one to readily identify central and peripheral positions by the very terms used to characterize organizational subunits such as battery, infield, and outfield. Moreover, one may differentiate those positions requiring the performance of independent and dependent tasks. It is somewhat more difficult to operationalize the degree of interaction associated with particular positions, and one might want to take issue with Grusky on his relegation of pitchers to the peripheral category. The greatest difficulty, though, comes when one tries to apply Grusky's model to other professional sports. McElvogue and I were never enchanted with our forced fit of Grusky's model to professional football, and we have found it virtually impossible to apply the model to many other kinds of sport. In sum, general sociological models provide useful initial frames of reference for exploratory investigations of social processes in sport situations, but these models must soon be modified to fit specific sport settings. If they cannot be adequately revised, then special models must be developed.

An innovative attempt at model-building is shown in Donald Ball's (1973) comparative analysis of stacking in professional football. Ball applied the Loy-McElvogue model to racial segregation in Canadian football and found a fair fit between data and theory. However, the fit was not as good when he examined stacking in terms of national origin. For the latter case Ball developed a new model having greater explanatory power; in brief, he distinguishes between *primary* and *supporting* positions. Offensively speaking, primary positions include quarterback, running backs, and pass catchers; center, guards, and tackles represent supporting positions. Defensively speaking, primary positions include tackles, ends, and linebackers; members of the secondary (i.e., cornerbacks and safeties) hold supporting positions. A further refinement within the primary offensive positions is the distinction between those which are *proactive* (initiate goal-directed activity and/or carry it out independently) and those which are *reactive* (dependent upon the activities of other primary positions for participation). Examples of proactive positions are quarterback and running backs; flankers, wide receivers, and ends represent reactive positions.

Ball's distinction between proactive and reactive personnel in professional football is not unlike McElvogue's distinction between initiative and receptive interactors in professional baseball. Among infielders, who typically interact to a high degree in contrast to outfielders, a shortstop would be considered an initiative interactor (he generally starts a putout), whereas a first baseman would be considered a receptive interactor (he generally receives the ball for a putout from another player). Perhaps these examples will suffice to illustrate ways in which new models might be developed to account for social processes such as racial segregation in sport situations.[1]

Let me say in conclusion that Madison and Landers have thrown light on another aspect of stacking in professional sports and I am certain that their work will stimulate still other investigations.

---

1. Other perspectives of structural segregation and racial discrimination in sport situations include Brower 1972; Edwards 1969, 1973; Jones and Hochner 1973; Olsen 1968; Smith and Grindstaff 1970; Worthy and Markle 1970; Yetman and Eitzen 1971, 1972.

REFERENCES

Ball, Donald W.
  1973   "Ascription and Position: A Comparative Analysis of Stacking in Professional Football." *Canadian Review of Sociology and Anthropology* 10, 2:97–113.
Blalock, Hubert M., Jr.
  1962   "Occupational Discrimination: Some Theoretical Propositions." *Social Problems* 9 (Winter): 240–247.
  1967   *Toward a Theory of Minority Group Relations.* New York: John Wiley and Sons.
Brower, Jonathan J.
  1972   "The Racial Basis of the Division of Labor among Players in the National Football League as a Function of Racial Stereotypes." Paper presented at the Pacific Sociological Association Meeting, Portland.
Edwards, Harry
  1969   *The Revolt of the Black Athlete.* New York: Free Press.
  1973   *Sociology of Sport.* Homewood, Ill.: Dorsey Press.
Egan, Pierce
  1812–29   *Boxiana.* 5 vols. London: G. Smeeton (and others).
Gordon, Milton M.
  1964   *Assimilation in American Life: The Role of Race, Religion and National Origins.* New York: Oxford University Press.
Grusky, Oscar
  1963   "The Effects of Formal Structure on Managerial Recruitment: A Study of Baseball Organization." *Sociometry* 26:345–353.
Jones, James M., and Hochner, Adrian Ruth
  1973   "Racial Differences in Sport Activities: A Look at the Self-Paced Versus Reactive Hypothesis." *Journal of Personality and Social Psychology* 27:86–95.
Loy, John W., and McElvogue, Joseph
  1970   "Racial Segregation in American Sport." *International Review of Sport Sociology* 5:5–24.
McIntyre, Thomas D.
  1970   "A Field Experimental Study of Cohesiveness, Status, and Attitude Change in Four Biracial Sport Groups." Ph.D. dissertation, Pennsylvania State University.
Olsen, Jack
  1968   *The Black Athlete—A Shameful Story.* New York: Time.
Peterson, Robert
  1970   *Only the Ball Was White.* Englewood Cliffs, N.J.: Prentice-Hall.
Smith, Gary, and Grindstaff, Carl F.
  1970   "Race and Sport in Canada." Paper presented at the Canadian Association of Sport Sciences Meeting, Quebec.

Worthy, M., and Markle, A.
  1970   "Racial Differences in Reactive Versus Self-Paced Sport Activities." *Journal of Personality and Social Psychology* 16:439–443.
Yetman, N. R., and Eitzen, D. S.
  1971   "Black Athletes on Intercollegiate Basketball Teams: An Empirical Test of Discrimination." In N. R. Yetman, ed. *Majority and Minority: The Dynamics of Racial and Ethnic Relations.* Pp. 509–517. Boston: Allyn and Bacon.
  1972   "Black Americans in Sports: Unequal Opportunity for Equal Ability." *Civil Rights Digest* 5 (August): 20–34.

A Commentary on Racial Myths and the Black Athlete

ROSCOE C. BROWN, JR.

While the McPherson and Madison and Landers papers provide some evidence of racial discrimination, actually they do not deal directly with the topic. One point that you might be thinking about is "Why are we so concerned about race and sport?" We are not concerned about Czechoslovaks in sports, or Swedes in sports. Right now, we are concerned about race and sports. Obviously this is because race is a very sensitive concern in our society, and the predominantly white society generally attempts to suppress any concerns about race which suggest that all is not well. Since sport has replaced religion as Marx's opiate, some people would like to believe that race does not affect sport very much. As a matter of fact, we have built up a tremendous number of myths such as sport and mobility, and sport and equality. Nevertheless, anyone who has been in a locker room or has played in any kind of game involving blacks and whites knows that these myths are not true.

Generally the researchers who look at race and sport are white scholars; there are very few blacks who deal with this. Other than Harry Edwards, and a few black educators like myself who cried in the wilderness for years, there are few blacks talking about sport. In fact, it is only recently that white scholars like Boyle, Charnofsky, and Loy have discussed it. I personally am very pleased that these people are interested, since it is certainly true that discrimination in sport should be exposed, using the definition of discrimination as overt or covert inequities based on race. Racism in sport is an extension of the Kerner Report, "Racism in America." To suggest that racial differences in sport are due to physical structure, heredity, and certain basic racial lifestyles cannot obscure the racism that exists in sport, for sport, in a very real sense, is a microcosm of the larger society. Anybody who lives in a black skin and has ever played any kind of ball knows that there is discrimination in sport. A major question for black scholars is, why bother describing something you know is there? Rather, black scholars might want to de-

Roscoe C. Brown, Jr., is director of the Institute of Afro-American Affairs, New York University.

vote their energies toward trying to do something about the racism in sports.

It is quite apparent now that the white athlete's plight is not really much different from the black athlete's plight; the main difference is that the white athlete does not know how bad the situation is, and the black athlete does. Therefore, many of the generalizations about favoritism, stacking, and authoritarianism that relate to the circumstances of the black athlete also relate to the circumstances of the white athlete.

Scholars are always about three years behind what's actually happening. We talk about the radicals after the radicals have left the campus. We talk about resistance of some white athletes to black captains and black quarterbacks, but that occurred four or five years ago. We often indulge in self-fulfilling prophecies because we do not want to deal with the real issues. McPherson mentioned some concerns about interracial dating. While anyone should have the opportunity to date anyone he wants, interracial dating never has been (and to my knowledge is not today) a major issue to the black athlete. The probabilities are that most people will date those who have similar kinds of backgrounds ethnically, economically, and religiously; if they don't, what's the fuss about? Interracial dating is not the problem; it is just a camouflage for other issues. The real issue is the fact that some people in athletics use interracial dating as a way of keeping the black athlete in his place. When it begins to look as though blacks are moving to positions where they might be able to control certain significant segments of our society, various things are done to deter them. In these days of the civil rights movement and civil rights acts, however, it is difficult to make these deterrents obvious.

Some whites indulge in a kind of reverse Jensenism: blacks cannot think, but they can run! Some coaches tend to promote these stereotypes. Much of the research on race and physical performance, such as running and jumping, indicates that when socioeconomic backgrounds are matched, there are really no significant differences between the races in basic things like running and jumping. Stacking or grouping of blacks at certain positions is one outcome of the stereotypic thinking about black athletes. These various stereotypes have developed in the black athlete's mind, in the white athlete's mind, in the coaches' mind, and even in the fan's mind. The objections to stacking usually come from the average performer, because just as the majority of white athletes are average, so are the majority of black athletes average. Since the average performer is discriminated against, he wants these practices to be exposed, and black athletes have led the challenge.

When you look at the large number of blacks participating in certain sports, you wonder if the disproportionate representation is brought about by physical circumstances, economic circumstances, or social circumstances. We should remember John Loy's admonition that "year after year we debunk some myth that blacks cannot do something." I can recall when blacks were not supposed to play basketball (they couldn't shoot!). So we develop our own myths and then we perpetuate them. Whenever you see that black participation in a given sport is disproportionately high or low, you should investigate to see what's bringing about this disproportion—particularly since men are probably the same physically, from their blood pH to the number of neurons in the cerebrum. When we look at differences in the degree of participation of blacks in various sports we must consider the reasons why they are excluded.

Are there circumstances where race is not a factor in sport? Are there certain things in team interaction and team togetherness that tend to supersede racial considerations? I once played at West Point and was called all kinds of racial epithets; I was manhandled on the lacrosse field by a well-known All American football player, and was generally given a rough time by the Army team. Our team was all white except for me, and the team set out to take apart the Army team in response to the treatment I was being subjected to. There are certain things about team loyalties and awareness that cross racial lines. I happen to still be involved in sport on my weekends as a coach in a Pop Warner Football League for youth from fourteen to twenty-five years old on three different teams. I have seen a lot of fights on teams that have black players and white players, and generally it is not the blacks fighting the whites; rather it is the blue jerseys fightintg the red jerseys. In other words, there are certain things that transcend the racial factor. Recently a western football team was protesting against the discrimination of the Mormons against blacks; they expressed their concerns by having all players wear black armbands. When the team got out of the bus in the opponent's territory, they were verbally assaulted causing both the white and black players to join together to play one of their strongest games and to almost defeat a high-ranking team. Again the togetherness of a team overcame the racial differences existing among them.

Does a black player block less hard on another black player when he is playing a ball game? Does he block harder on a white player? Does a white player charge harder on a black player? I seriously doubt that this happens to any significant degree. A person might do this on the playground when he first starts playing ball, particularly if he comes from a very prejudiced background. However, after you have been hit a few times, regardless of race, you realize that competition is the name of the ball game.

Many things should be seen in a larger context of race and opportunity in society—leadership positions and other positions that have been previously sacrosanct, like cheerleading. I am amazed to go to some schools even now where half of the football team and three-fourths of the basketball team are black and there are a hundred black students in the stands and yet they do not have any black cheerleaders. When I begin to investigate this situation, I find out that it is defended by the allegation that "Blacks never come out." Of course they never come out if they have never been asked, or if they come out once and are not given much attention. Much of our concern about race in sport has to do with the defensiveness of many Americans concerning race. Racism is not just in a textbook; unfortunately, it is in some people's hearts and minds. My major concern is what is done about it.

What does the research about the black athletes' situations suggest about solutions? What impact does the social revolution of today have on the black athlete's status in society? Three or four observations or generalizations emerge from the data. First, *the black athlete has power.* It is no longer a question of whether he will get power; he has it. Whether the black athlete is able to use this power effectively in every situation depends not only on the type of racism he is facing, but also the level of his own sophistication, the forces behind him, and the way he is able to manipulate these forces in order to change the situations that line up against him. Certainly, the example of John Mackey leading the NFL football players union and being able to mobilize that group, both white and black, to put the NFL against the wall is an indication of what can be done if black and white athletes collectively use their power. If black players responded to various forms of discrimination by refusing to play, the sports establishment in this country would not continue to exist. Some years ago when the Boston Celtics went down to North Carolina (which now, interestingly enough, has 300 black freshmen and several black athletes on the University of North Carolina teams), the black players were not able to sleep in the same hotel as the white players. Red Auerbach, to his credit, pulled the team out and said that we are not going to play ball. All of a sudden things began to happen; they found accommodations for the black players, because the promoters could lose thousands of dollars since they couldn't make money on games not played. The black athlete has a tremendous amount of power. This power is related not only to helping the athletes themselves, but also to things like black cheerleaders, black coaches, and black trainers, as well as seeing to it that the black athletes get the kind of education they should.

Second, *the black consumer has tremendous economic power* which can be used to change things. Through secondary boycotts the black consumer could keep thousands of fans away from several professional sports activities. Appropriate use of this power could help change some of the situations that exist.

One weakness in all of these papers, including my own, is the fact that too frequently we refer only to racism in professional sports. Many of the circumstances which we describe here exist not only in college (which I call semi-professional) sports, but also in high schools, junior high schools, and even in club sports. In other words, some of these racist practices exist everywhere. So when we talk about racism in sport, we should recognize that racism is a pervasive societal phenomenon; it just does not begin and end in high-level college and professional sport; it permeates the entire sport establishment. Both whites and blacks who are intimately concerned with sport need to be aware of the tremendous implications of racial interactions in the sport situation for the entire society.

Some people are concerned about the efforts to see that blacks get what's coming to them. Along these lines, some whites have formed an association referred to as SPONGE—Society for the Prevention of Negroes Getting Everything—"What's the matter with those blacks, they want everything." Since the move from one status to another means changes in existing role relationships, change to another new role for blacks does seem to be giving everything, in the eyes of whites who are prejudiced.

Third, *the black athlete is particularly concerned about his education.* In my opinion every athlete, white or black, who comes to a university should get the necessary tutoring and counseling to help him earn his degree. While not everyone can get a college degree, it should be possible for most students to get one. Black athletes are now demanding the type of tutoring and courses that are necessary in order to obtain a college degree. Of 800 or more football players in college who were drafted last year, I think 120 or 130 made the teams. That means there are a lot of men who are going to collect unemployment checks for 36 weeks if they don't get their degree. As McPherson pointed out in his paper, the consequences of not getting an education, through the opportunities provided by athletics, are obviously far more dire for the blacks than for whites. I have discussed this with Jackie Robinson, and

I am a colleague of Dan Dodson, the sociologist who has been working in the field of human relations for many years; Dodson's activities with the Mayor's Committee on Unity in 1945 led to Branch Rickey's final decision to crack segregation in baseball. They worked out a number of techniques to help Jackie through the first year, and they were pretty well assured that he was going to be accepted. Jackie Robinson came into baseball in 1946, which was eight years before the *Brown* decision which outlawed school segregation. It was Jackie's education that attracted Mr. Rickey to him. Jackie's presence attracted more and more black fans to the ball parks, and soon other baseball owners saw that this was good business; thus blacks started a new era of sports.

Many myths about the black athlete are still prevalent today. For example, the Atlanta Hawks basketball team alleged that they needed a white star, Pete Maravich, on their first team because it was believed that the Atlantans would have stopped coming if Maravich hadn't been hired. I believe that people respect excellence in sports regardless of sex, skin color, or height. They will come to games if the level of performance is good. Although some people tend to perpetuate some of these myths, we cannot afford the luxury of believing them. It is very important when we are dealing with data on race and sports to recognize that we always should be aware of the details of a particular situation before saying that the situation is due to discrimination. But it is certainly true that race is a major factor in most things in our society; the fact is that sport and race are very closely linked because of the depth to which racism has permeated our society. I think that all of us, black and white, should try and deal with the core issues of sport and racism rather than the peripheral issues, such as dating and dress. In other words, we must always be alert to the causes and the solutions to racism in sports.

Sport and New Left Criticism

Introduction

The broadest coverage of a single topic is found in the essays contained in this final section dealing with "Sport and New Left Criticism." Throughout the essays in the preceding sections, continual reference was made to traditional American values. Many of the authors were critical of some of the societal value orientations permeating athletics and other institutionalized aspects of American society. Although varying levels of discontent were expressed with the way societal values are mirrored (and often magnified) in athletics, few have suggested alternative value systems. The essays in the present section advance the case against many of the traditional American values—a case popularized by members of a subculture whose continuing social movement has become known as the counterculture. As Yinker (1970) points out, members of the counterculture have consciously and deliberately rejected the value system of the larger society within which they exist, attempting to substitute a series of inverse or counter values. During the 1960's the tentacles of this social movement spread to sport in what became known as the Athletic Revolution. In the seventies the debate over alternative value systems continues to capture the attention of contemporary investigators as the counterculture influence has spread to previously neglected areas (e.g., enhanced intramural programs, and alternative forms of sport involvement for women).

To better comprehend the contrasting value orientations of the American middle-class and those of the counterculture, the instrumental-expressive paradigm of structural-functional analysis is employed here. There is general agreement among sociologists that the dominant middle-class value structure in American society is instrumental in nature. Three components are regarded as comprising the major foci of the instrumental pattern; the first, as characterized by Parsons and White (1964), is "instrumental activism," wherein all Americans, regardless of background, are predominantly committed to the construction of a "good society" through continual, goal-oriented, ascetic effort. As pointed out by Spates and Levin (1972:329), "This commitment, a product of the long-term secularization of the Protestant Ethic, has as its primary focus a ceaseless and generalized obligation to 'worth-while' achievement." The second element of instrumental value preferences has been referred to by Williams (1960) as the "cult of secular rationality." Here one's actions in each situation must be constantly and completely guided in a rational manner so that the probability of success will be enhanced. This emphasis prompts those guided by the instrumental value orientation to control their emotions and "be realistic" so that irrationality does not deter their achieving the symbols of instrumental success: wealth, status, and power. Finally, through the last component of instrumental values—economic behavior—the elements of achievement and rationality are both mediated. Williams, (1960:418), for instance, has noted that a "comparatively striking feature of American culture is its tendency to identify standards of personal excellence with competitive occupational achievement." This helps to explain why Americans, while recognizing success in the professions as noteworthy, attribute the greatest prestige to the businessman and, in turn, evaluate the social positions of others in occupational-economic terms.

The other polarity of the intellectual model used herein is the orientation characterizing the counterculture. To members of the counterculture the instrumental system into which they were socialized has become, in their words, corrupt, dehumanizing, inauthentic, and alienating. Summarizing from the writings of others (Hedgepeth and Stock 1970; Yablonsky 1968) Spates and Levin (1972:330) sum up the counterculture position thus:

> The middle-class value system, by its overbearing emphasis on all forms of achievement (which produces persons enslaved to a "rat race"), rational behavior (which qualifies anything not specifically directed toward the attainment of sanctioned goals as being "irrational"), and economic endeavor (which produces a system of continually expanding "exploitation") has now developed to the point where it continually denies or represses other, more vital, human values and needs: the most important of these being the need of each person to develop his own humanness through his own personalized life-style; the need to be personally and meaningfully concerned for the welfare of others; the need to be affective, loving and trustful with other people; and the need for self-realization and spiritual development through religious and/or philosophical inquiry.

The varying themes running through the counterculture position have been subsumed under what has been termed an expressive pattern of behavior. In general, this pattern, unlike the instrumental pattern, is present-oriented, satisfying immediate needs rather than delaying gratification to a goal outside the immediate situation. This view, i.e., the valuing of an activity as an end in itself, is materialized by means of the components of the expressive value orientation. These components include self-expression (the do-your-own-thing ethic), concern for others (the love ethic), and a religious-philosophical belief system often associated with mysticism and the occult.

The essays contained in this section attempt to determine the place of athletics along the continuum of instrumental-expressive values. In the first essay, Schafer sees athletics functioning within the American schooling process to enculturate youth into traditional (instrumental) American middle-class values. His underlying assumption at the outset is that athletics contributes "to the stability, maintenance, and perpetuation of the Established Society." With the employment of Charles Reich's *The Greening of America* as a model, Schafer contrasts the counterculture socialization with that of athletics. Schafer's analysis of the contrasting socialization patterns suggests several hypotheses that will surely engage the attention of researchers as well as those who are either directly responsible for, or concerned about, the ways in which our athletic policies and practices ultimately influence American youth. Following is an empirical study by Rehberg and Cohen which provides some empirical support for the Schafer hypothesis that athletics fosters a conservative socializing influence upon those who participate. To test this hypothesis, only the political dimension (the conservative-radical continuum) is examined. The results, for this one indicator of conservatism, tended to support the hypothesis. Their conclusion, however, is tempered by the fact that many of the differences found were smaller than might be expected and were conditional in that they were dependent upon the intelligence level of the respondents.

The third essay in this section was developed by Spady to serve both as a formal critique of the two preceding essays and as a more general commentary on problems inherent in social scientific investigations attempting to assess the value domain of athletics. Some alternative ways in which mainstream social values are rejected are clarified in this essay. The second part of his essay contains an explanation of several methodological problems that need to be overcome before data, such as that obtained by Rehberg and Cohen, can be accepted with assurance.

The next essay is a theoretical paper which advances a very novel hypothesis that is certain to evoke much controversy. Petrie argues that the athlete, who was once considered to be a high-status figure among males in the high school setting (Coleman 1961), is now considered to be deviant in value orientation from the majority of high school youth, who in recent years have been moving more and more toward the expressive value orientation of the Radical Left. Deviance in the context of this hypothesis is behavior or attitudes that are a violation of peer group standards; that is, behavior "inconsistent with the value structure of the majority, or of the dominant student group, and which is provided with a negative loading of those individuals." With a direct test unavailable at the time when his hypothesis was formulated, Petrie was forced to rely upon indirect evidence derived from comparative studies of athletes and non-athletes in each of the following areas: attitudes toward work and the competition-achievement syndrome; attitudes toward individual rights; the athletic personality; and political ideologies in the educational setting.

The Petrie essay can be evaluated both on empirical grounds and on its logical merits. Many of the conceptual problems which arise are pointed out by Ingham in the final essay in this section. Ingham reacts to the nature of the concepts used by Petrie, and also to problems inherent in the arguments offered by many of the New Left critics of sport (e.g., Hoch 1972). Petrie's failure to specify the type of Left/Right polar subcultures as well as the type of conservatism that athletes are alleged to represent are regarded by Ingham as unfortunate omissions in analysis. Without such specifications, the notion of the New Left, for instance, may easily be confused with the concept of opposition where individuals use the rhetoric of the Left on certain issues but in general are not accepting of the ideology of the Left. Additionally, the conceptual distinction between activity and role is unclear in Petrie's analysis, as well as in other analyses by many of the critics of contemporary sport (Hoch 1972). In these analyses opposition to the role of athlete is often expressed, but frequently a social theory is lacking which delineates how the social role is to be reconstructed. Ingham argues that without clearly separating activity from role, the end result is often interpreted as a desire to abolish the activity itself, when all that was really intended was to abolish alienation in the social role.

Petrie concludes his essay with a plea for the type of research that would elicit a decisive test of his hypothesis. The kind of evidence needed, of course, is that which not only considers differences between athletes and other groups, but also examines the desirability of these differences within the athlete's peer group. Although it is not general practice to introduce current evidence as a part of an introduction, findings of recent studies were judged to best illustrate the importance of Petrie's analysis as well as the directions in which researchers might focus their attention in the future. Since the advancement of the Petrie hypothesis, at least two pertinent studies have emerged. The first was a survey of 87 high schools throughout the United States; in this study Johnson and Bachman (1973) found that both teachers and students agreed that in actual practice the school objective "to develop athletes" ranked first of fourteen school objectives. When asked to rate the *ideal* school objectives, the "develop athletes" objective[1] declined to the lowest ranking among teachers and students, while the objectives "to develop political and social concern" and "to motivate students to learn" ascended to the highest ranking for both groups. Before these findings are taken as somewhat supportive of the Petrie hypothesis, it is necessary to further determine the current prestige of the athlete among his adolescent peers. While it is evident that male adolescents desire a rearrangement in priority of educational objectives, the question that remains unanswered is whether the athlete has really declined in prestige in the status system of adolescent American males. Judging from the results of another study (Eitzen 1973) the answer to this question is currently no, but certain indicators suggest that the decline in the athlete's prestige may occur in the future. Ratings from a sample within each of nine high schools showed that male adolescents in 1973 were just as enthusiastic about sports as Coleman (1961) had found them to be in the late 1950's. The "athlete but not a scholar" type was rated most popular (46 percent), while the "scholar but not an athlete," the "ladies man but neither a scholar nor athlete," and "member of the counterculture" received considerably lower popularity ratings— i.e., 16.4, 19.8, and 17.5 percent, respectively. At first glance these data negate the predictions derived from the Petrie analysis. However, additional data provided by Eitzen suggest that the Petrie essay may forecast what could arise in the future. The social variables modifying the above student ratings of the athletes' prestige and their implications for future trends are summed up in the following way:

> . . . The strongest support for sport is found among some of the under-educated, in small schools, in schools with a strict authority structure, and among students at the center of the school's activities. . . . Thus, several trends suggest that the enthusiasm for sports may wane in the future. School unification makes schools larger, a larger proportion of youngsters attend suburban schools each year, each generation is

1. It should be noted that the discrepancy between perceived actual and ideal ratings of the schoolboys was very small for the objective "to develop athletes."

better educated, and schools are generally more permissive than in the past. If these conditions lead to somewhat less enthusiasm for sports, as our data indicate, then sport participation as the dominant criterion for social status will diminish in the future (Eitzen 1973: 8–9).

REFERENCES

Coleman, J. S.
1961   "Athletics in High School." *Annals of the American Academy of Political and Social Science* 338:33–43.
Eitzen, D. S.
1973   "Athletics in the Status System of Male Adolescents: A Replication of Coleman's *The Adolescent Society*." Paper presented at Midwest Sociological Society, Milwaukee.
Hedgepeth, W., and Stock, D.
1970   *The Alternative: Communal Life in America*. New York: Macmillan.
Hoch, P.
1972   *Rip Off the Big Game: The Exploitation of Sports by the Power Elite*. New York: Doubleday.
Johnson, L. D., and Bachman, J. G.
1973   In Adams, J., ed. *Understanding Adolescence*. 2nd ed. Boston: Allyn and Bacon.
Parsons, T., and White, W.
1964   "The Link between Character and Society." In Parsons, T., ed. *Social Structure and Personality*. New York: Free Press.
Spates, J. L., and Levin, J.
1972   "Beats, Hippies, the Hip Generation, and the American Middle Class: An Analysis of Values." *International Social Science Journal* 24:326–353.
Williams, R. M.
1960   *American Society: A Sociological Interpretation*. New York: Alfred A. Knopf.
Yablonsky, L.
1968   *The Hippie Trip*. New York: Pegasus.
Yinker, J. M.
1970   "Contraculture and Subculture." In: David O. Arnold, ed. *The Sociology of Subculture*. Berkeley, Calif.: Glendessary Press.

Sport and Youth Counterculture:
Contrasting Socialization Themes

WALTER E. SCHAFER

Investigators are beginning to focus on several problems related to sport and socialization. First, the *structure* of athletics as a socialization setting. What differences are there in structural characteristics between different sports? Between the same sport in different host settings? How do scholastic and collegiate athletics differ structurally from other socialization settings like the classroom, the peer group, the family, or other extracurricular activities? A second problem involves the intended and actual *content* of socialization within athletics. What is transmitted from one generation to the next through athletics? What cultural themes (e.g., attitudes, values, beliefs, norms) are emphasized? What skills and personality qualities are stressed and in fact developed? What is intended but not transmitted? Also important are the *processes* of socialization within athletics. How is the socialization content transmited? What is the role, for instance, of the coach's leadership style and personality? What part is played by the rules and behavior patterns of the game itself? By the structure of rules and the informal expectations among athletes? By the treatment athletes get in the host school and community? Finally, there is the problem of the individual and social *consequences* of socialization through athletics. What difference does it make to a person to have been an athlete? What difference does it make for the host school, the community, and the larger society?

In this paper I will focus on the second problem, the content of socialization. Specifically, my purpose is to sharpen our understanding of the socialization content of scholastic and collegiate athletics by contrasting different stances taken by athletics and the youth counter-culture toward a number of attitudes and actions. This discussion will be followed by remarks about implications for the individual athlete,

Walter E. Schafer is visiting associate professor of sociology at the University of California at Davis and co-director of a private alternative school for adolescents. This paper was written while the author was partially supported by a grant from the National Institute of Mental Health (MH 1925–01) to the State University of New York at Binghamton, Richard A. Rehberg, Project Director.

the athletic program, and the larger system. It has been said that intelligent speculation, careful research, and the development of formal theory all have a place in social science. Perhaps this exercise in speculation will prove useful for both theory development and practice related to sport.

In another recent paper I argued that sport is an important agency of enculturation within the American schooling process (Schafer 1971). In a number of important ways, athletics contribute to fitting the athlete into established mainstream cultural and behavioral patterns of the society and in this way contribute to the stability, maintenance, and perpetuation of the established society. I speculated (correctly I believe) that athletics contribute to an instrumental or goal orientation, to achievement as a virtue second only to godliness, to a commitment to hard work, to learning to adjust oneself to others within a formal organization, to accepting standards of personal conduct defined as desirable by the mainstream, dominant part of the adult population and passed on by the coach, to the development of an apolitical or politically conservative stance toward social problems, to an elitist stance toward sport (participate only if you are an expert), and to conditional self-worth. I contended that as a result of these probable effects, scholastic and collegiate athletics have the effect of conserving the established society by assimilating athletes into its ways and by idealizing for spectators some of its prevailing value patterns. I also questioned the extent to which, in contrast, school sports contribute to the maturity and independence of the athlete himself.

Here I want to begin where I left off in that paper, and perhaps extend our understanding—or at least raise new questions—about the socialization influences of scholastic and collegiate athletics by contrasting some of the stances taken by youth counterculture, as described by Charles Reich in *The Greening of America*, and by the athletic system toward self, social relations, and the society. I contend that the counterculture socializes its members toward rejection of many of the tenets of the established society, while athletics help reinforce many established cultural and behavioral patterns, thereby contributing to the social assimilation of athletes into the mainstream adult society. My approach will be speculative rather than definitive, in the dual hope of stimulating hypotheses for further study and stimulating those involved in athletics to ask new questions about the effects of what they are doing.

I will not go into the question of how accurate Reich is in his description of the counterculture, nor into the issue of the pervasiveness of what he describes. Rather, I will assume that there probably is a constellation of actions, thoughts, and feelings which in many ways stand in opposition to established patterns of action, thought, and feeling, that an increasing minority of youth participate in it, and that Reich probably is relatively accurate in his depiction of that constellation—at least for some youth some of the time. I recognize that there are important distinctions within the counterculture, but time precludes dealing with them here.

SPORT AND YOUTH COUNTERCULTURE AS SOCIALIZATION SETTINGS: CONTRASTING THEMES

Reich contends in his book that Consciousness III, a profoundly far-reaching new stance toward self and society, had its roots long ago in the thinking of such persons as Thoreau, but that only in the late 1960's did it appear on a wide scale—not just among the Holden Caulfields and the isolated beatniks of the fifties, but among millions of young people "who had endured no special emotional conditions, but were simply bright, sensitive children of the affluent middle class" (Reich 1970:222). He argues that a cultural revolution of the first magnitude and significance is well underway and cannot possibly be reversed, since the present corporate state, the embodiment of Consciousness II, carries its own seeds of transformation. This revolution is occurring, not directly through political action, but indirectly through profound changes, first of all in the consciousness of great numbers of people. From these shifts in consciousness—ways of thinking, personal goals, value priorities, ways of perceiving and ordering the world outside the person—ultimately will emerge profound changes in the objective social, political, and economic structures of the society. Contrary to many writers, Reich contends that structural change of any lasting and pervasive kind can only follow large-scale changes in consciousness (Reich 1970: ch. 9).

It must be noted that *The Greening of America* is intended not just as an objective description of such changes but as an apology, a defense of them, a stimulus for even more widespread and rapid movement toward Consciousness III. Reich often idealizes and overstates in his enthusiasm for what is happening among youth. If my own remarks about the counterculture sometimes seem overdone, it is as much a result of Reich's treatment as of my own evaluation of the counterculture, though I share a good deal of his enthusiasm. I must hasten to add, however, that Reich romanticizes in a fashion which ignores many unfortunate features of countercultural lifestyle: the transience and superficiality of many relationships, rampant anti-intellectualism, ravaging of mind and body with drugs, sponging off others, failure to live up to one's commitments, failure to stick to a thing long enough to do it well and to get many lasting satisfactions from it. In short, there are aspects of the counterculture which I find objectionable personally. But, as I shall point out later, there is much worth paying attention to in what many countercultural youth are attempting.

Consciousness III opposes not just one political party or another, but the very ideological and structural foundations of contemporary society. It is not all negative, however; rather, it is optimistic and positive, according to Reich, leading the individual toward patterns of thought, feeling, and action which are expressive of life, individuality, and true community—conditions not often expressed in the prevailing technocracy (a term used by another observer, Theodore Roszak [1969]). I contend that scholastic and collegiate athletics are likely to socialize the athlete more toward the technocracy, the established society, and the corporate state than toward the world of tomorrow which Reich contends is emerging from Consciousness III. A brief look at the themes of Consciousness III and of corresponding themes in the world of sport will illustrate what I mean.

TABLE 1. Contrasting Socialization Themes in Youth Counterculture and Sport

Theme	Counterculture	Sport
Self as means and end	self as end	self as means
Self-acceptance	unconditional	conditional
Source of identity	existence	roles
Wholeness of self	unified	fragmented
External control	rejection	acceptance
Meaning of excellence	individuality	comparative merit
Goal attainment	process, not outcome	outcome, not process
Hierarchical relationships	rejection	acceptance
Role-specific relationships	rejection	acceptance
Competition	rejection	acceptance
Participation in formal organizations	rejection	acceptance
Schooling	opposition or indifference	encouragement
Upward mobility	indifference	encouragement
Evaluation of established society	rejection	acceptance

SELF AS MEANS AND END

In the counterculture, the beginning and ending point is the self. Fundamental tenets are, "Thou shalt not do violence to thyself" and "Be true to oneself" (Reich 1970:225). It does not mean a full-time ego trip or sheer selfishness, but simply that self is the ultimate end, the ultimate value. If in fact every individual has absolute worth, then it is immoral within the counterculture for individuals to use others or to let themselves be used for ends or goals which contradict what that person wants or to what is good for him in the long run. In fact, there is revulsion against conceptualizing or experiencing self as an instrumentality, a means to another end, objective, or purpose.

In contrast, scholastic and collegiate sports place greatest emphasis on the team, the common goal, the victory. Especially in team sports like basketball, football, and hockey, the person must learn to view himself as secondary to the goal of winning, to the best interest of the team. His talents, energies, and time are means to the end of victory. What may develop in the way of self-worth, or a feeling of wholeness, dignity, or enjoyment are less important than how the person contributes to winning. Of course, the coach seeks to join individual interest with the common good, just as do supervisors in a factory. But whenever there is potential conflict between the two, it is in the nature of intense competition that the individual must submerge the personal parts of himself to his role as a team member. This view of self is illustrated by the locker room slogans reported by coaches and athletes in a recent study in Ohio by Eldon Snyder: "'Ask not what your team can do for you, but what you can do for the team. Self-sacrifice. There is no I in team" (Snyder 1971). The self, then, is a means in the world of athletics, an end in the counterculture described by Reich.

SELF-ACCEPTANCE

In the counterculture, unconditional self-worth is stressed, while in the world of competitive sport, self-worth is contingent on performance. Because the counterculture defines the individual as unique and entirely worthwhile by virtue of his simply being or existing, individuals come to treat one another with unconditional personal regard, to use Carl Rogers's words, and hence the individual comes to view himself in the same way—often after overcoming the conditional self-worth he has felt for years at home and in school. He learns that he need not perform, measure up, or please others to accept himself as worthwhile and good. His self-worth is not contingent or conditional on anything, but is (or at least can be) inherent and constant (Reich 1970:226).

Within sport, on the other hand, self-acceptance necessarily is contingent on performance, winning and improvement—understandably so, since self-satisfaction would lessen his improvement and commitment to victory. Conditional acceptance from the coach is an important contributing influence to conditional self-acceptance. In this spirit the slogans say, "Are you better than yesterday? If you don't intend to improve tonight, don't come! Never be willing to be second best. When you're through improving, you're through! Be good or be gone" (Snyder 1971). As a result of these influences, the athlete learns to rely on external roles and standards for his sense of worth. If this is true, then athletics contribute to the situation described by Reich where the typical adult male experiences a "terrible fear of failure in the competitive struggle." (Reich 1970:84). Whereas the counterculture exerts an influence toward unconditional self-acceptance, athletics generate conditional self-worth, a quality prevalent and perhaps even essential in the technocracy of Consciousness II.

SOURCE OF IDENTITY

Closely related is a key difference in the source of identity. For the member of the counterculture, identity comes from his very existence, from the unique combination of his human qualities (Reich 1970:226). He need not depend on social position, evaluation of his performance, or anything outside himself for answers to the question, Who am I? Rather, it comes from within, based on how he experiences himself. The athlete, on the other hand, is likely to learn to base his sense of identity on his athletic role, especially if he is successful and if that success is won in a host school and community which gives high prestige and honor to the star athlete. This is likely in turn to develop a more general and lasting tendency to establish one's identity from external position. This may well contribute to the situation in adult America portrayed by Reich, whereby the individual "relies on institutions to certify the meaning and value of his life, by rewarding accomplishment and conferring titles, office, respect, and honor." (Reich 1970:68). Reich also points out that it is often difficult for an athlete whose personal and public identity has come to depend on his success as an athlete to shed the role and to develop independent selfhood: "The high school athlete-leader, cool, competent, straight, finds it a tremendous effort to free himself from this role; he must learn to approach people instead of waiting to be sought after, make himself emotionally vulnerable, wear absurd clothes, spend time with people who are definitely not part of the accepted crowd. Fighting off a role makes for conflict with parents, school authorities, coaches; it is a prime source of misunderstanding, but is essential to get rid of the imposed response." (Reich 1970:256).

WHOLENESS OF SELF

Another emphasis in the counterculture is on wholeness and unity of the self. Life is not to be fragmented, with different selves or facets of the personality emerging in different situations. Reich contends that unity is illustrated by the kind of clothes worn by many of the young. "There is not one set of clothes for the office, another for social life, a third for play. The same clothes can be used for every imaginable activity, and so they say: it is the same person doing each of these things, not a set of different masks or dolls, but one manysided, *whole* individual." (Reich 1970:235).

In athletics, one necessarily becomes a very different person from what he is at home, in the classroom, on a date, or at work. With his date in a parked car after the football game, he must try to become tender, gentle, and empathic, following an evening of trying to be aggressive, fierce, and tough. While it is the same person, the parts of himself do not necessarily integrate or mesh well and may even conflict or grate upon each other. Since adult life usually is separated into unrelated segments (home, work, golf course, and church), learning to move easily into and out of different roles, identities, and behavior patterns may be good preparation for the dominant lifestyle of today's technocracy.

EXTERNAL CONTROL

In the counterculture, outside discipline or control is anathema, while in scholastic and collegiate athletics it is greatly emphasized. According to Reich, "The foundation of Consciousness III is liberation. It comes into being the moment the individual frees himself from automatic acceptance of the imperatives of society and the false consciousness which society imposes. . . . The meaning of liberation is that the individual is free to build his own philosophy and values, his own lifestyle, and his own culture from a new beginning." (Reich 1970:225). The idea of abiding by the edicts of another person or an authority runs directly counter to the stress on liberation and self-direction. This is illustrated in drug use—that drugs happen to be illegal is bothersome and inconvenient, but certainly not a deterrent to many countercultural youth.

The athlete, especially in high school, must conform to the standards of behavior set forth by the coach. He must accept discipline; he cannot question or challenge it. This is true within the sport itself, of course, for clear reasons—an athletic team is a complex organization of the first order, requiring coordination and leadership if victory is to be the goal. Thus the slogans say, "The boy who isn't criticized should worry. It's best to remain silent and to be thought a fool than to open one's mouth and remove all doubt" (Snyder 1971). But it is also true of behavior outside training for and participating in the contest itself, partly as a result of a mission of most coaches to "civilize" and build good character in their athletes. In this respect, the slogans of coaches and athletes proclaim, "Live by the code or get out. Stay out for sports and stay out of courts. The way you live is the way you play. Profane language never made a man out of a boy. Good behavior reflects team behavior" (Snyder 1971). A participant in the counterculture would cringe upon being confronted every day by such pronouncements, but the athlete becomes accustomed to them, accepts them, and perhaps is influenced by them. Such external control through sport may help account for the lower rates of dropout and delinquency which have been reported for athletes (Schafer and Armer 1968; Schafer 1969). On the other hand, of course, it simply may be that conforming types go out and stay out for sports.

MEANING OF EXCELLENCE

The counterculture rejects the idea that excellence should be judged by some standard outside the person or by comparison with the performances of others, while in competitive athletics excellence can only be judged in terms of comparative merit. According to Reich, youth in the counterculture refuse to evaluate people by general standards, to classify them as superior, mediocre, better, or worse. Where intrinsic worth is stressed, there are no external governing standards. "A person who thinks very poorly is still excellent in his own way . . . because there are no governing standards, no one is rejected. Everyone is entitled to pride in himself, and no one should act in a way that is servile, or feel inferior, or allow himself to be treated as if he were inferior." (Reich 1970:227).

In the world of athletics, the conception just described is unthinkable, since it runs counter both to the idea of improving performance for the sake of victory and to the idea of winning and losing. By the very nature of the game, the winner is more excellent than the loser. In track and field, the four-minute miler is, very simply, better than a 4:10 miler. Excellence, then, is judged either by performance in relation to an opponent or in relation to an external standard such as height, weight, time, distance, or score. As the slogan says, "Man shows what he is by what he *does*" (Snyder 1971). While in the counterculture excellence is synonomous with existence, it is judged only by comparative merit in athletics. It is only reasonable to expect these different conceptions to have a carry-over effect in time and place (Snyder 1970).

GOAL ATTAINMENT

The pursuit and attainment of goals are unimportant in the counterculture but central to athletics. In the counterculture, process matters more than product or outcome. Strong motivation arises out of enjoyment of acting, rather than from anticipation or realization of the thrill of victory, as in sport (Reich 1970:232). Quite different stances toward the future result: the counterculture is more oriented toward now, athletics toward later. Reich's description of the typical Consciousness II male fits many athletes well. "His motivations are constantly directed toward the future, because it is not inner satisfaction that moves him but something extrinsic to himself." (Reich 1970:73). Moreover, "life consists of a position achieved and not in living-in-process." (Reich 1970:131). This stance is not inherent in sport activity itself, but is a central element in highly competitive, victory-above-all athletics as practiced in nearly all schools and colleges. Hence the slogans read, "Winning isn't everything, it's the only thing. Aim for the stars. We aim to achieve high goals. The determination to succeed is better than any single thing. Be a champ. They ask not how you played the game but whether you won or lost" (Snyder 1971). Athletics, then, are likely to reinforce and help generate high achievement motivation. As a result, the athlete will be much better prepared in terms of motivation and commitment to enter and succeed in the established technocracy.

HIERARCHICAL RELATIONSHIPS

The counterculture stresses lateral relationships, while athletics stress both lateral and vertical relationships. In the counterculture, there is a great reluctance to relate to someone else as higher or lower in power, prestige, or position. Since each man is regarded as worthwhile and self-directed, vertical relationships are avoided, both within the counterculture and in roles in the larger system that might be necessary. As Reich states, "III also rejects relationships of authority and subservience. It will neither give commands nor follow them; coercive relationships between people are wholly unacceptable." (Reich 1970:228). This is a point of substantial tension with parents and teachers, of course, as well as a possible source of disorganization tension and turmoil in communes where organization and direction are avoided but perhaps needed.

In the world of sport, the athlete learns early to cooperate with teammates in lateral relationships, partly through such messages as "Teamwork means success. Work together, win together. Good players help others to be good players. United we stand, divided we fall. Teamwork. Cooperation—remember the banana, every time it leaves the bunch it gets skinned" (Snyder 1971). But he also learns early in his career to accept or at least accommodate vertical relations with the coach. Perhaps that is one intended meaning of the slogan in a basketball locker room: "Position for athlete and Christian: knees bent, eyes up" (Snyder 1971). The athletic situation, then, is a simulation of life in formally organized work settings and hence probably serves as a useful training ground for later work roles in the established society.

ROLE-SPECIFIC RELATIONSHIPS

While the counterculture generates a strong aversion to role-specific relationships involving only a limited part of the personalities of those involved, athletics by their very nature emphasize such role-specific relationships. Reich puts it this way: "III also rejects any relationships based wholly on role, relationships limited along structural, impersonal and functional lines. *There is no situation in which one is entitled to act impersonally*, in a stereotyped fashion, with another human being; the relationship of businessman to clerk, passenger to conductor, student to janitor must not be impersonal." (Reich 1970:228). Rather, there is stress upon only participating in relationships that are relatively close and personal, involving as much as possible of the person's "inside self." Masks and impersonal games are rejected out of hand.

In contrast, athletics by their nature are limited to the situation at hand and to the part of the person relevant to that situation. To be sure, basketball players may well develop deep on-court empathic ties during a season, but that still entails only a small part of the other's total life space and personality. The same is true of the coach-player relationship. Each is most likely to know little of the inner thought and feelings or of the happenings in other parts of another's life; players may get to know one another well through friendships and common travel, but then again they may not, especially where racial differences exist. In any case, the relationships required in the activity itself are role-specific—which may be good practice for role-specific actions and relationships in which most of the young eventually will participate in the established society.

COMPETITION

Except when carried out in fun, competition usually is abhorred by those in the counterculture, while it is inherent in sport (Reich 1970: 226). Those in the counterculture believe that intense competition generates conditional self-worth, role-specific relationships, goal orientation, excellence based on competitive merit, self as a means, and subjection of self to external control—all of which are to be avoided. Certainly there is an aversion to the kind of intense winning-is-everything sport practiced in most schools and colleges, where competition is the name of the game. There it is highly valued, stressed as healthy for mind and spirit, as well as body. Development of competitiveness is justified not just on the ground that it will generate successful athletic performance, but also on the ground that it will prepare the person for success in the competitive world of work in adulthood. Competitiveness as a virtue is reflected in such locker room slogans as these: "A quitter never wins, a winner never quits. When the going gets tough, the tough get going. Hustle. Win. The difference between winning and losing is hustle. It's not the size of the dog in the fight, but the size of the fight in the dog. The greatest thing in life is to succeed." (Snyder 1971). To the extent that such messages have an effect, they prepare the athletes well for the established society in which "Consciousness II sees life in terms of a fiercely competitive struggle for success." (Reich 1970:75).

PARTICIPATION IN FORMAL ORGANIZATIONS

Members of the counterculture avoid participation in formal organizations which are bureaucratically structured to achieve goals. The reasons for dislike of such participation are similar to those creating an aversion to competition. Formal organizations such as a factory, business, government agency, or church generally involve a goal-orientation, segmental relationships, hierarchy, an authority, universal criteria of success, and so on—factors the counterculture rejects. As noted earlier, the athletic system simulates formal organization, both in structure and in personal qualities which make for success. In order to succeed, one must learn to accept authority, follow institutionalized procedures and rules, and adapt to the ways of complementary role partners. Athletes, especially those in team sport, are quite likely to develop a positive attitude toward participation in formal organizations, while they are participating and in later life. In fact, this similarity may help account for the higher rates of extracurricular participation, community leadership, and occupational success reported for athletes.

SCHOOLING

Whereas the counterculture takes an indifferent or opposing stand toward formal education, scholastic and collegiate athletics strongly support it. In the counterculture, schooling usually is seen as embodying much of the worst of Consciousness II and the corporate state which has grown out of it. Since the present and the process of doing are more important than the future or the product, many counterculture persons drop out as soon as they can. Grades, gold stars, praise, promotions, degrees—none necessarily lead to the kind of lifestyle valued within the counterculture and, in fact, may be counterproductive, to use a slightly punned Corporate State term (Reich 1970: 130).

But in athletics, schooling is stressed on several grounds: continued enrollment and conformity to school rules are necessary for continued athletic eligibility and for a possible collegiate scholarship; achievement is inherently good anytime, anywhere, including in the classroom; education is a virtue simply because it is defined that way by the dominant adult majority. Recent findings to the effect that athletes tend to attain higher levels of educational achievement suggest that this emphasis on schooling may have some effect (Schafer and Armer, 1968; Rehberg and Schafer 1968; Schafer and Rehberg 1971; Bend 1968). Since scholastic athletics are a part of the school itself, such an emphasis is entirely understandable. Athletics and the counterculture, then, are likely to have quite different effects on promoting the educational progress necessary for successful occupational placement and advancement in the established society.

UPWARD MOBILITY

It should not be surprising that the counterculture and athletics stress quite different attitudes toward mobility, with the former taking an indifferent or oppositional stance, and the latter a supportive one. Within the counterculture, it is usually believed that high position carries with it sacrifices that are too great in human terms: "The goals of status, a position in the hierarchy, security, money, possessions, power, respect, and honor are not merely wrong, they are *unreal*. A person whose life is one long ego trip or power trip has not necessarily chosen one kind of satisfaction in preference to others; he has chosen goals that have no relationship to personal growth, satisfaction or happiness." (Reich 1970:239). In reaction, the counterculturist is more likely to remain flexible, not plan too far ahead, or deliberately not strive for high position.

Sport promotes quite a different attitude toward mobility. Many of the slogans reported by Snyder could just as well be intended for aspiring executives as for athletes. Yet whether athletic participation in fact generates greater mobility—and if so, how—is still open to question, as pointed out by Spady (1970) and also by Ogilvie and Tutko (1971), who recently concluded from their years of research that "athletic competition has no more beneficial effects than intense endeavors in any other field. Horatio Alger success—in sport or elsewhere —comes only to those who already are mentally fit, resilient and strong." Despite their doubts, though, it seems likely that the higher levels of occupational attainment and monetary success reported for athletes may be partly a result of the development, through many years in sport, of personal qualities selected for in the occupational world, if not from occupational sponsorship or the halo effect flowing from athletic prominence (Schafter 1975).

EVALUATION OF ESTABLISHED SOCIETY

Many of the values and premises of the counterculture already described lead its adherents to a radical criticism of society, while athletics generates acceptance. Reich points out that many young people who participate in or are influenced by the counterculture are not simply critical of one or another governmental official, administration, political party, or policy; rather, they reject some of the most fundamental premises, values, and structural characteristics of the technocracy, calling instead for a whole new way of life and new personal and public priorities. (Reich 1970:229). While the emerging alternative cannot clearly be seen yet, the critique is clear, as reflected in the words of another recent observer, Theodore Roszak (1969:4):

> . . . it is the American young, with their underdeveloped radical background, who seem to have grasped most clearly the fact that, while such immediate emergencies as the Vietnam war, racial injustice, and hard-core poverty demand a deal of old-style politicking, the paramount struggle of our day is against a far more formidable, far less obvious, opponent, to which I will give "the technocracy"—a social form more highly developed in America than in any other society. The American young have been somewhat quicker to sense that in the struggle against *this* enemy, the conventional tactics of political resistance have only a marginal place, largely limited to meeting immediate life-and-death crises. Beyond such front-line issues, however, there lies the greater task of altering the total cultural context within which our daily politics takes place.

Athletics, on the other hand, generate a fundamental acceptance of the established society, partly through promotion of the attitudinal and behavioral patterns already described. Although no studies have been reported on the political attitudes and behavior of coaches, there is some evidence that college physical education faculties are highly conservative and accepting of present government policies. And anyone who has been around at all certainly knows they are not often out on the vanguard of criticism of the technocracy or of movements aimed toward social or cultural change. The same holds for high school and college coaches whom they help professionalize and for whom conformity and patriotism are next to godliness and loyalty to the team. As Ogilvie and Tutko (1971:63) remarked, "Most coaches believe that a truly good athlete is also, by definition, a red-blooded, clean-living, truth-telling, prepared patriot. A top-notch competitor who disagrees with national policy is a heavy thing for a coach who undoubtedly believes that the wars of England were indeed won on the playing fields of Eton." One can only wonder about the effects of such influences from coaches on the relative passivity, docility, and silence among most Americans toward the violence in Vietnam.

There are several reasons why athletes are likely to be drawn in the direction of fundamental acceptance of the status quo. For one thing, athletes have little time to think about or get actively involved in social criticism. For another, they often believe they have a good deal to gain personally from the way things are. Too, athletic competition is likely to promote more of an individualistic than a systemic interpretation of such social problems as racial conflict, poverty, and crime, a stance whose effect is to minimize discontent with the established order itself. Finally, athletes are more likely to have grown accustomed to accepting authority and not questioning its existence or effects. In short, then, the counterculture and athletics draw their adherents in quite different directions in relation to the society—one toward criticism and alternative lifestyles, the other toward acceptance and assimilation.

IMPLICATIONS

I am contending then, that, in contrast to the youth counterculture, athletics are an important mechanism for generating loyalty to, support for, and assimilation into what Roszak calls the technocracy, Reich calls the corporate state, and I refer to as the established society. In this sense, the counterculture stands in fundamental opposition to the status quo, while scholastic and collegiate athletics play a conservative role in the society. Whether this is good or bad depends, of course, on how one evaluates the present state of affairs. My own frame of reference tells me that the technocracy, while affording much that is good, also has produced much that is dehumanizing within many of us, between us, in our sense of progress, in the way we relate to other nations, in the way we treat our criminals, in the use of our free time. Within this same frame of reference, I wonder more and more about the redeeming value of highly competitive, spectator-oriented, elitist, win-above-all-else, conform-or-quit sport as it currently is practiced in most schools and colleges. Perhaps it is entertaining and ego-building in the short run. But, in the long run, are such programs contributing to self and society in a way that will generate the greatest personal satisfaction and the greatest humanly beneficial social progress? I must admit to serious question in my own mind as to the merit of the present narrow base of involvement and the feverish pitch of competition in major sports when the same resources might be used for the development of inclusive, attractive life-time sport programs in which sport would be carried on for fun, recreation, fitness, and friendship.

I want to make two points. First, coaches, athletes, and everyone else connected with sport must be clear about what they are doing. How many coaches, for instance, have ever heard of the technocracy, conditional self-worth, excellence-based-on-existence, or wholeness of self? Few, I suspect. Wisely taught new courses on the sociology and social psychology of sport might help. And how many athletes blindly use sport only as a means of gaining fame, of combatting deficiencies of self-worth, failing all the while to think about what they are doing or to learn anything at all about their inner selves or the cultural context in which they compete—learning which might make them much more satisfied persons in the long run and, in the short run, lead to involvement in sport as a way of expressing self?

Second, just as schools and colleges must avoid indoctrinating and conventionalizing, scholastic and collegiate sports must do likewise, as parts of those institutions. Coaches are unjustified in requiring conformity to a particular set of moral or political standards having no relationship to training or performance. As I have stated elsewhere,

> To some extent, sport will by its very nature enculturate youth, since participation in many ways is like participation in the adult community at large. But much greater stress ought to be placed on questioning, inquiring, making individual choices as to values and life style, and protecting the rights of persons to be different. The mission of the school—and of athletics carried on within it—ought to be not to indoctrinate but to develop independent-minded, autonomous, self-aware persons with a basic unconditional sense of self-worth—qualities depending in part on the extent to which coaches convey a deep sense of acceptance and dignity to each athlete. (Schafer 1971)

Finally, the counterculture is having and will continue to have numerous important effects on scholastic and collegiate athletics, including decreased attendance, reduced financial support by student governments, smaller numbers turning out for sports, drug use by athletes, challenges to the authority of the coach in relation to off-the-field conduct, revulsion by many athletes to surrendering themselves to victory-above-all, pressures to increase support for more open club sports. The influence of the counterculture in one school is reflected in the following excerpt from a student-composed litany recited at the school's baccalaureate exercises:

Leader: Many adults got upset at the rejection of traditional school spirit. They seemed to measure the success of a school by the number of organized rooters at a football game.

Class: In our sophomore year, pep assemblies were made no longer mandatory.

Leader: One of the biggest changes in the past three years has been in the school's attitude toward sports. Athletes are recognized for their outstanding achievements without being put on a pedestal.

Class: It's not that being an athlete is bad, but there are many areas in which a student can excel: in drama, music, Junior Achievement.

Leader: Blind school spirit no longer has meaning. These years have been years of transition from an inward to an outward view.

Class: The crises of the world have become important to us and we seek involvement in political movements outside the school.

The future cannot be predicted in detail, but it is clear that the counter-culture will continue to grow, affecting the world of scholastic and collegiate sport in a variety of ways. I hope that this discussion will generate greater understanding—or at least new kinds of questioning—about the effects of athletics on the individual and his society. Only through enhanced awareness can we hope to channel sport toward truly humanistic ends.

REFERENCES

Bend, E.
   1968   *The Impact of Athletic Participation on Academic and Career Aspiration and Achievement*. New Jersey: National Football Foundation and Hall of Fame.
Ogilvie, B. C., and Tutko, T. A.
   1971   "Sport: If You Want to Build Character Try Something Else." *Psychology Today*, October, p. 61.
Rehberg, R. A., and Schafer, W. E.
   1968   "Participation in Interscholastic Athletics and College Expectations." *American Journal of Sociology* 63:732–740.
Reich, C. A.
   1970   *The Greening of America*. New York: Random House.
Roszak, T.
   1969   *The Making of a Counter Culture*. New York: Anchor.
Schafer, W. E.
   1969   "Some Social Sources and Consequences of Interscholastic Athletics: The Case of Participation and Delinquency." In: Kenyon, G. S., ed. *Sociology of Sport*. Chicago: Athletic Institute.
   1971   "Sport, Socialization and the School: Toward Maturity or Enculturation?" Paper presented at the Third International Symposium on Sociology of Sport. Waterloo, Ontario.
   1975   "Athletic Success and Social Mobility." In Yiannakis, A., ed. *Socio-Cultural Aspects of Sport*. New York: Associated Educational Services.
————, and Armer, M. J.
   1968   "Athletes Are Not Inferior Students." *Transaction*, November, pp. 21–26, 61.

————, and Rehberg, R. A.
    1971   "Athletic Participation, College Aspirations and College Encouragement." *Pacific Sociological Review*, Summer, pp. 38–44.
Snyder, E. E.
    1970   "Aspects of Socialization in Sport and Physical Education." *Quest* 14:1–7.
    1971   "Athletic Dressing Room Slogans as Folklore: A Means of Socialization." Paper presented at the annual meeting of the American Sociological Association, Denver.
Spady, W. G.
    1970   "Lament for the Letterman: Effects of Peer Status and Extracurricular Activities on Goals and Achievement." *American Journal of Sociology* 75(4):680–702.

Political Attitudes and Participation in Extracurricular Activities

RICHARD A. REHBERG AND MICHAEL COHEN

The past decade has seen a historically unprecedented rise in political and social awareness, involvement, and protest among athletes in the United States. The actions of black trackmen in 1968, the writings of former football pro Dave Meggysey, and the protests of athletes from Berkeley to the Ivy League are selected instances of the growing political and social conscience of those who participate in sports, whether it be on the playing fields of the local high school or the stadium of the metropolis.

Events of the past decade aside, however, many observers continue to maintain that those who participate in sports are more conservative than their nonparticipating counterparts. Former Kennedy aide Joseph Califano (1970), writing of his impressions from a worldwide study of youth unrest, noted a particular affinity in Japan between the political right and athletes. Schafer and Phillips (1970) reported for their sample of secondary school students that, in comparison with the student body, athletes were both more accepting of general school norms and traditions and more intensely regulated by their own athletic subculture norms. Schafer (1969) and Schafer and Phillips (1970) have also reported that interscholastic athletes have lower rates of juvenile delinquency, more negative attitudes toward marijuana, greater support for strict control by the coach over athletes, and more support for stringent school rules.

In essence, then, athletics as an intra-educational institution "serve first and foremost as a social device for steering young people—participants and spectators alike—into the mainstream of American life through the overt and covert teaching of 'appropriate' attitudes, values,

Richard A. Rehberg is associate profesor of sociology, State University of New York, Binghamton. Michael Cohen is now with the National Institute of Education. The research reported herein was supported by an initial grant from the State University of New York Research Foundation (40–220–A), a subsequent grant from the National Science Foundation (GS01950), and a current grant from the National Institute of Mental Health (MH 1925).

norms, and behavior patterns. As a result, school sports tend to exert more of a conservatizing and integrating influence in the society than an innovative or progressive influence" (Schafer 1971).

THE RESEARCH PROBLEM

In an effort to test empirically the proposition that athletic activities within the secondary school exercise a conservative socializing influence on participants, we shall examine the responses of varsity athletes—as well as of other appropriate categories of students—to a set of political attitudinal items employed by the research firm of Daniel Yankelovich in its 1969 nationwide survey of American youth for the Columbia Broadcasting System's series "Generations Apart."

THE SAMPLE

Respondents for this study consist of the 937 male students who were present in eight public and parochial, urban and suburban school systems in the southern tier region of New York for the freshman year (1967), sophomore year (1968), and senior year (1970) survey panels of a four-wave, five-year longitudinal panel investigation of adolescent behavior. While restricting the sample to those students present throughout the four-year span of secondary school tends to bias certain statistics upward, the extent of such a bias is minimal. Comparing the retained four-year sample with all students who were present for the freshman year panel, regardless of whether those present for the first wave persisted or not, we find the mean Hollingshead two-digit Index of Social Position score for the retained sample to be 39.85, in comparison with 40.35 for the freshman-panel-only sample; measured intelligence for the retained sample is 110.88, compared with 109.77 for the freshman-panel-only sample; level of educational expectation, freshman year, on a scale where a score of 1 indicates graduate or professional school and 4 indicates completion of high school, is 2.50 for the retained sample in comparison with 2.63 for the freshman-panel-only segment.

THE VARIABLES

Political attitudes. Four domains of political attitudinal variables were selected from those included in our senior-year survey questionnaire for analysis in this paper.

1. *Acceptance of authority*

   This is an index comprised of responses ranging from "accept easily" to "reject outright" to four separate items: (a) abiding by laws you do not agree with; (b) conforming in matters of personal clothing and dress; (c) the power and authority of the police; and (d) the power and authority of your teacher and principal.

2. *View of American society*

Respondents were asked, "Which one of the following views of American society and American life reflect your own feelings?" Alternatives were: (a) the American way of life is superior to that of any other country; (b) there are serious flaws in our society to-day, but the system is flexible enough to solve the flaws and problems; (c) the American system is not flexible enough—radical change is needed.

3. *Position on military draft*

This item read: "Which one of the following statements comes closest to your own point of view?" (a) resisting the draft is basically wrong—a citizen is obligated to serve his country regardless of his personal views about the justness of a war; (b) an individual should obey his conscience—if he feels that he is being drafted to fight in a war that is morally wrong, he should resist in any way he can.

4. *Definition of personal role in bringing
about social change in school and society*

The question read: "With respect to your own personal role in seeking to bring about changes in your high school and/or in other institutions of our society, which one of the following statements best describes your own position?" (a) I consider myself an activist; (b) I am in sympathy with most of the activists' objectives, but not with all of their tactics; (c) I am not emotionally involved, one way or the other; (d) I am not sure that I approve of what the activists are trying to do, but I have no strong objections to letting them try; (e) I am in total disagreement with the activists.

Participation in extracurricular activities and athletics. Basic data for categorizing the sample into various classes of participation in extracurricular activities are derived from a yes/no matrix listing some fifteen activities. In response to each the student was asked to indicate whether he had or had not participated during the final year of secondary school. Included among the activities was "Athletics: *inter*scholastic (varsity or junior varsity)." Cognizant of and consistent with Spady's (1970) caveat regarding the pitfalls of a facile two-fold categorization of students into participants and nonparticipants in sports, we have employed a four-fold system of classification: participation in no extracurricular activities (26 percent of the sample); participation only in non-sport extracurricular activities (28 percent); participation both in sport and non-sport activities (35 percent); and participation only in sport activities (12 percent).

PROCEDURE

Inasmuch as participation category differences in political attitudes may represent either selection or socialization influences (or some combination of selection and socialization), our first effort is directed toward identifying those variables associated with both participation and political attitudes. Zero-order and multiple correlation are employed to identify and measure sources of variation in extracurricular participation. Correlation and percentage analyses are used to identify sources of variation in political attitudes. The results of this latter effort, however, are reported in a separate forthcoming paper and hence have not been reproduced here. Assessment of participation category differences in political attitudes with an antecedent source of variation in both participation and attitudes controlled is executed with multivariate tabular percentage analysis.

DATA

VARIABLES ASSOCIATED WITH PARTICIPATION AND
POLITICAL ATTITUDES

Inasmuch as differences in political attitudes between these four categories can represent the products of *selection into* each category or *socialization within* the category, or some combination thereof, we attempt first to identify and then to control for those selection variables. Though an analysis of between-category differences in political attitudes with statistical controls for such selection variables does not insure that those differences manifest the socialization experiences within the category, it does increase the probability that such differences can be understood as the consequences of the participation experience.

Considering the plausible sources of variation in overall participation in extracurricular activities, an analysis of zero-order correlation coefficients indicates that the number of activities in which a student participates is positively associated with:

Family socioeconomic status . . . . $r = .17$
Measured intelligence . . . . $r = .21$
Parental stress on continued education
    beyond high school . . . . $r = .18$

Supportive, nurturant parental socialization practices . r = .21
Value of education to the student himself . . . . . r = .21
The degree to which the student is future-oriented . . r = .15
The degree to which the student has a sense of
    environmental (social) mastery . . . . r = .24
The student's own educational goal as a freshman . . r = .35

When these separate sources of variation in senior-year participation are placed in a multiple regression equation, the multiple correlation coefficient is .40 for an accounted-for percentage of the variance of 16.

If we restrict the analysis to sources of variation in participation in senior-year interscholastic sports, the number of predictor variables and the degree to which most are associated with participation diminishes. Participation in senior-year interscholastic sports is positively associated with:

Family socioeconomic status . . . . r = .10
Measured intelligence . . . . r = .07
Parental stress on continued education
    beyond high school . . . . r = .10
Supportive and nurturant parental socialization
    practices . . . . r = .11
The degree to which the student is future oriented . . r = .09
The degree to which the student has a sense of
    environmental (social) mastery . . . . r = .10
The student's own educational goal as a freshman . . r = .17

Combining these variables into a multiple correlation equation yields an r of .20, accounting for some 4 percent of the variance in senior-year interscholastic sport participation.

Although these two analyses reveal that senior-year participation in extracurricular activities generally, or in interscholastic sports specifically, is associated with seven or eight antecedent selection variables, other analyses, to be reported under separate cover, have revealed only one of the above sources of variation in participation to be meaningfully associated with political attitudes: namely, measured intelligence. Consequently, measured intelligence is the only variable we shall control in our efforts to assess the degree to which political attitudes and behavior are associated with participation in extracurricular activities, particularly in sports.

POLITICAL ATTITUDES AND PARTICIPATION

Acceptance of authority. Certainly, the literature on the socialization consequences of sports suggests that the very structure of athletics would instill in participants a respect for and acceptance of authority. The table displays, by each of the four participation categories, the arithmetic means of authority acceptance, where a score of 1 designates most and a score of 9 least acceptance.

While those who participate in no activities whatsoever are consistently least accepting of authority, without IQ controlled (mean = 4.29) and with IQ controlled (mean = 4.26 low IQ, 4.34 high IQ), those who participate only in interscholastic sports are not the most accepting; rather, they tend to be tied for second place with those who participate only in non-sports activities. Thus, without a control for IQ, the sports only and the non-sports only participants each have means of 4.02. For those with IQ's below the median, the mean scores for these two categories are 3.82 and 3.81 respectively, while for those with IQ's above the median, those who participate in sports only are somewhat less accepting of authority (mean = 4.23) than are those who participate in non-sports activities only (mean = 4.18). Most accepting of authority (and consistently so) are those who participate in both sports and in other types of extra-curricular activities, i.e., zero-order mean = 3.69; first-order mean low IQ = 3.60, high IQ = 3.74.

To a degree, then, the generalization that athletes are more accepting of authority than others is contingent upon whether the athlete participates in other types of activities (in which case he *is* most accepting of authority), or whether he participates only in athletics (in which case he falls somewhere between the most accepting "collegiate-scholar," to borrow Bob Ellis's term for the "well rounded" student, and the least accepting complete non-participant).

View of American society. Defining as "traditional" the response that "the American way of life is superior to that of any other country," our data reveal that students who participate in interscholastic sports are slightly more traditional, conventional, or conservative than those who do not so participate. This difference is most pronounced when the comparisons are made without a control of IQ: 28 percent of those participating only in sports, 23 percent of those participating in both sports and other activities, compared with 19–20 percent of those who participate only in non-sports activities or in no activities at all, stated that "the American way . . . is superior." A somewhat more dramatic

Specified Responses to Specified Political Attitudinal Items by Category of Extracurricular Activity participation, senior year, with Measured Intelligence Controlled*

Predictor variables		Political attitudinal item							
Measured IQ	Extracurricular activity participation	Acceptance of authority (mean) Index score	View of American Society		Military draft: One should:		Personal role in social change: I am:		
			Conservative %	Radical %	Obey the law %	Obey conscience %	Activist %	Uninvolved %	Opposed %
Above the median	No participation	4.34	20	13	33	66	6	37	2
	Only non-athletic	4.13	20	11	30	69	15	16	5
	Both athletic and non-ath.	3.74	21	7	41	56	14	17	5
	Only athletic	4.23	21	9	38	62	2	30	0
	All	4.05	21	10	36	63	11	22	2
Below the median	No participation	4.26	19	15	43	56	6	37	7
	Only non-athletic	3.81	18	18	53	45	13	31	5
	Both athletic and non-ath.	3.60	27	6	52	46	14	28	5
	Only athletic	3.82	34	14	68	30	8	50	6
	All	3.89	23	13	52	47	10	35	6
All	No participation	4.29	20	14	39	60	6	37	5
	Only non-athletic	4.02	19	14	39	59	14	22	5
	Both athletic and non-ath.	3.69	23	7	45	52	14	21	5
	Only athletic	4.02	28	11	53	45	5	40	4
	All	3.97	22	11	43	55	11	28	4

*Responses are for the 809 of the 934 male students who were present for the freshman, sophomore, and senior year panel surveys of the Career Preference Research project. IQ-participation category n's are: high IQ: 94, 131, 170, and 47, respectively; low IQ: 113, 93, 111, and 50, respectively; All: 207, 224, 281, and 97 respectively. The difference between 934 available and 809 analyzed respondents is due to exclusion from this analysis of the no response data to measured intelligence.

picture emerges in the below-the-median control level; 34 percent of those participating only in sports and 27 percent of those participating in both sports and other activities endorse the traditional response, vis à vis 18–19 percent of the non-sport participants and the non-participants. Counterbalancing the more extreme percentage differences found in the low IQ control level are the all but absent percentage differences in the high IQ control level, where sport-participants are but one percentage point more "conservative" than non-sports participants and non-participants.

If we use as a criterion the percentage checking the statement that "the American system is not flexible enough; radical change is needed," we find that those who participate both in interscholastic sports and in other activities are least likely to view radical change as necessary (6–7 percent). Those who participate in no activity at all or only in non-sports activities are *most* likely to regard radical change as necessary (11–18 percent); falling between these two extremes are those participating only in interscholastic sports, where between 9 and 14 percent (depending upon the control level for IQ) believe that American society requires radical change.

In summary, then, when appraised by their response to a single item tapping an overall evaluative view of American society, interscholastic athletes are somewhat more likely than non-athletes to endorse a conventional response, and somewhat less likely to endorse a radical response calling for fundamental structural change. Remember, however, that the magnitude of our percentage differences is minor to moderate, never exceeding twelve points.

View of the Draft. Among the more salient issues of the past decade of youth activism has been the posture of American young men with respect to the military draft. By a somewhat moderate percentage margin of five or more points, interscholastic athletes, especially those who participate only in sports, regard "resisting the draft as basically wrong." Without regard to IQ, 53 percent of those who participate only in sports and 45 percent of those who participate in both sports and other activities endorsed the "resisting the draft is wrong" alternative, compared with 39 percent of the students not participating in athletic activities.

For those with IQ's below the median, the percentage difference separating the athletes-only from those who participate in no activities at all increases—68 percent of the athletes-only, compared with 43 percent of those participants in no activities, feel that to resist the draft is basically wrong; while the difference between those who take part in other activities and do or do not also take part in sports all but disappears—52 and 53 percent, respectively. To some degree the pattern changes when those with IQ's above the median are examined: an average of 40 percent of all athletes, compared with 31 percent of all non-athletes, endorse the response that draft resistance is basically wrong.

Self-definition as an activist. Social psychological theory regards the conception of the self both as a reflector of past and as a generator of present and future behavior. In an effort to ascertain how students view themselves politically vis à vis social change, our respondents were asked to locate themselves on a five item scale ranging from "I consider myself an activist" through "I am not emotionally involved, one way or the other," to "I am in total disagreement with the activists."

Since a cursory inspection of the last column in the table reveals almost no meaningful between-category percentage differences in "opposition" to activists, this end-point response category shall be disregarded in our analysis.

When attention is focused solely on the two response levels: "I consider myself an activist" and "I am not emotionally involved . . . ," two distinct profiles of extra-curricular participants emerge, regardless of IQ. On the one hand, those who participate only in sports are similar to those who participate in no activities at all. A very small percentage of either participation category regard themselves as activists (2–8 percent, depending on category and IQ level), and a fairly high percentage of either participation category regard themselves as not emotionally involved one way or the other (37 to 50 percent, depending on category and IQ). On the other hand, those who participate in sports and other activities resemble those who participate only in non-sport activities in that a modest percentage classify themselves as activists (13–15 percent, depending on category and IQ), and a fairly small percentage assess themselves as not emotionally involved (16 to 31 percent). It is important, however, to observe that almost twice the percentage of low IQ respondents assess themselves as not involved (31 to 28 percent) as do those in the high IQ level (16 to 17 percent).

Those who participate only in interscholastic sports or in no activities at all can be characterized as non-involved and apathetic, while those who participate only in non-athletic activities, or in both athletic and nonathletic activities, can be characterized as involved and non-apathetic.

CONCLUSION

In the introduction to this paper, we noted the reasoning of those who cogently and persuasively argue that the socializing experience of sports, particularly the experiences encountered by those who participate in varsity sports in the American secondary school, exercise a conservative influence on the athlete.

With data from 937 senior male students from eight school systems in the southern tier region of New York, we have sought to test the socialization proposition by focusing on the political dimension of the multi-dimensional conservative—radical ideological continuum.

Given that athletes were somewhat more conservative than non-athletes in three of the four domains measured (more accepting of authority, more traditional in their view of American society, and more likely to regard the military draft as a legal obligation rather than as a matter of personal moral conscience), we conclude that there is some empirical substance to the model of sports as, in the words of Schafer, "a social device for steering young people—participants and spectators alike—into the mainstream of American life." We would urge, however, that the theoretical import accorded this model not exceed its empirical base. In each of the three differentiating variables analyzed, not only were the margins separating the athlete from the non-athlete of minimal magnitude, but the relationship between political attitudes and participation was often itself a conditional one—dependent upon the level of measured intelligence. Considering the comparative youth of the sociology of sport and the eagerness with which the lay public seizes our data to support their various interests (as per the dispute which raged over the proposed abolition of varsity sports as an austerity measure in the Philadelphia public school system), we would be wise to keep our theoretical reach well within the realm of our empirical grasp.

REFERENCES

Califano, J.
    1970 *The Student Revolution: A Global Confrontation.* New York:
          W. W. Norton.
Schafer, W. E.
    1969 "Participation in Interscholastic Athletics and Delinquency: A
          Preliminary Study." *Social Problems.* Summer: 40–47.
    1971 "Sport, Socialization and the School." Paper presented at the
          Third International Symposium on the Sociology of Sport.
          Waterloo, Ontario.

———, and Phillips, J. C.
 1970 "The Athletic Subculture: A Preliminary Study." Paper presented at the annual meeting of the American Sociological Association. Washington, D.C.
Spady, W. G.
 1970 "Lament for the Letterman: Effects of Peer Status and Extracurricular Activities on Goals and Achievement." *American Journal of Sociology*, 75:680–702.

A Commentary on Sport and the New Left

WILLIAM G. SPADY

Given the rather different orientations and styles of the Schafer paper and the Rehberg and Cohen paper, I find it simpler to react to each separately, according to its particular frame of reference and approach. Later I shall attempt a brief synthesis of their common elements. First, however, I must raise an important issue that pertains directly to both papers: that is the ambiguity surrounding terms such as "mainstream of American life" and "dominant social values," and the attendant problems in specifying their antonyms. Presumably these mainstream or dominant values include an entire constellation of beliefs involving the importance of individual effort and accomplishment in defining one's status and worth, both economic and social. I also assume that built into this diffuse complex of values are beliefs in both the ultimate legitimacy of the law and in the special privileges of those in positions of authority and responsibility.

One of my major difficulties with these terms concerns what might be called the boundaries of this conglomerate. Where, for example, does individualism end and conformity begin as a dominant Western value—or do we believe in both simultaneously? Are there limits to the achievement-status-individual worth syndrome—or does the accumulation of wealth, power, and influence reach no point of marginal return? A lengthy list of similar questions could be raised.

Another of my difficulties with this notion is really more germane to my central thesis, which involves the variety of stances one can adopt toward these "core values," and the implications which these variations have for understanding things like the counterculture, the New Left, activists, hippies, Consciousness III, and all of their relatives. Even if we could all come to some agreement on the dominant values and lifestyle of the society, we would still be faced with analyzing the various stances which people or groups take toward them. For example, apparently

William G. Spady is senior research sociologist, National Institute of Education, Washington, D.C.

some rather large group actively embodies and supports this "way of life"; otherwise it would not be mainstream or dominant. In addition, presumably others more or less conform to this pattern, albeit in a less enthusiastic fashion. Rehberg, Cohen, and Schafer are all arguing that athletics typically promotes one of these two stances, but usually the former. I generally concur. The real issue, then, is adequately differentiating among the distinct ways that individuals or groups can "reject" these values, for these modes of rejection define the rubrics with which athletes are being compared in these papers.

Allow me to suggest four oversimplified patterns of rejection that are commonly confused in our haste to deal with "the counterculture" or "activists" as one homogeneous group. These are: apathy, rebellion, withdrawal, and protest. Although my definitions of these terms will probably not hold up under critical examination, they are a way of illustrating the complexity of this issue. I regard the latter three—rebellion, withdrawal, and protest—as distinctive forms of activism, although we have come to associate the term "activism" mainly with what I call protest. Protest usually involves the deliberate organization and mobilization of individuals around some issue for the purpose of demonstrating an objection to some established practice. Most social or political protests remain within the boundaries of the law, although they often violate what others regard as the unofficial norms of the society. There are, of course, cases in which laws are deliberately broken in the name of "higher principles" and in which violence is committed in the name of these same principles, but extreme cases of violation and violence on the part of protesters are not as common as they are conspicuous. Although many critics would argue to the contrary, I regard protest activity as having permanent changes in social or political structures and processes as its major goal, and this remains its basic feature.

Protest is conceptually quite distinct from what I mean by rebellion; the latter usually involves the violation of norms or laws without regard to the consequences of these actions for others. Some would argue, of course, that the more serious incidents of protest have degenerated into rebellion, but the important distinction involves not only the means used to achieve ends, but the nature of the ends as well. Typically, rebellion involves striking out against the society for the purpose of changing one's immediate circumstances (such as an armed robbery, to improve one's economic state of affairs) with little if any intention of precipitating wider social change. On the other hand, some acts of rebellion may appear to have no purpose beyond the venting of one's frustrations against the people or conditions that symbolize the perceived sources of that frustration.

Withdrawal, in contrast, typically implies an attempt to remove oneself from a given society, either physically or psychologically. Western history is replete with examples of cultural or religious conflicts precipitating the migration of peoples to new surroundings in which their values and lifestyle would not clash with that of their neighbors. The attempts of some contemporary Americans to realize themselves by forming agricultural communes far removed from what they regard as the artificial and inhibiting nature of modern urban existence are examples of this countercultural phenomenon. Such a mode of adaptation implies neither reforming nor striking out against "mainstream society," but removing oneself from it as far as possible. For some, withdrawal is possible even within the framework of urban life, but it often involves a periodic psychological retreat into alcohol or drugs.

Apathy exists in those individuals whose rejection of "mainstream values" is not accompanied by any distinctive form of action to change their circumstances. They neither confront nor withdraw from the society, but essentially cope with their state of normative incongruity, often with resignation. In theory at least, they are the potential allies of the protesters. What is required, of course, is a change in their consciousness which allows them to believe that their efforts can make a difference in the struggle for social reform.

I have tried, by means of this digression, to clarify a few distinct ways in which rejection of mainstream social values manifests itself. Naturally, individuals and groups change their basic mode of adaptation from time to time, which implies that the boundaries of these modes are often indistinct and permeable. Nonetheless, it should be clear from the outset that the two papers under discussion here deal with these modes not as distinct analytical types, but as diffuse manifestations of countercultural orientations. This makes analytical clarity difficult to achieve and direct comparability between papers problematic.

With these four modes of "rejection" in mind, let me turn to Rehberg and Cohen's analysis of political attitudes and patterns of extracurricular participation by discussing their research design, variables, and analysis. From my perspective, two major issues of design are raised in their paper. The first involves the assumption, which they address quite explicitly, that their data reflect the socialization influence of extracurricular activities rather than selection biases. In simple terms, it is the difference between athletics (for example) actually influencing students to be more conservative, and having more conservative students choose athletics in the first place. This issue cannot be resolved without longitudinal data (which they have not presented in this paper), and even then considerable care would have to be taken in dealing with change scores over time. Their argument concerning possible contaminating variables is instructive in suggesting which other factors may be associated with either participation or political attitudes, but such variables do not help us to untangle the causal question regarding attitudes influencing participation, participation affecting attitudes, or (as is most likely) the two reinforcing each other.

The second issue of research design actually overlaps issues involving the choice and operationalization of variables. There are always potential gains as well as losses implied in the decision to use items or tests that have been used in other major studies. By using standardized or published instruments, one can begin to build a comparative data base across samples and over time, thereby linking his findings directly with those of others. However, if these instruments contain poorly worded questions with limited or questionable alternatives (as I believe is true of the Yankelovich items used to measure political attitudes), the researcher must suffer the consequences of having comparable but bad data. For example: the item on the American way of life has an overly restricted number of alternatives whose meanings are somewhat ambiguous and which logically allow for multiple responses; the item on the draft forces responses toward one of two extreme positions without allowing for some middle range of opinion; and the item on activism falsely implies that efforts toward change are exclusively a phenomenon of the left, whereas activism of both left and right are present in our society. In my opinion, Rehberg would have been better off designing his own items. I say this with a prejudiced view of his ability: I know he could have done a better job of item construction on his own.

In addition, there are grounds for arguing that the criteria used in categorizing patterns of extracurricular participation should have taken into account the presumed nature of the socialization experience in those activities. The range of possible effects implied in "other" (i.e., non-athletic) activities could easily be so diverse that the liberalizing influences of some particular activity could be offset by the conservatizing effects of others. Very simply, we do not know what "other" means except in its distinction from athletics and from "none." Since the most conservative answers are often found among the athletes who are also in "other" activities, it would be of considerable interest to know what "other" means in those cases.

A final word about variables before turning to the data themselves: IQ should be thought of in this analysis as both an *explanatory variable* (i.e., brighter students tend to be less authoritarian or conservative; therefore the activities they choose may reflect this liberalism) and as a *conditional variable* (i.e., the socializing effect of a given activity may vary, depending on the student's intelligence). I believe that the findings in their table suggest that both processes are at work.

If my reconstruction of Rehberg and Cohen's raw numbers is correct, approximately 55 percent of the low IQ boys are engaged in some non-athletic activity (30 percent are in both), compared with 68 percent of the high IQ boys. Thirty-one percent of the low IQ boys are in no activity compared to only 21 percent of their brighter classmates. Simply stated, *brighter students are more likely to be active, especially in non-athletic activities.* The following table, summarizing the findings pertaining to the military draft, also suggests that *brighter students are more likely to be liberal, regardless of their activity.* These figures show the percentage of students who report that they would follow their conscience in dealing with the draft.

	Athletics			
	No		Yes	
	Other		*Other*	
	No	Yes	No	Yes
High IQ	66%	69%	62%	56%
	(94)	(131)	(47)	(170)
Low IQ	56%	45%	30%	46%
	(113)	(93)	(50)	(111)

Sixty-six percent of the 94 high IQ boys in no activity at all would follow their conscience rather than the law. Of their 113 low IQ counterparts, only 56 percent chose the "liberal" answer. Note also that these non-active boys are the *most* liberal of all of the low IQ students in the sample, yet they compare exactly with the *least* liberal high IQ boys (those in both sports and other activities). Inspection alone suggests, in fact, that *more variability in student responses is due to IQ differences than to variations in participation.* When weighted appropriately by the n's for each category, these differences average 17 percent across the whole table. Nonetheless, there is also considerable variability across participation categories, *particularly among lower ability boys.* The most conspicuous category involves those who are athletes only: *the combination of only being an athlete and having a low IQ mitigates most strongly against having liberal attitudes* (i.e., their 30 percent is 15 percentage points lower than any other group in the sample).

Further inspection of Rehberg and Cohen's table also reveals that this same group held the most conservative views of American society and were by far the most likely to express no emotional involvement regarding the issue of bringing about change in their school or society. Half of them claim to be uninvolved in the issues surrounding them, and over two-thirds place the law above conscience. Among the high IQ students, the athletes-only are also the most likely to be uninvolved, but their apathy is exceeded by that of students who are not active in anything. This latter group, regardless of ability level, appears to have comparatively strong liberal attitudes but a decided degree of detachment from the life of the school. It is perhaps among these students that the withdrawal and apathy noted in my earlier remarks is most clearly manifested.

To summarize: despite the limitations in the variables under examination, it appears that conservative attitudes are more prevalent among athletes than among non-athletes. But even more important is the consistent effect of ability; all things being equal (which they are not), less able students tend to be more conservative than brighter ones. They are also more likely to be uninvolved or uncommitted regarding issues of social change, particularly if they are in athletics and nothing else. On the whole, however, political uninvolvement is also comparatively common among those who are uninvolved in other arenas of school life.

As a further clue to sorting out the causal ordering implied by these findings, I would encourage Rehberg and Cohen to control simultaneously for family socioeconomic status (SES) as well. Presumed "effects" of IQ may actually be due to the socioeconomic origins of these students, since higher SES families have brighter children. If current assumptions regarding the greater "permissiveness" of middle-class parents are true, the liberalism associated in these data with higher IQ may actually be the result of less authoritarian and conservative socialization practices in the homes of these brighter students. Then again, they may not. It may require a more facile mind to look beyond the simplicities inherent in many conservative political and social ideologies. In either event, treating SES as a dichotomous variable is unlikely to be very revealing, for this would tend to clump the upper and lower middle classes into one category, thereby merging groups whose political orientations and socialization practices are believed by some sociologists to be quite dissimilar. A better strategy would involve treating SES minimally as a trichotomous variable with a somewhat disproportionate middle category. This would assure that upper-middle-class and working-class families would be clearly differentiated, not only from each other but from the more typical "Middle American" group comprising the lower-middle and upper-working classes.

Perhaps this discussion of extreme versus middle groups provides a convenient opportunity to shift attention to Schafer's analysis of socialization themes, since his paper clearly differentiates between the normative extremes embodied in competitive athletics and Reich's Consciousness III. One cannot be anything but impressed with the extreme contrasts in values and orientations represented in Schafer's characterizations of athletic culture and the "counterculture." At first glance, it would appear that the two have virtually nothing in common.

While this may be true, it would be premature to draw any conclusions about the future character of society at large from an extrapolation of Schafer's analysis. Clearly he is decribing the ideal-typical features of these two extreme groups, which leaves most of the real world (us included) somewhere in the middle. It is probably safe, though hardly profound, to suggest that no society based exclusively on one or the other of these extreme models is likely to survive for long in the world as we know it. One demands too much from its individual members in order to assure collective success, while the other too readily sacrifices unity of the whole in order to maintain the integrity of the individual. The simplest implication to draw from this point is that social life is a highly complex struggle between the individual and the collectivity which demands compromises from both. Schafer's description of Sport I (if I may be allowed the privilege of naming the phenomenon) and Consciousness III certainly allows little room for compromise or overlap between these two theoretical constructs, yet experience suggests that these two are rarely manifested in such extreme form. Their more moderate manifestations no doubt have features in common (as do, I believe, the ideal constructs themselves); I would like to discuss these common features, and particularly the paradoxes they generate.

The most conspicuous set of paradoxes raised by Sport I and Consciousness III emerge from a juxtaposition of the terms "individuality" and "community." As I have suggested above, one way of interpreting Schafer's analysis is to equate Consciousness III with a strong impetus toward individuality, and Sport I with compliance to community (i.e., team or collective) norms. However, it is certainly obvious that athletes contribute to the welfare of their team only to the extent that their individual skills and contributions are highly developed and efficiently exercised. In other words, one must make a considerable investment in himself and exercise his skills imaginatively and effectively before he can be of value to the collectivity. Group welfare depends largely on strong individuals; this is as true in the symphony orchestra (which does not operate according to strict competitive conditions) as it is on a basketball team (which does). The real issue, then, is the balance between individual and group needs that the team athlete must attain in exercising his highly individual skills. The fine line between self and selfishness may determine who gets to play, regardless of batting average or passing ability.

In the case of the team, however, the entire meaning of community may become distorted. The team as a collectivity may help to symbolize and thereby unify a given community of individuals, but the resulting feelings of identification and pride tend to foster highly localistic and particularistic loyalties, since other teams from other communities are seen as "the enemy" that must be defeated. Solidarity within the team and within the community that supports it may be gained at the expense of more open and cooperative relations among communities. Encouraging this openness in a more cosmopolitan way is an important aspect of Consciousness III.

Some critics regard the athlete not as the altruistic member of a group more significant than himself, but as the supreme egotist whose satisfactions derive mainly from his domination and superiority over others. In individual sports, where the harmonious coordination of individuals is not important, he must be completely self-reliant and totally self-disciplined. This may lead not only to the conditional self-acceptance about which Schafer speaks, but certainly to a major preoccupation with self as well.

The latter, however, may not only be a dominant characteristic of Sport I; it also seems to be a striking feature of Consciousness III. There is no doubt that Reich is describing a psychological state in which individual desire and satisfaction are paramount. Consciousness III rejects the imposition of external controls and rewards and stresses the autonomy and gratification of the individual. The only adequate measure of the individual is himself; through self-initiated activity one is fulfilled.

At this point, I must confess, the paradoxes within paradoxes are becoming too much for me to handle, for Reich claims (even though Schafer remains a bit skeptical) that it is through this process of self-discovery that Consciousness III also discovers the oneness of man and the capacity for generating a true sense of community. As a sociologist

I lack both the expertise and sensitivity of psychologists and psychiatrists to comprehend how one so apparently effortlessly makes the transition from complete absorption with oneself (which directly implies a rejection of the standards, values, and expectations of others) to acceptance of and integration into a total human community (which implies just the reverse). Community implies shared values and expectations which Consciousness III basically rejects in favor of autonomous behavior. For community life to sustain itself, there must be a system of shared norms and values which members basically agree and adhere to. This seems highly inconsistent with Reich's continual emphasis on individuals "doing their own thing" and rejecting external standards.

Before I leave this particular morass of paradoxes and apparent inconsistencies, let me raise two brief questions. First, have we been discussing individualism or egotism? In the case of both Sport I and Consciousness III, it may be more of the latter than the former, but that is for you to judge. Second, which of the adaptive modes of rejection discussed at the outset seems to be most characteristic of Consciousness III? I do not mean to be cynical when I suggest that the most prevalent mode is probably apathy followed by some types of withdrawal and, perhaps, rebellion as well. It is certainly not protest, and for this reason I question how much either Schafer or Reich's analysis actually applies to the New Left.

What I am suggesting is simple, if not simplistic. Protest, if it is to be at all effective, demands the formulation of goals, the rational development of means to achieve those goals, and the marshaling of forces and influences to implement the means selected. In other words, effective protest requires thinking, planning, and organization, all of which are intellectual activities in which individuals must reach a consensus and diligently apply their efforts if they are really serious about changing things. I do not see how this combination of intellectual and pragmatic activities could be carried out by Consciousness III, with its strong non-intellectual and consummatory biases. Consciousness III people may be willing to attend the rally (if they feel like it), march (until their legs get tired), sit in (until they get bored), or get arrested (because they couldn't run fast enough to evade the police), but they are not likely to be leaders and organizers of protest activities.

The implication, of course, is that Reich has attempted to cast his countercultural net too widely, claiming the membership of all who wish to reject various aspects of Consciousness II, but he fails to recognize the qualities that one must possess to be either an activist or, perhaps, a real individualist. This also leaves the door open for skeptics to argue that it is precisely because so many protesters are steeped in Consciousness III that protest activity seems to have run its course: they have no staying power and can no longer get their apathetic, self-indulgent friends involved now that the glamor has worn off and only hard work lies ahead. Although this argument (with which I agree only in part) stands as a serious indictment of New Left motivation and commitment, there are a host of other factors that help to account for the current lull in protest activity. Nonetheless, I think that members of both the New Left and the NCAA will have to take my earlier point seriously: being effective in a competitive arena and doing one's own thing are generally incompatible alternatives in a zero-sum game in which only one can flourish at a time.

The issues and ambiguities that I have raised regarding the real dimensions of Sport I and Consciousness III can certainly not be confined within the parameters of any one rubric. I have touched on several themes which apply in varying ways to both phenomena: individuality versus community, leadership versus passivity, and instrumental versus consummatory involvement. Let me suggest in passing that equally important questions could be raised about external versus internal control, self-improvement versus group improvement, independence versus dependence, and schooling versus intellectual introspection.

However, I wish to address myself briefly to a theme with which many of these others overlap: self-fulfillment versus achievement. On the surface it is easy to see that Sport I is immersed in an achievement syndrome in which competing and winning rather than achieving excellence for its own sake is the dominant feature. Similarly, it is easy to be persuaded that Consciousness III represents quite the opposite: a rejection of competitive and comparative pressures, and an engagement in activities for their own sake. I would like to argue, however, that both Sport I and Consciousness III stand in need of critical self-examination and "consciousness reform." The athlete needs to accept a new set of standards for evaluating his engagement by replacing winning (which is inherently extrinsic and comparative) with a more intrinsic form of reward for competent performance in its own right. Until then he will remain dependent on dominating others for gratification and on the limitations of conditional self-acceptance which it implies.

Since self-actualization requires that the individual derive gratification from his engagement in an activity, my Consciousness I upbringing and training lead me to believe that the better he can do it, given his physical or mental limitations, the more exhilarating and rewarding the activity becomes. This bit of interpretive bias implies two things. First, self-actualization means self-realization, and realization is attained through some degree of effort and mastery. Second, mastery implies that initially, at least, there are standards of adequacy that lie outside of the individual to which he must become attuned and aspire. In other words, fulfillment implies the capacity to perform an activity well, rather than just to engage in it per se. This in no way requires that the activity be selected by others or meet their approval; hence one may readily do his own thing. The critical condition, however, is in being able to do that thing well enough to find it intrinsically rewarding.

For example, I seriously doubt that the novice guitarist, whom Reich would seem to admire, is fulfilled by his plucking and strumming until his technical mastery of the instrument enables him to express the tones, chords, and moods he desires. I also doubt whether he can afford to reject all external standards of excellence and criteria regarding his performance if he ever expects anyone to listen or to sing along. Being self-actualized may imply having done one's thing, but it also requires working at that thing long enough to develop the mastery necessary for self-fulfillment. Consciousness III's preoccupation with doing one's own thing while readily dismissing standards of excellence and achievement as important components of self-generated activity may be a grave mistake. The consequence could be a lot of unguided and sporadic attempts at a variety of activities whose outcomes might be the occasion for more disappointment and disillusionment than fulfillment. This might further reinforce a tendency toward apathy and withdrawal, thereby ensuring that the gap will widen between Consciousness III and Consciousness II (or Sport I) on the one hand and the activists we call the New Left on the other.

In closing, it may be appropriate to link these points to my initial remarks and to Rehberg and Cohen's work. I suggested at the outset that rejection of the (ambiguous) dominant values of the society could take several forms including protest, rebellion, withdrawal, and apathy. It is now clear that Consciousness III is only a partial reflection of the total countercultural scene, for it describes a cohort who are men neither of serious introspection nor of action, thereby eliminating both the creative artist and the political activist. The diversity of this scene is also suggested by Rehberg and Cohen's data in which some highly liberal students are engaged in a variety of different activities, while others are not active in anything. Similarly, a small percentage describe themselves as activists, and a much larger percentage consider themselves uninvolved in the concerns of the former.

The lesson to be learned, I think, involves the danger of trying to simplify our theoretical conceptions before adequately exploring their diversity and complexity. Despite broad, general trends in our theories and data, there may be as much variability among counterculturists and among athletes as there is between them. The answer will depend not only on more detailed scrutiny of the data and interpretations currently available, but on greater imagination in planning and executing future work as well.

The Athletic Group as an Emerging
Deviant Subculture

BRIAN M. PETRIE

In the past, the athletic subculture has been provided with considerable support and prestige within the educational setting. So much support was provided that many educators contended that the true purposes and goals of education were being lost in the glamor of and community support for interscholastic and intercollegiate teams. As Coleman (1961:88) found,

> Among the freshmen in each of the four schools studied for leading cliques, the one attribute shared by every boy in every leading clique . . . was being out for either football or basketball. No other attribute— in background, activities, or attitudes—so sharply distinguished the leading cliques. In the latter years of school, the leading cliques were found to be less uniformly athletic, but, among freshmen, they were found to be totally so.

Apart from the importance of athletics in the status system of the school, it was also apparent that it was regarded as having definite significance by the faculty and administrators.

> Few principals would seriously consider dispensing with these games. Yet, it is also indisputable that athletic contests create serious problems for the schools. Perhaps the most serious problem is the change they engender in the institution itself. Their very importance to the life of the school transforms the school from an institution devoted to learning into an institution focussed, at least partly, on athletics. (Coleman 1961:95)

Within colleges and universities the situation was much the same. The athlete was granted a considerable degree of prestige by virtue of his role in presenting a favorable image of the university in a sector of social life that was highly visible and strongly supported by the student body and the outside community. This image as a representative of the

Brian M. Petrie is associate professor of physical education at the University of Western Ontario. This article was originally presented in 1971. It does not reflect subsequent changes in American universities.

students in an us-versus-them situation provided the opportunity for the students to identify with their colleagues on the sporting fields and feel the development of a strong emotional attachment to the alma mater.

This effect continued after graduation, with the successful and highly publicized performances of the sporting teams providing a continued and positive link between the individual and his college. The link could then be translated into financial support by the alumni for the institution, with contributions apparently correlated with athletic success in the major sports.

Considerable social change has occurred in American society since those relatively unsophisticated days. One of the changes has related to the importance of athletics in the educational institutions. Athletics still have strong support, but the student population, and a few of the athletes themselves, have begun to question whether interscholastic and intercollegiate athletics merit such tremendous attention and support when other priorities appear more crucial. The days of unquestioning support and automatic high status for the participants of the major sports have been replaced by a new set of standards, many of which are related to concerns with the directions being taken by society itself.

During the times of campus turmoil, it was common to see various references in the mass and underground media to the identification of athletic groups with antagonism toward radical or liberal social action. Most of us are familiar with the actions attributed to members of a well-known athletically oriented fraternity and to members of intercollegiate athletic teams in precipitating action against black students at Straight Hall at Cornell; with physical attacks by "jocks" at Michigan State, San Francisco State, and Columbia on student sit ins, demonstrations, and campus protest marches; and with the attempted ejection of sit in demonstrators during the early stages of the Kent State troubles by "jocks" and "Greeks." Whether or not these events were actually precipitated by members of the athletic groups on the campuses concerned may be subject to some debate, but it is certainly evident that the "jocks" have been placed in a role of campus scapegoats and have been blamed for any physical attack against liberal or radical groups. The athlete has been identified as excessively oriented to the defense of the status quo, as an establishment man, and as an unquestioning supporter of conservative or reactionary political positions. To be a "jock" on many campuses is to be regarded as out of step with the new politics, the new humanism, and the youth culture.

It is possible, then, to perceive a trend in the adolescent and university society toward the acceptance of the athlete as a member of a deviant subculture. To the extent that the main body of the student population continues to accept elements of the philosophies, lifestyles, behavior codes, and techniques for social action of the more radical elements of the youth culture, this trend will magnify to create definite acceptability problems for athletes. Any analysis of the assumed trends toward redefinition of values among adolescents, and the location of the athlete within the social milieu of the school or university, must tap a multitude of dimensions which represent areas of concern in the student population.

It is tempting to restrict one's analysis to the investigation of political ideologies held by different groups within the educational setting, but to determine the influences leading to negative expression toward athletic groups, one must include many other features. The acceptance of more general values relating to the expectations for individual participation within society, such as orientations toward achievement, competition, success, status, and materialism, are prime areas for the assessment of differences between groups. It would also be valuable to consider whether the differences in personality structures that have been found to exist between athletes and non-athletes could possibly contribute to a separation of the athletic group from the rest of the student body.

This paper contends that there is an ongoing redefinition of values in the youth culture, and that the members of the athletic group are often located on a different end of the ideological continuum from those in the vanguard of this reorientation. As more of the largely uncommitted middle group accept (as indeed they appear to be doing) the value structures of the social activists, the athletic group will be further separated, and the nonathletes' perception that athletes represent a deviant subculture will increase.

DEFINITIONS OF TERMS

In the context of this paper, deviance is regarded not as some form of behavior that violates institutional expectations, but as behavior which violates the expectations of the client group (students) in the social system of the school or university: in effect, violation of peer group standards on an attitudinal or behavioral dimension.

From this perspective, the expectations of the faculty, administrators, and others in positions of power in the educational institutions would be of less significance to the evaluation. Deviance, then, is behavior that is inconsistent with the value structures of the majority, or of the dominant student group.

Frantz's (1969) definition of a student subculture has utility here. He wrote that it was a group which held "a shared set of expectancies producing a pattern of student behavior which distinguishes it from other groups of students."

A deviant subculture would be one with expectancies so far removed from the acceptance or tolerance of the dominant or majority group that the subculture was regarded as a group of outsiders for whom little support, encouragement, or emulation should be provided without some risk of disapproval.

It is useful to assume that three subcultural groups are present in the educational environment, with each of interest in the present discussion. They are: the athletic subculture; the subculture identified with the counterculture, made up of individuals seeking redefinition of societal goals through some level of radical activism; and the student subculture, made up of the mass of students representing the predominant values of society itself. The interaction of these three groups, two of which are definite minorities, presents interesting opportunities for analysis of potential and actual deviance in the educational setting. Certainly, the minority subculture which appeared to have the greatest connection with the mainstream would be provided with some degree of support and lifestyle imitation, while the other would be regarded as different, if not deviant. What is of crucial interest, then, is the direction of movement of the mass of students in terms of tolerance for a particular set of expectancies which are regarded as acceptable but distinctly different from their own.

ATTITUDES TOWARD WORK AND THE COMPETITION-ACHIEVEMENT SYNDROME

One task we have is to separate the concept of productivity from work. Work is money. Work is postponement of pleasure. Work is always done for someone else: the boss, the kids, the guy next door. Work is competition. Work is linked to productivity to serve the Industrial Revolution. We must separate the two. We must abolish work and all the drudgery it represents. . . . [Competition led to productivity] during the Industrial Revolution but it won't do for the future. . . . Cooperation will be the motivating factor in a free society. I think cooperation

is more akin to the human spirit. Competition is grafted on by institutions, by a capitalist economy, by religion, by schools. Every institution I can think of in this country promotes competition. (Hoffman
1968:57)

The only way out of the dilemma of our society is to say that in the
short run, everyone is entitled to a guaranteed income—and this is
the very short run, and then very rapidly move into a society in which
you simply go into a store and take what you want. (Theobald 1967)

Although it appears that the numerically dominant group in the
schools is still strongly identified with the occupational sector, and
that the educational experience is used for securing a desirable job, a
definite movement in the schools seeks to reevaluate our approaches
to work. Regardless of their political orientations, students see that
automation and cybernation are significantly affecting the structure of
the work force and creating social problems with respect to unemployment, job displacement, and occupational redundancy.

The counterculture takes this awareness one step further, looking to
the replacement of work as a major social force by a new social necessity based upon individual self-realization and autonomy in leisure.
Neville, attempting to delineate the major ideological positions of the
International Counterculture, has indicated that the predominant attitude of the youth underground is to regard work as redundant: "The
Underground has abolished work. There are no Positions Vacant col-
umns in the Underground press. Hippie hands do not say housework.
No one takes vacations—do children holiday from play?" (Neville
1971:212). He draws attention to the fact that differences could be
observed in the game patterns of counterculture members. One such
game is Frisbee: "It is somehow divinely appropriate that this game is
favoured by drop-outs. Frisbee is non-competitive. It has no rules. No
one could sell tickets for it. Like a child taking its first steps, members
of the Underground are learning how to live in that future where work
is rendered obsolete. They are re-learning how to play" (Neville 1971:
222).

Neville emphasizes the fact that modern society appears to have
reached the stage in the socialization process that precludes the opportunity for play:

Play has been abolished in contemporary society—except in children,
until we knock it out of them—and in its place there is recreation—
human maintenance. . . . Children learn at peak capacity during play
days. Soon such spontaneity is diverted into the factory process known

as education. As with their parents, work becomes compulsory and examinations parody work incentives. Organized sport isn't play either; it's a ritualized, legitimized aggression narcotic; hard work, competitive, corrupt. Ever seen an Olympic contestant smile?

Those most caught up in the syndrome of work/family/machine sport/success/failure/guilt . . . are those most outraged by the evolving Underground alternative. At student sit-ins, it is the "jocks" who try to toss the anarchists out. (Neville 1971:223)

This, then, is the counterculture position on work and its related values. While assuming that this position is adhered to by the representatives of the counterculture in the educational setting, how strong are achievement orientations and success syndromes among student representatives of the mainstream and the athletic subculture?

In a study of student attitudes and value structures toward features significant in play, Webb surveyed over 1,200 children drawn from grades 3, 6, 8, 10, and 12 of a major school system in Michigan. He found a developing emphasis upon the importance of achievement criteria in the play situation. The transition into high school marked the beginning of a surge of preference for achievement criteria in the evaluation of the play experience. Differences were evident, however, in the responses of the males and females in his sample.

This would seem to be consistent with the different experience both groups acquire with respect to ascriptive and achievement criteria. For the males, expected job experience will dictate some submission to the latter, one of whose constituents is "success," thus the emphasis on it illustrates its importance in attitudes developed in play by age, at the same time it illustrates its utility in providing attitudes consistent with later adult activity. For the females, on the other hand, such participation is neither as likely nor as expected, with the prime concern being choice of husband, and, . . . this is likely to occur on ascriptive bases rather carefully cultivated. (Webb 1969:168)

A similar study in the university environment reinforced these findings (Petrie 1970).

Although the Webb study looked at the student population as a whole and only utilized social background variables in order to investigate differences between subgroups, several studies have looked for differences on the basis of athletic participation. A recent study by Mantel and Vander Velden (1971) showed that "the professionalization of attitude toward play among preadolescent boys is directly related to participation in organized sport. Specifically, participants in organized sport regard skill or victory as the most important factor in play while nonparticipants emphasize fairness." Although that study employed a rather small sample, a recent large-scale study in a Canadian school system provided considerable support for their findings. Sampling a total of 567 students in Grades 8, 9, 10, and 12, Maloney and Petrie (1971) determined that

(a) the males were more professionalized in their attitudes toward play than the females because of their greater emphasis upon achievement oriented evaluative criteria; (b) the professionalization of attitude toward play increased among the male students as they progressed through school; (c) those respondents involved in minor levels of athletic involvement were most likely to hold a play orientation toward physical activity; (d) those respondents who had the greatest degree of involvement in athletic participation were more professionalized in their orientations toward physical activity; (e) participation in intramural athletics programs appeared to act as a damper upon the development of a professionalized attitude toward play, regardless of the level of personal involvement in other sport forms.

Feldman sampled a group of 335 high school males classified in terms of increasing involvement with athletics. One group of students had no participatory or spectator involvement with athletics; another was made up of students whose predominant involvement was as spectators, while a third group was comprised of participating athletes. He determined that the non-participant, non-spectator group was more likely to have higher standards of sportsmanship, and that interscholastic athletics did not contribute significantly to the development of the desirable but nonspecific value structures of responsibility, loyalty, honesty, friendliness, moral courage, or selflessness, all of which are associated with the use of intrinsic criteria for the evaluation of satisfaction in the game situation (Feldman 1969).

On the basis of the evidence presented, one can agree with Webb's conclusions regarding the effect of the development of work-oriented values in the game situation. He felt that to continue to insist that play contributes to the development of desirable but nonspecific social development characteristics "is to ignore its structural and value similarities to the economic structure dominating our institutional network, and the substantial contribution that participation in the play area makes to committed and effective participation in that wider system" (Webb 1969:178). The development of such values in the sporting group does not appear to be regarded as dysfunctional in the schools by any except committed counterculturists. The counterculture ideology would probably be perceived as deviant by most students, but, in view of the fact that this value has recently developed adherents, there is some likelihood that it will intrude into the belief structures of the mainstream.

There is, of course, a tendency to question the emphasis on interscholastic and intercollegiate athletics. One consistent element of such complaints appears to concern the fact that athletics requires great selectivity which results in a disproportionate amount of funds being directed to the participation of a few. Those who make this objection stress the need for expansion of intramural programs and for redirection of money to such activities, indicating a need for the democratization of sport and for the reduction of the success syndrome prevalent in representative athletics.

A link with the ideology of the counterculture can be perceived here. The spirit of play must be brought back into sport; the ritualism, competition, and work-related value structures must be replaced by a new orientation toward self-realization and fun in physical performance.

ATTITUDES TOWARD INDIVIDUAL RIGHTS

"There are two great national institutions which simply cannot tolerate either internal dissension or external interference: our armed forces, and our interscholastic sports programs. Both are of necessity benevolent dictatorships" (Rafferty 1971:15). Considerable attention has been directed recently to the allegation that sport, as presently constituted, is dehumanizing. Players are sometimes regarded as objects which can provide for successes, in the form of social or financial profit for the group in control. Sporting success is regarded as a means for securing individual prestige for coaches and institutional prestige for schools; as a means of developing positive identification among the nonparticipants for the institution; as a means of allowing some socially acceptable release of tensions and anxiety; and as a way of achieving personal and institutional financial gain.

One feature of dehumanization is the disregard of coaches for the individual rights of the players. Such disregard has been expressed through restrictive dress, behavior, and dating codes that act against any move toward conformity with the prevailing trends of the youth culture.

Additionally, individualized training programs and forms of democratic decision-making for teams have not been readily accepted as desirable modifications by the coaches. "In an age where students are making strong requests for recognition of their individuality, their right of self-expression, and a personal involvement in their school, it is incongruous for sport to drag its feet by holding to antiquated traditions and crew-cut stereotypes" (Melnick 1969:33).

A study by Puretz (1969) indicated that significant differences were evident in the attitudes of collegiate athletes and non-athletes toward the expression of individual rights in the athletic situation. His initial interpretations of the data suggested that athletes value their personal rights and the individual rights of others to a significantly lower degree. He continued by stating: "We have endeavored to treat athletes for so long as a special group that we may be in danger of succeeding. Unfortunately, it appears that while they may indeed be identified by their fellow students as members of a special group, they are unlikely to be perceived as being members of a desirable social group" (Puretz 1969:7).

One major tenet of the youth movement is the establishment and protection of individual rights. Authority that places unacceptable bonds upon the expression of individual freedom is to be denied and thwarted. There is a belief that society has become incapable of responding positively to expression of the individual freedom upon which it was based. This pressure upon freedom has been caused by the continued and uncontrolled application of technology, and by the pressure of such technology and supporting institutions upon all members of society. According to Keniston,

> The technology created to serve society has come to dominate it, and now threatens to destroy it. The institutions founded to express the popular will and serve the public interest have come to manipulate public opinion and exploit public anxieties. Probably no one has a precise, detailed, and accurate prescription for reversing these trends. But it is clear that to do so will not be the work of one apocalyptic moment, one revolutionary spasm, or one brief outcry of opposition. It will be the task of a lifetime, of a generation of men and women dedicated to the hard work of making the best visions of the youth culture real throughout the entire society. . . . (Keniston 1971:210–211)

Keniston clearly indicates that he feels that the methods of the youth revolution espoused by Rubin (1970, 1971) and Hoffman (1968, 1969, 1971) are unlikely to succeed. However, it is clear that the youth movement and its philosophies with regard to freedom have considerable support.

In a news release from the Institute for the Study of Sport and

Society, Scott (1971b) indicated that "professional athletes are not going to be in the forefront of the movement to radically change the nature of American Sport. Though few sports writers choose to publicize it, the athletic movement is alive and thriving on the grade school, high school and college levels." Although this belief is supported by the declining interest in West Coast interscholastic competitions, few schools appear to have reached the stage of abandoning their programs because of a lack of recruits. Those schools which have cut back or eliminated their programs have done so because of budgetary problems, or because student groups have voted to divert money from athletic budgets to more socially relevant causes.

Those who are attracted to the traditional programs are apparently willing to trade away some of their individual freedoms in order to achieve goals which they deem to be realizable through athletics. Although it has not been demonstrated that authoritarianism and the denial of athletes' rights are necessary concomitants of successful coaching, it has been shown that coaches have little interest in the dependency needs of others, and that they frequently manifest extreme conservatism which limits the use of new techniques and perceptions with respect to new problems (Ogilvie and Tutko 1966:23–24).

There is, of course, nothing wrong with the pursuit of excellence in physical activity, but if such involvement carries with it a willingness to be less concerned with personal rights, it is clear that (on this dimension) the athletic subculture is out of step with the counterculture, and may also be out of step with the belief structures of the mainstream.

THE ATHLETIC PERSONALITY

Many studies have hypothesized that crucial aspects of personality must be present or emphasized if an individual is to become a superior performer; the works of Ogilvie and Tutko (1966, 1971) and the review by Husman (1969) have established where these differences lie. In the latest example of this research, Ogilvie and Tutko have denied the existence of a beneficial influence of sport upon the development of character:

> Athletes who survive the high attrition rate associated with sports competition are characterized by all or most of the following traits:
>
> 1) They have a great need for achievement and tend to set high but realistic goals for themselves and others.
>
> 2) They are highly organized, orderly, respectful of authority, and dominant.

3) They have large capacity for trust, great psychological endurance, self control, low resting levels of anxiety, and slightly greater ability to express aggression.

Most athletes indicate low interest in receiving support and concern from others, low need to take care of others, and low need for affiliation (Ogilvie and Tutko 1971:61).

Although there has been some concern expressed regarding the intrusion of personal value systems in the works of these authors (Scott 1971a:131–142), the features of dominance, ascendency, and self-sufficiency appear in association with the personality structures of athletes in a variety of studies.

The personality profile expressed here does not appear to embody the features provided with positive reinforcement within the youth culture. In this latter group, at least as far as its ideological positions indicate, there is low emphasis on achievement secured at a cost to others, a distrust of authority and of those who seek dominance, and a willingness to cooperate and provide assistance to others. Since athletes are significantly higher on personality dimensions regarded with disfavor by the youth culture, once again the athletic group emphasizes characteristics which work against their possible integration.

POLITICAL IDEOLOGIES IN THE EDUCATIONAL SETTING

Athletics has consistently regarded itself as an apolitical institution, but recent events are causing a reevaluation of this position. This claim that sport is free of political influence has usually cloaked the basic conservatism of the institution. Certainly, as Melnick (1969) has indicated, sport is such a major component in the life of the school, college, and community that there is a natural reluctance to accept any change. The very conservatism of the athletic environment, and of the authority figures within it, would lead one to expect that the major influences would be toward maintenance of the status quo. The extreme negative reactions to such "symbols of extreme radical belief structures" as long hair, moustaches, beards, and beads indicate an attempt to protect the stereotyped image of the clean-cut athlete.

Athletes in the educational environment would be expected to differ from their nonathletic peers on the political activism dimension; given an appropriate issue, students in the mainstream have shown that they are willing to cooperate with regard to certain political causes, and to eagerly utilize radical techniques in the expression of their concern. Indeed, the strong support of Canadian students for closure of border crossings into the United States in opposition to the Amchitka atomic warhead test provided a recent indication of this tendency. The willingness to actually become concerned with liberal or radical causes is a major area separating the mainstream and counterculture from the athletic subculture. Most athletes appear more concerned with adhering to the expectations of the athletic establishment than with becoming involved with the concerns of their peers. Preliminary data released by Rehberg (1971) has provided some support for these contentions. Scott (1971a), however, has pointed out that a move to reject the apolitical atmosphere associated with athletics is particularly active in West Coast and Ivy League universities.

There is little solid evidence to support the contention that mainstream and counterculture groups view athletes as a deviant group. Much research has been directed toward establishing evidence of difference, while little has been aimed at determining whether these differences were perceived as desirable within the athletes' peer group. Now is the time for such an examination to take place.

Face validity appears to support the contention that athletes are being placed in defensive positions because of damaging stereotypes and the scapegoat effect. The prime task of those involved in serving the athletic group is to make certain that the athletes are not forced to accept and magnify tendencies which will lead to a strong separation from the youth culture.

REFERENCES

Coleman, J. S.
  1961 "Athletics in High School." In Sage, G. H., ed. *Sport and American Society*, pp. 84–98. Reading, Mass.: Addison-Wesley.
Feldman, M.
  1969 "Some Relationships between Specified Values of Student Groups and Interscholastic Athletics in Selected High Schools." Ph.D. dissertation. University of Massachusetts.
Frantz, T. T.
  1969 "Student Subcultures." *Junior College Student Personnel.* January: 16–20.
Hoffman, A.
  1968 *Revolution for the Hell of It.* New York: Dial Press.
  1969 *Woodstock Nation.* New York: Vintage Books.
  1971 *Steal This Book.* New York: Pirate Editions.
Husman, B. F.
  1969 "Sport and Personality Dynamics." In NCPEAM, eds. *Na-*

tional College Physical Education Association for Men, 72nd Proceedings, pp. 56–70. Minneapolis.

Keniston, K.
　1971　"The Agony of the Counterculture." *Educational Record* 52(3):205–211.

Maloney, T. L., and Petrie, B. M.
　1971　"Professionalization of Attitude toward Play among Canadian School Pupils as a Function of Sex, Grade, and Athletic Participation." Research paper. Department of P.H.E., University of Western Ontario. London, Ontario.

Mantel, R. C., and Vander Velden, L.
　1971　"The Relationship between the Professionalization of Attitude toward Play of Preadolescent Boys and Participation in Organized Sport." Paper presented at the Third International Symposium on the Sociology of Sport. Waterloo, Ontario.

Melnick, M. J.
　1969　"Footballs and Flower Power." *JOHPER* 40 (October):32–33.

Neville, R.
　1971　*Playpower*. London: Paladin.

Ogilvie, B. C., and Tutko, T. A.
　1966　*Problem Athletes and How to Handle Them*. London: Pelham Books.
　1971　"Sport: If You Want to Build Character, Try Something Else." *Psychology Today* 5(October):60–63.

Petrie, B. M.
　1970　"Physical Activity, Games, and Sport: A System of Classification and an Investigation of Social Influences among Students of Michigan State University." Ph.D. dissertation. Michigan State University.

Puretz, D. H.
　1969　"Athletics and the Development of Values." Paper presented at the AAHPER National Convention. Boston.

Rafferty, M.
　1971　"Interscholastic Athletics: The Gathering Storm." In Scott, J., ed. *The Athletic Revolution*, pp. 13–22. New York: Free Press.

Rehberg, R. A.
　1971　"Preliminary Data: NIMH 1925." Department of Sociology. SUNY—Binghamton.

Rubin, J.
　1970　*Do It*. New York: Ballantine Books.
　1971　*We Are Everywhere*. New York: Harper and Row.

Scott, J.
　1971a　*The Athletic Revolution*. New York: Free Press.
　1971b　"*Sauer Power: Part II*." News Release. Institute for Study of Sport and Society. Oakland, Calif.

Theobald, R.
1967 *Los Angeles Free Press* article of Sept. 19, 1967. In Hoffman, A. *Revolution for the Hell of It*. P. 175.
Webb, H.
1969 "Professionalization of Attitudes toward Play among Adolescents." In Kenyon, G. S., ed. *Sociology of Sport*, pp. 161–178. Chicago: Athletic Institute.

Sport and the "New Left": Some Reflections upon Opposition without Praxis

ALAN G. INGHAM

In the past decade there has been at least a modest revival of radicalism in America. Once again our attention has been turned to the ideological debates which characteristically define the relationship of the individual to his society. Institutionalized behavior of all kinds has come under close scrutiny, and since sport is a social institution, it came as no surprise when sport too was called into question.

At the ideological level, sport's place in society was viewed as anachronistic, just as the social criticisms of the early 1900's found sport to be an area of arrested social development. To use the invectives of Thorstein Veblen (1931), sport was viewed as an outmoded remnant of capitalistic predatory exploit. That is, sport was open to criticism because it apparently had not kept pace with the social and economic changes that had occurred in industry. Implicit in such criticism was the notion that sport still reflected the ideological premises of a bygone era; namely, the laissez faire capitalism of the turn of the century which was so successfully legitimated by the philosophy of Social Darwinism as espoused by William Graham Sumner.

At the structural level, there was increasing recognition that sport was becoming more rationalized and bureaucratic. Sport was seen as mirroring the "formalized, hierarchical, rule-laden, and efficiency-seeking type of social organization" (Page 1973) of modern business enterprise. Such a trend could only be regarded as inimicable to the quest for humanism which characterized the social movements of the 1960's. Rationality and bureaucratization were viewed as trends, the outcome of which could only be an increasing suppression of personal autonomy. As Robert K. Merton explains in his essay, "Social Structure and Anomie," the increasing emphasis upon victory through

Alan G. Ingham is assistant professor of physical education at the University of Washington. This paper is a modified version of his oral presentation. Although originally intended as a reaction to Brian M. Petrie's paper, "The Athletic Group as an Emerging Deviant Subculture," the present version is a more general analysis of ideology as it relates to sport at all levels of participation, rather than a specific analysis of the role of the athlete in the educational institution.

efficient means could only result in the primacy of expedience as a behavioral norm (Merton 1957). Sport, then, emerged as yet another performance-oriented activity in social life, in tune with the ideology of meritocracy rather than the ideology of democracy intrinsic to the values of the New Left. Such criticisms apply not only to professional athletics. The 1960's revealed an increasing suspicion that the thrust of rationality was permeating lower levels of participation: the increasing emphasis upon victory at the expense of fairness seemed also to characterize high school athletics.[1] Concomitant with the suspicion of the diffusion of rationality was an increasing concern that the primacy of expediency might result in the athlete sacrificing not only his own human rights, but also the rights of his opponents. The New Left came to reemphasize the notion of alienation: Marx's social and philosophical writings, rather than his economic writings, came into vogue (Bottomore 1966).

Sport produced anomalies. In a decade which was euphemistically heralded as the onset of "The Golden Age of Leisure," sport's continued emphasis upon the Protestant ethic of hard work and productivity could only be viewed as outdated. Sport became viewed as a repressive social institution where athletes "work for an apparatus that they do not control, which operates as an independent power to which individuals must submit if they want to [continue in their work role]" (Marcuse 1955). In a decade which emphasized the miseries accrued in the separation of man from the products of his labor, the sport role became a prime target for social criticism. The ascetic commitment to work advocated by sport's ideologues was brought into question as the work ethic was transformed to the leisure ethic.

The New Left revolted against degradation, exploitation, and dehumanization in all forms; the buying and selling of athletes as entertainment commodities conflicted with the optimistic sentiments for a more humanized existence. At the professional level, athletes became envisioned as pawns" having utility in providing for successes that can be translated into some form of social or financial profit" (Petrie 1971).

1. Several papers emerged from the initial study performed by Harry Webb which was entitled "Professionalization of Attitudes toward Play among Adolescents" (in G. S. Kenyon, ed., *Sociology of Sport* [Chicago: Athletic Institute, 1969]). See, for example, B. M. Petrie, "Physical Activity, Games, and Sport" (Ph.D. dissertation, Michigan State University, 1970); R. C. Mantel and L. Vander Velden, "The Relationship between the Professionalization of Attitude toward Play of Pre-adolescent Boys and Participation in Organized Sport" (Paper presented at the International Symposium on the Sociology of Sport, Waterloo, Ontario, 1971).

As sport increasingly reflected the rationalized practices of business enterprise, the work role of the athlete became labeled as alienating: like other workers, athletes were seen as selling their labor.

As the New Left reaffirmed the commitment to liberation, the socialization of the athlete into the athletic role became viewed as analogous to the socialization of inmates in total institutions (Goffman 1961). An emphasis upon conformity, with a corresponding loss of self-identity, appeared characteristic in both cases. Not only did sport critics assume that the athlete was mortified in the socialization process, but they also envisioned that the outcome of such a process was the unquestioning commitment of the athlete to his social role. Since the 1960's was a decade of cynicism, commitment to social roles in existing social institutions could only leave the athlete as part of an "emerging deviant subculture." The athlete emerged as one who would conform to institutional demands, who would succumb to authoritarianism in order to reap social and economic rewards. Unfortunately for the athlete, the social institution of sport has traditionally been associated with conservative elements of society; therefore the athlete was envisioned as a conformist to an ideology out of step with the values of the New Left.

The New Left also envisioned sport as a reaffirmation of the ethic of undiluted competition. Since competition was seen as a primary cause of alienation, the commitment of athletes to such an ethic could only separate them from their New Left peers, who were stressing the virtues of cooperation and sociability. Sport, from the viewpoint of the Left, had ceased to be play; it had become a work situation in which the athletic role had emerged as a service occupation[2] with extrinsic rather than intrinsic rewards. From this perspective, the athlete again emerged as a member of a deviant subculture.

I would now like to raise some problems which I find with such arguments. In so doing, I shall also attempt to provide some criticism of Brian Petrie's paper.

Perhaps the first problem is whether or not a Left/Right antithesis exists in North America in the classical sense; if so, where does the athlete stand in relation to these polar ideologies? In other words, is there a conservative power elite celebrating the virtues of capitalism,

---

2. I have discussed the notion of the athletic role as a service occupation and its ramifications for the athlete in greater detail in an article co-authored by Michael D. Smith, "The Social Implications of the Interaction between Spectators and Athletes," in J. Wilmore, ed., *Exercise and Sport Sciences Review* (New York: Academic Press, 1974), II, 189–224.

to use the ideas of C. Wright Mills, and a socialistic left wing which is attempting to undermine the existing economic and political structure? Or has the liberalized capitalism of America been so successful in raising the living standards and working conditions of the average individual that a socialist revolution is unnecessary, and indeed impossible, in a nation of "one-dimensional men"? The one-dimensional man is one who possesses "Happy Consciousness": "the belief that the real is rational and that the system delivers the goods," reflecting "the new conformism which is a facet of technological rationality translated into social behavior" (Marcuse 1964:84). Continuing to use the ideas of Marcuse (1972:5), "Why should the overthrow of the existing order be of vital necessity for people who own, or can hope to own, good clothes, a well-stocked larder, a TV set, a car, a house, and so on, all within the existing order?" Has a new and altogether different type of Left/Right antithesis emerged in the 1960's, as T. B. Bottomore (1966:66–81) has claimed? That is, perhaps the New Left has ceased to align itself with classical socialism, since the practical applications of this ideology have not measured up to its espoused ideals. Instead, the New Left has turned to "humanism allied with skepticism, or at least with an experimental and empirical approach to problems: an egalitarianism which repudiates the exposition of some orthodox doctrine by infallible teachers; and a strong belief in the importance of moral choices" (Bottomore 1966:74). If the New Left has ceased to align itself with classical socialism, the existing Right has never really aligned itself with the classical conservatism found in Europe. Since America was founded on liberal ideals, the existing Right (if it is a celebration of status quo) is celebrating, at least on the level of rhetoric, "People's Capitalism"[3] and not ascriptive elitism. If a New Right is emerging, it is also critical of the existing order and is urging the creation of an upper-class establishment "which would produce and perpetuate 'a set of traditional standards which carry authority and to which the rest of society aspires' " (Bottomore 1966:80). In the new Left/Right antithesis, both the New Left and the New Right emerge as opposed to the notion of the "one-dimensional man" as popularly portrayed in the Mass Society hypothesis.

To the question whether a Left/Right antithesis exists in the classical

---

3. The idea of "People's Capitalism" is taken from Herbert Aptheker's astute analysis of C. W. Mills's *The Power Elite* contained in his book, *The World of C. Wright Mills* (New York: Marzani and Munsell, 1960). Essentially the term "People's Capitalism" refers to the notion that the ownership of the American corporate system is widely dispersed.

sense, I think we should answer in the negative. America was born out of a revolutionary rejection of the conservative traditions of the *ancien régime*, and Americans have always been suspicious of socialism traditionally associated with the classical Left, especially since socialism became tarnished under the guidance of Stalin (see Harrington 1972). The best choice between the other two alternatives outlined above is difficult. Both the Mass Society hypothesis and a redefined Left/Right antithesis possess elements of truth. Mythical[4] "People's Capitalism" coupled with the inroads made by bourgeois socialism (commonly called the welfare state) may be in the process of producing—at least on the level of belief, if not in actuality—a mass society in which the middle class becomes all-encompassing. This trend toward *embourgeoisement* may be producing opposition, not only from the ranks of the New Left, who see it as a facade glossing over serious problems, but also from the ranks of those who see the trend as a threat to existing lifestyles. Certainly there is evidence to suggest that the notion of a mass society is anathema to those who regard themselves as patrons of "high-brow" culture, since a mass society implies the standardization of lifestyle and taste. Standardization, they fear, will result in the production of a "middle-brow" culture somewhat inferior to their professed cannons of taste. If an antithesis exists in American society, it cannot be conceived of simply in terms of New Left versus New Right. The notion of antithesis should also describe a loose coalition concerned over the loss of pluralism which stands in opposition to those celebrating a status quo characterized by a belief in gradual *embourgeoisement* through a meritocratic system of "People's Capitalism."

I have digressed from a discussion of sport in order to claim that to view the 1960's as a decade of revived antagonism between the Left and the Right is somewhat naive, unless that antagonism is redefined or qualified. Such a digression was necessary if we are to take an enlightened approach to the question, "Is the athletic group emerging as a deviant subculture?"

In his paper, "The Athletic Group as an Emerging Deviant Subculture," Brian M. Petrie suggests several criteria for distinguishing be-

4. I use the word "myth" guardedly. However, it is the case, as C. Wright Mills has pointed out in *The Power Elite*, that "the idea of a really wide distribution of economic ownership is a cultivated illusion. . . . At the very most 0.2 or 0.3 per cent of the adult population own the bulk, the pay-off shares of the corporate world." For more recent figures refer to Gabriel Kolko, *Wealth and Power in America* (New York: Praeger, 1962); H. P. Miller, *Rich Man, Poor Man*, (New York: Crowell, 1971).

tween athletes on one hand and the New Left on the other.[5] Using such criteria Petrie creates an antithesis between two polar subcultures on the basis of their ideology. Implicit in his discussion is a rejection of the claim made by Daniel Bell[6] that ideology has come to an end after the 1950's. Yet nowhere in Petrie's paper is there an adequate discussion of whether the polar subcultures reflect a classical Left/Right antithesis, a redefined Left/Right antithesis, or a loose coalition which is opposed to those celebrating status quo. Consequently, when he suggests that the athletic subculture represents a conservative minority, there is no real specification of the type of conservatism which they represent. If the athletic subculture is to be classified as deviant, there ought to be an analysis of how this subculture differs from the mainstream as well as from the New Left, since, by his own definition, to be deviant is to be "inconsistent with the value structure of the majority."

In order for the athletic group to be considered as an emerging deviant subculture, Petrie must presuppose that the mainstream is forming a loose coalition with the New Left, or that they are ideologically aligned. Since he chooses the latter, I think he should be criticized for confusing the New Left with the notion of opposition. That is, a true left wing always stays left wing (even if it becomes the dominant ideology), whereas opposition can fluctuate, depending upon who is holding authority or upon specific social issues (Aron 1962). Had Petrie chosen the former alternative, I would have found his argument more in tune with real events. In a time when the executive branch of government was viewed by some as becoming increasingly despotic, opposition to government action, to authoritarianism, and to the loss of individual rights may be constituted by a variety of social groups without these groups necessarily sharing ideological conviction. The 1960's might be viewed as a decade in which the liberals aligned themselves with the New Left, but only on certain issues—the anti-war campaign, the questioning of executive power and privilege, the unconstitutional bombing of Cambodia, the handling of student protest movements, etc. Whether sport was an issue which engendered such an alignment is debatable. Possibly Petrie attributes "Left-wing ideology" to the notion of opposition primarily on the basis of rhetoric—the main-

5. I have summarized most of these criteria in my introduction and so I will not reiterate them again at this point. However, it should be noted that my summarization is much more general than that contained within Petrie's paper.

6. I am referring here to the title which Daniel Bell gave to a collection of essays which appeared under his editorship in *The End of Ideology: On the Exhaustion of Political Ideas in the Fifties.*

stream may be espousing opposition to certain issues in terms of the rhetoric of the Left, and yet be far from accepting its ideology. In this sense, the rhetoric does not reflect the feelings which the majority has toward their place in the economic or political infrastructure. Rather, the rhetoric is a deflection of basic conviction.

If one is to assert that the athlete is deviant, one must ask who is defining him as deviant. If one is to assert that sport is anachronistic, one must ask to which subcultural group should such assertions be attributed. If the athletic role can be stereotypically conceived of as lacking personal autonomy; as embodying willing submission to arbitrary authority; as exhibiting unwitting commitment to a dehumanized condition of existence, then, in a time of revived interest in Marx's theory of alienation, the New Left would certainly regard those committed to such a role as deviant. And if sport is becoming increasingly viewed as rationalized, bureaucratized, and divorced from player control, and if those in economic and social control are viewed as exploiters of the players as commodities, the New Left might label athletes as falsely conscious dupes who are unaware of their conditions of existence. Should some athletes be seen as suspending good consciousness and cynically performing their roles to reap the rewards, they are still open to charges of hypocrisy. If we accept these assertions as valid, we are left with the impression that athletes are rejected men in an institution rejected by the New Left.

Yet such assertions do not recognize the dialectical nature of the athletic role (or any role, for that matter). They portray it as a predefined entity having control over the volitions of the individual. Consequently, they obviate the possibility that a social role can be analyzed both in terms of personal commitment and non-commitment or role distance. To quote Natanson (1972:221), "the paradox of the role lies in the necessary distance between acceptance and performance, between affirmation and reflection"—and it is precisely this paradox that is neglected by eristical assertion. The athletic role is paradoxical: the athlete can be committed to athletics and at the same time be cynical about the ritualized ways in which he is required to perform. Failing to conceive of the role in this paradoxical fashion results in the inability to distinguish between the activity and the role which circumscribes it. Neglecting the paradoxical nature of the social role, therefore, results in a naive interpretation of Marx's theory of alienation. That is, by viewing activity and role as a single idea, there is no distinction made between the activity as an embodiment of human subjectivity (i.e., a direct expression of human needs) and the role as an institutionalized mediation between the activity and the system of rewards. Such reasoning will not do since it rules out the possibility of transcendence, a concept which Marx used to describe how alienation might be superseded without destroying human institutions.[7] Without a distinction between activity and role, those who would abolish alienation in the social role end up by abolishing the activity as well.

There is another danger in failing to recognize the paradoxical nature of the athletic role: it might be assumed that, by taking the athletic role, a person's total self has been invaded by his athletic identity. From this perspective, it might be assumed that the adoption of the sport role results in the adoption of a world view determined by the ideologues in the sport establishment. In a sense, the failure to analyze the sport role in terms of role distance results in the interpretation of commitment in terms of false consciousness. The athlete is perceived from the perspective of "the oversocialized conception of Man" (Wrong 1961); by virtue of his commitment to his athletic identity, he is described as one who is also committed to the "occupational charter"[8] which legitimates sport as a social institution and is willingly compliant to the situational and occupational demands made upon the role. While this description may characterize some athletes, there is danger in using it as a stereotype since it violates empirical reality. Athletes do engage in role distance. Athletes do distinguish between their public and actual identities. Athletes are not all falsely conscious; some are very aware of their conditions of existence and the uses to which their labor is put. The danger of stereotyping is that it leads to rejection. Since the New Left critics of sport cannot stereotypically conceive of the athlete as capable of transcending the alienation of his social role, they reject not only the role but also the individual who performs it. Historically, the trend toward rejecting those who are alienated, possibly out of feelings of impatience, has led to the attempted imposition of a new order without their consent. Yet such an imposition reveals a poor understanding of Marx's premises. "His profoundly democratic realism led him to argue that the good society would be fashioned, not by the dictates of some intellectual's plan, but according to the needs and creativity of the people themselves" (Harrington 1970). A revolution imposed on athletics from without will not allow the athlete to transcend the aliena-

7. For a more erudite discussion of the relationship between alienation and transcendence I would suggest that readers consult István Mészáros, *Marx's Theory of Alienation* (London: Merlin Press, 1970).

8. I am using the concept "occupational charter" to describe the value-laden statements made by the athletic establishment which serve to justify the place of sport in the community and which attempt to guarantee its continued existence.

tion of his social role; indeed, it is only a change in dictatorial face. Should the athlete accept this new order in an unquestioning or uncritical fashion, how has this change of face elevated him from his position of ideological servitude? Criticism which fails to confront the inherent paradoxes in the playing of a social role does not generate answers to questions concerned with the relationship between commitment and transcendence. Such criticisms fail to confront the notion that athletes can be committed to the activity of athletics and yet may wish to bring about changes in the economic and social structure of sport. In this sense I am accusing the critics of sport as opponents with no view on praxis.[9] The critics constitute an opposition which lacks a social theory; lacking such theory, it becomes impossible to ask whether athletes are emerging as a deviant group, for to be deviant is to be deviant from something, and what that something is has never been specified.

If, however, we agree that athletes are deviant from whatever the New Left is proposing, it is still a major leap to regarding the athlete as a deviant from the viewpoint of the mainstream. Sport attracts large segments of American society both as participants and spectators. Indeed, it might be suggested that the growth of sport reflects a trend toward *embourgeoisement* indicative of the transition of America into a mass society. The myth of "People's Capitalism" which suggests that Americans are as a whole becoming better off is nowhere better served than in sport. Indeed, one author has concluded that "in no area of American life more than in its leisure activity is the outdated concept of class made apparent" (Kaplan 1960). Since the working man of today may own his own boat, play golf, or engage in other once-exclusive sports, and since such opportunities at the behavioral level lend support to the ideological hegemony[10] of the *embourgeoisement*

9. "The concept of praxis in Marxism refers to the activity of man which aims at transforming the world as well as aiding his own self-development. Man is not a passive product of external influences, but instead participates, through his own practical activity, in shaping the conditions for his existence." See Jaromer Janousek, "On the Marxian Concept of *Praxis*" in J. Isreal and H. Tajfel, eds. *The Context of Social Psychology: A Critical Assessment* (New York: Academic Press, 1972), pp. 279–294.

10. Ideological hegemony refers to the thesis that "in class differentiated societies, a major source of undisturbed elite dominance is control over the ideological institutions of that society. By using their power to define what is good, true, just, reasonable, practical and inevitable, the ideological institutions are able to purge interpretations based upon deviant, dissident or revolutionary traditions" (D. L. Sallach, "What Is Sociological Theory," *American Sociologist* 8 [1973]:134–139).

hypothesis, it may be difficult for him to regard these newfound privileges as deviant. Consequently, the working man may not regard as deviant those who are exemplars of athletic performance. And since the privileged elites of society have access to sport and can use it to propagate their values to a population which is largely unaware of alternatives, those who populate the stadia or spend much of the weekend watching sports on television are not likely to align themselves with critics of sport as a social institution. Sport has traditionally been associated with American ideals of hard work, competition, self-challenge, free enterprise, striving for excellence. If it is the case that the ideology of *embourgeoisement* through meritocracy is becoming hegemonic, then political socialization leading to widespread belief in this ideology would certainly militate against any alignment between New Left and the majority in a criticism of sport. Since sport reflects the traditional values of American society, criticisms of sport represent a challenge to the social fabric of the society[11] and can lead only to confrontation, *not* alignment, between the New Left and the majority. If we ask who is defining the athlete as deviant, we must conclude that it is not the majority. And if we use Petrie's definition that a "deviant subculture would be one whose expectancies were so far removed from the acceptance or tolerance of the dominant or majority group," we must conclude that to be an athlete does not constitute a position which may be regarded as outside their tolerable limits.

I have not intended in this paper to compromise the arguments of the Left. I have simply suggested that if sport is to be reconstructed in a way which transcends the alienation of the athletic role, then social criticism without social theory is not going to facilitate the reconstruction process. Second, I have suggested that any attempt to impose an athletic revolution from without is not only a contradiction of Marxist premises, but also an imposition which would lack popular support. Athletes are beginning to reconstruct the social and economic structure of sport through membership in players' unions, willingness to strike, and challenges of the sporting oligarchy via the reserve clause. Their efforts should not be dismissed lightly. However, such efforts may not necessarily lead to the transcendence of alienation; they may simply be attempts to reevaluate the worth of their labor, which in no way elevates this labor from its status as a commodity. That is, while such efforts may induce quantitative changes, they may not necessarily pro-

11. This position was adopted by Spiro Agnew in his speech to the Touchdown Club of Birmingham, Alabama. Implicit in this speech is the idea that this view reflected the feelings of the "silent majority."

duce the qualitative changes intrinsic in the notion of transcendence. Finally, cynical criticism alone is not the way to good consciousness. To ask athletes to become merely cynical, without a concern for transcendence, is to ask them to indulge in schizophrenia. It would result in an unmanageable separation of self from role—their athletic identity would be a fraud.

REFERENCES

Aron, Raymond.
    1962   *The Opium of the Intellectuals*. New York: Norton Library.
Bottomore, Tom
    1966   *Critics of Society*. New York: Vintage Books.
Goffman, Irving
    1961   *Asylums*. Garden City, N.Y.: Anchor-Doubleday.
Harrington, Michael
    1970   *Why We Need Socialism in America*. New York: Norman Thomas Fund.
    1972   *Socialism*. New York: Saturday Review Press.
Kaplan, Max
    1960   *Leisure in America*. New York: John Wiley and Sons.
Marcuse, Herbert
    1955   *Eros and Civilization: A Philosophical Inquiry into Freud*. New York: Vintage Books.
    1964   *One-Dimensional Man*. Boston: Beacon Press.
    1972   "Socialism in the Developed Countries." *International Socialist Journal*. Cited in P. Mattick, *Critique of Marcuse: One-Dimensional Man in Class Society*. London: Merlin Press.
Merton, Robert
    1957   "Social Structure and Anomie." In R. Merton, ed. *Social Theory and Social Structure*. New York: Free Press.
Natanson, Maurice
    1972   "Phenomenology and Social Role." *Journal of the British Society for Phenomenology* 3 (October):218–230.
Page, Charles
    1973   "Pervasive Sociological Themes in the Study of Sport." In Talamini, J., and Page, C., eds. *Sport and Society: An Anthology*, pp. 14–37. Boston: Little, Brown.
Petrie, Brian
    1971   "The Athletic Group as an Emerging Deviant Subculture." Presented to the Conference on Sport and Social Deviancy. Brockport, N.Y.
Veblen, Thorstein
    1931   *The Theory of the Leisure Class*. New York: Viking Press.
Wrong, Dennis
    1961   "The Oversocialized Conception of Man in Modern Sociology." *American Sociological Review* 26 (April):183–193.

Index

Achievement: as a value in sports, 23–24; emphasis in play, 229; level in bowling hustlers, 90

Achievement motivation, 13, 50, 191

Activism, 209, 213

Adult control: for children's games, 46

Aggression. *See* Hockey violence

Affiliation: expressed by new left, 239; in competition, 240

American society: competition in, 50; sport norms in, 71–72; structural change in, 208

Arousal, 14

Athletes: as a deviant subculture, 180, 226–27, 243; assimilation of, 160, 184; conservatism of, 210, 217, 225; political attitudes of, 201, 203, 205, 214–17

Athletic identity, 245, 248

Athletic role. *See* Social role

Athletics: and scholarships for blacks, 130; counterculture attitudes toward, 191–200; importance in education, 130, 225; individual rights in, 232; involvement in, 230

Attitudes: changes in, 30; for an outgroup, 33–34; for counterculture, 195, 197–98, 227–28; political, 202–5, 210, 214–15, 234; toward work, 227

Backyard baseball: as a learning model, 48; described, 47–48; peer relations in, 48. *See also* Little League baseball

Black athletes: as role models, 124, 139, 152; discrimination against, 134–42, 151, 161–63, 169, 170–71; education of, 130, 160–61, 172; racial myths concerning, 168; role conflict for, 143–44, 162, 172–73; social mobility of, 131–32, 161; sport involvement of, 122–27, 157–59; team positioning for, 139, 152–55, 163–64

Capitalism: laissez faire, 238; liberal, 241

Cheating: absence in children's games, 75–76; and association, 68; competence in, 75; outcome uncertainty and reward, 70; personality characteristics in, 70; regulation of, 71, 73–74; sanctioned, types of, 68; social class standing, 71–72; social system characteristics for, 68

Children's learning: competition and, 20–23; Little League baseball and, 47, 49; sex roles and, 23

Collective action. *See* Intergroup competition

Competence: in cheating, 75; in hustling, 78–79; theory of, 12

Competition: American society and, 23, 50, 227; and educational reform, 51; as a social process, 12–13; benefits of nonparticipation, 52; cooperation related to, 19, 51; counterculture values toward, 51; definitions of, 10–12, 14, 25; development of, 22; prolonged over time, 31–32; psychological effects of, 26–29; racial integration and, 116; social facilitation and evaluation related to, 12–14; theory of, 15

Conservatism: classical, 241; in attitudes, 217

Consumer sport, 60